A Book of Country Houses

a book of
Country Houses

edited by Miles Hadfield

With contributions by
Alec Clifton-Taylor
Geoffrey Beard
St John Gore
Kenneth Garlick
Christopher Gilbert
Charles Lines

Country Life London/New York/Sydney/Toronto

Half-title illustration: an *œil de bœuf*
at Shugborough, Staffs.
Title page: Blickling Hall, Norfolk.
Contents page: Dyrham Park, Glos.

Published for Country Life Books by
THE HAMLYN PUBLISHING GROUP LIMITED
LONDON · NEW YORK · SYDNEY · TORONTO
Hamlyn House, Feltham, Middlesex, England
© Copyright The Hamlyn Publishing Group Limited
and Miles Hadfield 1969.

Printed offset litho in Great Britain
by Cox & Wyman Limited,
London, Fakenham and Reading.
Design by Christopher Pow.

SBN 600 43027 8.

Contents

List of Illustrations

Foreword

The usually admirable guides that can be bought when visiting country houses have certain inevitable limitations. While they can, for example, enlarge a little on some of a house's more singular occupants, they can expand little if at all on the details of the house itself. Shortage of space makes it inevitable that they should be written on the assumption that the visitor is acquainted with the general background and history of architecture. Thus we may read that such-and-such a house is in the Palladian manner, designed by a certain architect for a certain nobleman on his return from the Grand Tour, that the decoration is a fine example of Rococo, while the furniture and pictures are typical of the period.

The eccentricities of the original owner will be noted in the Guide; his character may be judged from a portrait hanging in the Yellow Room, his ancestry from the genealogical table. But as for the general architectural information–such as the meaning of Palladian or what other houses were designed by the same architect (you may like his work and want to see more of it) and what the Grand Tour was all about–well, there is no space for it.

Our aim is to provide a single-volume compendium that will give at least an outline of the information required. The procedure we have followed is this. First, an attempt is made to define the country house and its importance–for important in many ways it was and still is. Next, a brief outline is given of the fashions and styles that have overtaken it. This picks out in the sequence of time rather than of the alphabet the main figures in our *Biographical Index*, to which the reader is referred. Building materials play an overwhelming part in both the structure and appearance of a house, and these are considered by Mr Alec Clifton-Taylor. From the outer shell we move logically to the interior and its decoration–a subject which has long concerned Mr Geoffrey Beard.

And thence to those two major embellishments: first, furniture, glorified beyond mere utility, is discussed by Mr Christopher Gilbert; secondly, the pictures, whose historical and aesthetic qualities are examined by Mr St John Gore. So much for the fabric and its adornments.

There then follows an account of that singular and relatively short-lived feature of British civilisation–the Grand Tour, whose effects can be seen to this day. This is described by Dr Kenneth Garlick. Back to the principal creators, from architects to craftsmen, we turn again to Mr Beard, who has done his share in bringing hitherto nameless ghosts known only by their work back to life with names, workshops and dates of birth and death. Next, a list of houses is included in which Mr Charles Lines, whose personal inspection of them must be unexcelled, gives us an indication of the points of interest in each. Then we have a brief glossary explaining some of the many technical terms that the amateur of architecture encounters, and finally a short reading list.

An attempt has been made to refer only to houses open at least occasionally to the public. In these changing times, however, it is essential before planning a visit first to confirm that the house is accessible and secondly to ascertain the times at which it is open, by referring to such books as Historic Houses, Castles and Gardens in Great Britain and Ireland, *issued annually by Index Publishers, and lists of opening arrangements issued by the National Trust and the National Trust for Scotland. Lists of gardens open to the public for various charities are also often helpful.*

The Country House

Miles Hadfield

opposite. Ragley Hall, Warwicks.: the Great Hall decorated from designs by James Gibbs *c.* 1752.

Can we define a 'country house'? It is now difficult to do so. A century and a half ago it was easier. Guide books referred to 'seats' and 'residences'. A seat was, as it were, the headquarters of a landowning peer or squire, set in the midst of his estates. Though he might pass little time there, it was normal for him to spend 'the season' in his town house–it was in the neighbouring church that his ancestors were probably buried and where his own mortal remains would finally rest. It was more than likely that on one–or even more–occasions the head of the family would rebuild the house to glorify his and his family's name, an event which often coincided with a step up the ladder of the peerage. The house would contain his finest furniture and works of art, all of which would almost automatically be inherited by his heir. Splendour and display is the keynote of these houses; their owners have often played prominent parts at the courts of kings and queens and at high levels in politics and diplomacy. Above all, they could provide what no mansion in town, however grand, had at its doorstep–sport. Houses such as Woburn Abbey, Chatsworth, Ragley and Burghley are what can justly be called our stately homes.

Then there are many, many more which were truly classed as residences, the so-called manor houses, inhabited by squires and their families– perhaps descended from those who had originally made money in wool or as bankers. Such houses usually dominated not vast estates but little more than a village and its surroundings and were the homes of the families which officered the navy and the army and from which the clergy were recruited. Among them are some architectural gems.

It is tempting to believe that a house can be adequately described from one viewpoint alone– that of architecture. Yet this is not the case. Every house has a different character. It may be grandiose, placid, cheerful, disturbing or exquisite. Architecture may be its skeleton, but the soul which identifies it and the flesh and blood that clothe it are the legacy of those who have inhabited it, or indeed still live there. These inhabitants are in turn affected by the house's location and climate, and by special and economic pressures. Of these, the most important is often fashion–that eternally powerful driving force now known as keeping up with, or even triumphantly excelling, the Joneses.

Among the distinguishing features of the country house is its proximity to and relationship with the village. It has probably long dominated the village by which it stands and the broad acres around. It has therefore been a seat of power and inevitably has acquired an individual character, unlike the town house, however grand, which tends to be submerged among many. The 'big house' may, indeed, still deserve its title, and its occupants may still stand as protectors of the smaller, rural community.

It is easy to criticise the builders and owners of country houses and their estates for abusing their power in the past. It is much more important to contemplate the overwhelming contribution that the country seats and their occupants have made to our civilisation. Politically, until well into the present century, they were the places where informal behind-the-scenes meetings took place, at which were discussed the future policies of both parties of the time–Whigs and Tories–particularly during the days of the Whig supremacy.

From the days of Thomas Howard, 2nd Earl of Arundel (1586-1646)–though his own Arundel House was in London–the aristocracy, old and new, were the travellers who, often with an entourage that included prominent men of learning, linked our insular civilisation with that of the Continent, bringing back for their collections works of art and, more important, an understanding and knowledge of the lively and vital world of scholarship, learning and the developing sciences, largely emanating from Italy.

The country house was also intimately connected with our literature from early times. This association was particularly strong during that great period of building, the early 18th century, when Addison, Matthew Prior and Alexander Pope were closely linked with the country house set.

Music, too, is part of the heritage of the country house – from Tudor days, through Handel at Canons and to more recent patrons such as the 8th Duke of Marlborough with his organ and private organist, and the late Lord Howard de Walden.

Painting and furniture, which have their own special chapters, are further major features. And the whole existence of the sporting artist (of whom many consider Stubbs to be our finest representative) is bound up with the country house. Further, it has been said that Britain's most individual contribution to aesthetics is the landscape garden of the 18th century. In this, too, the country house owner played the key part.

So one could go on, concluding with the fact that many country houses and their owners still contribute much to the day-to-day life of the countryside. Their houses, with all their beauty and interest, are often thrown open to the public in aid of good causes. Many others help to maintain them by opening regularly and charging a fee for admission. The motor car has made visiting them a regular delight for a wide public. Country house visiting has, however, a very long history. Until excavations were carried out recently, we relied on accounts written by visitors (not guests), such as Paul Hentzner and Thomas Platter, who in the last years of the 16th century went to Nonsuch and Hampton Court, for a description of these buildings at that time. Later travellers – Celia Fiennes in the late 17th century, the Reverend Dr Alexander Carlyle in the mid-18th and the Reverend William Gilpin at the end of the 18th century – graphically described the routine of country house visiting. In 1738 Wilton was open at stated times. Later in the century Woburn was open on Mondays, Wanstead on Saturdays, and Chatsworth twice a week. With the coming of the railway, the social stratum of visitors was greatly widened. Formerly largely restricted to the gentry who toured on horseback or by carriage, it now included the inhabitants of the rapidly expanding industrial areas. This was particularly true at Chatsworth after August 10th 1848, when Mr Paxton (as he then was) arrived at the house in a carriage drawn by the people, having succeeded in getting the railway to pass through the park. In the evening, the 'bachelor' Duke of Devonshire sent beer for all the staff, speeches were made, and there was dancing and fireworks. In consequence, we learn, there arrived shortly afterwards on the new iron road a party of 1686 teetotallers from Sheffield, who made the routine trip round the house and garden. The love of the urban population for the homes of country aristocracy, and for the countryside generally, could now be fulfilled.

The theme of escape from the town to the joys of the countryside is an old one in our poetry. To quote Thomas Randolph's *Ode to Master Anthony Stafford to hasten him in Country* written in the days of Charles I:

> Come, spur away
> I have no patience for a longer stay,
>   But must go down
> And leave the chargeable noise of this great town:
>   I will the country see,
>   Where old simplicity,
>   Though hid in gray
>   Doth look more gay,
> Than foppery and plush in scarlet clad
>   Farewell, you city wits, that are
>   Almost at civil war –
> 'Tis time that I grow wise, when all the world
>   grows mad.
>
>   There from the tree
> We'll cherries pluck, and pick the strawberry;
>   And every day
> Go see the wholesome country girls make hay,
>   Whose brown hath lovelier grace
>   Than any painted face
>   That I do know
>   Hyde Park can show
>   Where I had rather gain a kiss than most
>   (Though some of them in greater state
>   Might court my love with plate)
> The beauties of the Cheap, and wives of Lombard
>   Street . . .

Chatsworth House, Derbyshire: the south front by
William Talman, begun 1686.

It is entertaining to consider the Caroleans making their way laboriously over dreadful roads to one of the great houses built during the last decades of the 17th century, embodying the first signs of the Renaissance in their architecture. Then to compare them with today's traveller from Cheap-side jammed, choked with petrol fumes, on the Exeter By-Pass, or on the crowded A5 escaping from the Black Country to the West. For an ever-increasing number of these modern motorists, on their journeys of liberation, the inspection and enjoyment of our country houses is an especial pleasure.

Inspirations and Fashions

Miles Hadfield

opposite. Oxburgh Hall, Norfolk: the gatehouse and moat from the north west.

It might be said that the English country house—at least well into the 18th century—can be broadly divided into three types. First there is the straightforward, more-or-less functional building, with little or no outside influence, aesthetic or otherwise. Its form is virtually dictated by the method of its construction, whether of wattle and daub, timber-framing and brick, stone, brick alone—or any other of the conventional materials. 'Frills', such as purely decorative ornament, are usually entirely absent, and in any case are largely applied and superficial. To this category belong vast numbers of small cottages and houses, from the early cruck houses, whose whole structure is dependent on the natural shape of two weighty oak branches, to the millions of plain, box-like small brick houses still being built today. Their appearance was and is arrived at unconsciously.

The second kind of house has something more— an element of display about it. Windows are not merely topped with a block of stone or a baulk of timber, but take the form of the pointed arch, that great achievement of the architecture commonly known as Gothic. Gothic decorative features are to be found in the grander houses up to Tudor times, and were later used, at first very fancifully and without true understanding, in the latter part of the 18th century; this 'gothick' phase was followed in the nineteenth century by a more serious antiquarian interest in gothic forms, which continued into the present century.

The next great influence on our architectural style originated in classical Greece—an incongruous backward glance far remote from the intervening styles of the middle ages. This classicism came to us not in its original form, but as employed and altered by the Romans. Greek architecture was trabeated— that is, a space was bridged by a horizontal beam and not an arch. It was an elaboration of a primitive post-and-lintel timber structure. However, it came to us via the Italian Renaissance, which harked back to Roman models, based on the arch.

Fundamental to the classical style are the three main Greek columnar forms of construction or 'orders'. In each, the column rises from a base, to carry an entablature surmounted finally by a pediment, whose proportions and details were worked out with mathematical accuracy; these component parts are repeatedly referred to in descriptions of all buildings inspired by the classical ideal. The three principal Greek orders built of stone are, in historical sequence, the Doric, Ionic and Corinthian. (For drawings illustrating their detailed parts, see the *Glossary,* p. 243). In the hands of the Romans, with a civilisation quite different from that of the Greeks, the principles went through numerous variations, permutations, combinations and elaborations. Indeed, in Asia Minor the Greek colonists themselves varied the designs of the orders.

The outstanding example of the Doric order is that of the Parthenon. It is massive and simple, appropriate to the character of the rougher Dorians from the North. Yet the massive appearance of the column may have to be quoted as just one of the many optical illusions discovered and incorporated by the Greeks in their architecture: its sides swell out a little, barrel-wise. If they did not, it would appear slightly concave and weak.

Looking at the building from the long side, each column rises direct from the three-stepped stylobate, with no base. They are fluted and on the top is mounted the capital, consisting of two parts, the lower circular (the echinus) and the upper square (the abacus) with sides as long as the diameter of the echinus. Along the top of the columns, resting on the abacuses, runs a long beam, as it were, called the architrave. This is the first division of the entablature, in effect the framework on which the roof stands. The next section consists of ornamentation, in the form of alternate triglyphs and metopes. The former are projections and are vestigial remains in stone of the ends of wooden cross-beams in earlier buildings. The metopes are intervening spaces decoratively carved. The final section of the entablature is the cornice consisting principally of the broad fascia, with moulding and ornament above.

Now, by turning and looking at the front of the building, it is possible to see the pediment, the flattened triangular facing of the roof with a carved panel at its centre, with the upper part of the cornice carried up to its apex.

From this description, it will be noticed that most of the technical terms named are still in use today, though with different applications. Yet they may still be largely explained by reference to the orders.

Next in time comes the Ionic order, the use of which in the north porch of the Erecthion is generally taken as a prime example. The most striking feature of this is the capital, which now consists of two spiral scroll-shaped ornaments (volutes). The column now stands on a distinct base set upon the stylobate. The constituents above the capital, architrave, frieze and cornice, are still there, but they are now more elaborate, their edges moulded into subtle curves and ornamented.

Finally comes the Corinthian order; its principal feature is the elaborate capital whose design is based on the acanthus leaf. The text-book example comes from the Choragic monument of Lysicrates at Athens. This again comprises the same main elements as the other orders.

The spread of the classical architectural style of Greece and Rome northwards reached England in a crude form in Tudor times. The earliest book in English on the subject was John Shute's *The First and Chiefe Groundes of Architecture*, published in the year of his death, 1563.

To summarise, then: until recent times the architecture employed in British country houses had three main sources. First, the purely vernacular, dependent largely on the requirements of those dwelling in the house, their way of life, economic circumstances, and the materials available for construction, with no conscious effort to achieve a 'style'.

Second, came the influence of the Gothic with its pointed arch and methods of construction, knowledge of which derived from our close connection with France, particularly at the time of the Norman conquest and during the medieval era. This style was later revived, first as the whimsical 'gothick' of the late 18th century and later in the carefully imitative and mechanically produced Gothic during Queen Victoria's reign.

Finally, the influence of Greece and Rome arrived here through our increased mercantile and political connections with Renaissance Europe from the reign of Henry VIII onwards. This influence was at its height during the great period of country house building and rebuilding – from the time, say, of William and Mary to the last of the Georges. During this period men such as Wren, Vanbrugh, Kent, the Adam brothers and Chambers enter our history.

It must be remembered that Britain, as a colony of the Roman Empire, possessed classical buildings in plenty. And yet the grandeur of Rome does not seem to have been much of a reality in our midst and appears to have had little influence on our own indigenous architecture. The Roman buildings crumbled away (or were pillaged) during the centuries known as the 'dark ages', and Anglo-Saxon structures were made of timber only and have therefore perished. Even the few Anglo-Saxon churches we still have show evidence of being transcriptions into stone of architecture and building methods originally conceived in terms of wood.

The first type of buildings that we can bring under the heading of 'country house' are the castles and fortified houses built at the time when the countryside was becoming more stable and less dangerous. The central government was beginning to find ways to control the disorderly members of the nobility and the bellicose element declined.

An example of a castle built during the transitional period is Thornbury, on the Severn estuary. It was begun in 1511 by Edward Stafford, 3rd Duke of Buckingham, a powerful nobleman and favourite of Henry VIII. Its exterior was in the traditional, war-like castellated manner. Like all castles, it was, for obvious reasons, built around a courtyard in which troops and the impedimenta of war could be safely sheltered in the event of siege. The scale of Stafford's building and the style in which he lived can be gathered from the fact that at one Epiphany his guests and their entourages numbered 459 per-

Penrhyn Castle, Caernarvonshire: the great keep
from the south (begun 1827).

sons. Thornbury differed from other castles in that its savage exterior concealed a façade to the owner's private quarters that was in the latest style of domestic architecture, with tall and beautifully wrought oriel windows, overlooking a garden. Outside the castle, too, was a pleasure garden, with fruit-trees, roses, and alley ways. Stafford was executed in 1521 and the last of the barons' castles, now an anachronism, remained uncompleted.

It was in Tudor times, too, that other medieval castles were transformed into homes in the grand manner rather than war-like establishments (though some, it is true, returned to their original purpose during the Civil War of the 17th century). For example, in 1587, Sir Edward Herbert, a son of the Earl of Pembroke, bought the ancient 'red' castle of Powis in Montgomeryshire and added a long gallery in the fashionable Elizabethan manner. And while on the subject of castles, it is as well to remember that a number of houses so named are not real castles in the sense of having any connection with medieval war: take, for example, Castle Howard, begun in 1701, and a whole range of houses imitative of the castellated style, such as Bolsover (Derbyshire) of 1612 and Eastnor (Herefordshire), Penrhyn (Wales), Caerhays (Cornwall) and Castlewellan (Northern Ireland), which are 19th century. Many also have been much added to or rebuilt in comparatively recent times; examples are Croft in the 18th century, Powis in the 19th, and Arundel, which is now almost entirely a 19th-century structure.

The Middle Ages to Oriana

From martial grandeur, we must now come down to earth and discuss those charming smaller, early houses, many of which, usually amended over the centuries and certainly modernised in recent decades, we still visit today. They have now often assumed without authority the epithet 'manor'. (The true manor house was the home of the lord of the manor, was usually surrounded by his own lands and situated not infrequently at the head of a small valley just below the rising of a stream.)

Such a house was, until Renaissance influence was felt, largely functional and unselfconscious as a work of art. Its beauty lay in the skill of the craftsmen that built it, and the way in which they made use of the great variety of local materials. It was constructed on a unit plan governed by the length of the beams available – that is, from 13 feet to 15 feet. The owner and his family ate and lived in one room, the great hall. In early times, the hearth was in the centre, the smoke rising through the roof, which might be, in the grander houses, of a complex structure giving a larger floor space. The entrance to the house was at one end of this hall by means of a passage running the whole width of the building; on one side of the corridor would be the entrance to the hall through the wooden 'screens', which pro-

tected it from the pantry, kitchen, buttery and domestic offices on the other. Often, above this passage and the screens was a gallery opening to the hall. At the end of the hall opposite the screens was a dais. Upon this sat the lord of the manor and his entourage. From this dais a narrow stairway led to the other important room, the solar, which was above a secondary chamber. The first floor, of no great consequence, was reached by a narrow, spiral stairway tucked into a corner.

A small and very simple example of this type of house is Old Soar, at Plaxtol in Kent (dating from about 1290), which also has a chapel. The old part of Penshurst Place, also in Kent, is a somewhat larger example (surrounded by extensive later additions). This was, in fact, built as a country house for a prosperous city merchant about the middle of the 14th century, a few decades after Plaxtol. In this the hearth in the centre of the hall floor can still be seen. The similarity of the doorways and windows in both of these houses to that of churches was also typical of the period. Glass was still not in common use, and it is still often possible to see how the wooden shutters were fitted.

By degrees houses became larger and more complex and the windows much bigger. The plan remained irregular and the exterior appearance haphazard. They continued to have elements of fortification, such as the moat when the water table was high – an efficient form of protection in a countryside still unfenced against animals both four and two-footed. This was crossed by a bridge often combined with a gatehouse. An example is Oxburgh (built in 1482), where the great tower and moat defend an entirely domestic house. On a much smaller scale, and of about the same period, is the typical and delightful little gatehouse at Lower Brockampton in Herefordshire, again bridging a moat. A little later, the decoration of these gatehouses, built on a huge and elaborate scale as symbols of affluence and power, sometimes hint at the arrival of Renaissance influence arriving here from the Continent. An example is Layer Marney Towers in Essex; it is the gatehouse of a proposed

Plan and elevation of a typical late-medieval manor
house showing the disposition of parts.

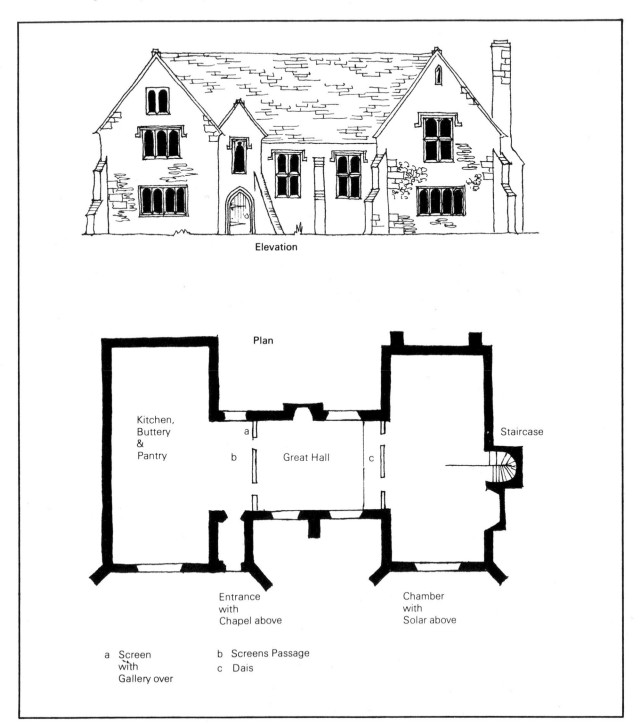

Elevation

Plan

Kitchen,
Buttery
&
Pantry

a

b   Great Hall   c

Staircase

Entrance
with
Chapel above

Chamber
with
Solar above

a   Screen   b   Screens Passage
    with   c   Dais
    Gallery over

The elaborate sky-line of Barrington Court, Somerset.

house that never materialised. This brings us to about 1520, a date which coincides with the first use of terracotta work in a foreign manner, under the influence of the European Renaissance.

It is often said that King Henry VIII and his Chancellor Wolsey first came face to face with this movement of classical revival, at their meeting with Francis I of France on the Field of the Cloth of Gold in 1520. But this is an oversimplification. At about that time, however, broad, though largely superficial, elements of it could be seen in architecture, some coming from Italy, more from Holland. The most singular early example was the country house that Cardinal Wolsey began to build himself at Hampton Court in 1515, which from 1525 onwards Henry VIII turned into a palace. Here was an early instance of a house consciously designed as a grandiose piece of architecture, no longer, like the last of the castles, demonstrating armed might, but a symbol of the new wealth, the arts and culture.

The Renaissance element was, however, largely confined to ornament, and such things as fireplaces.

Chimneys, too, became ostentatiously elaborate, as can be seen at Barrington Court in Somerset. The most frequently visited houses of this period are those of moderately large size built by those who prospered under the Tudor system, which, it will be remembered, included the redistribution of the wealth and lands of the monastic orders. The Tudor structure is usually the central or main body of the building, with later additions and alterations such as modernised windows. The eastern block of Barrington is a good early example, and this type of house is a development of the late medieval style with a greater number of rooms and two floors connected by a much more substantial stairway. The plan has one long side with projecting wings at each end and probably an entrance porch between them. The width throughout is about 15 feet, the length of the beams available. The windows are not large. Internally, the wall panelling consists of small panels, mostly of oak or other native timbers. The chimneys, at first rather heavy and elaborate, became in Elizabethan and Jacobean times slender

The entrance front of Hardwick Hall, Derbyshire.

or with simpler, more elegant decoration. These are distinguishing features of the Tudor and Jacobean periods.

Larger, but on the same general plan, is the Elizabethan Montacute House. (We now see the house back to front, the original entrance being through the central projection on the south front facing the courtyard with its pavilions.) Here the design is more highly refined and stylish; the delightful curved gable ends are typical of those just coming into fashion. The end wings project on both sides of the house. At Montacute, too, there is another remarkable feature, typical of the period – the long gallery in the upper storey. The screen through which one enters the hall is massive and heavily ornamented. Such houses were built by the successful men whose ambition wisely did not vault so high that it o'erleapt itself and royal displeasure. This power-seeking class built itself what Sir John Summerson called the 'prodigy house' of Elizabethan I's reign. Few of these now remain intact; several have additions or replacements. Examples

are Longleat in Wiltshire, Burghley House in Lincolnshire, and the rather less grand Burton Agnes Hall in Yorkshire. The most startling and best known is the amazing Hardwick Hall begun in 1590. The first impression is conveyed in the well known and justified jingle:

'Hardwick Hall, more glass than wall.'

This comment is one indication of the rapid improvement in the materials available during the Tudor period, and indeed, of structural methods. (The windows are also a feature at Burton Agnes.) The next point one notices is that the hitherto typical E-shape (which, incidentally, has nothing to do with the Virgin Queen's initial) is abandoned. The plan shows the main body of the house to be contained within a rectangle, the long sides of which are identical with tower-like wings projecting at right angles; the main projecting wings, again identical, are at each end. So it is that on all four sides there are batteries of windows, from which one can look out in every direction.

Another change is that the whole centre of the

Melford Hall, Suffolk: the lodge gateway and garden pavilion, with the turrets of the house beyond.

house is filled by the hall. The screen is now no more than a partition dividing it from the entrance. There is no dais. There are several stairways. Decoration is lavish—not perhaps refined—and includes motifs originating on the Continent. The designer of Hardwick was probably one of a remarkable and progressive family, the Smythsons.

These grandiose houses continued to develop during the reign of James I. Unlike the older houses, they were prominently situated, uninhibited and ostentatious cynosures. For the first time their settings were designed as complementary to the house. Not until Elizabeth I's reign was much attention paid to gardening. With our increased trade, and increasingly close connections with North America, many new trees, shrubs and plants were introduced from abroad. It became the fashion to grow them. (On the stairway at Hatfield is a carved figure that is almost certainly John Tradescant, a pioneer both of horticulture and foreign travel in search of new plants.) The gardens surrounding these houses were often designed by the same men that designed the buildings. They consisted of interlinked courtyards with fountains, pavilions (those at Montacute still remain), walks lined with trees, beds of plants and orchards of fruit trees. The latter were also trained against the tall walls that invariably surrounded these gardens. (Those surrounding Melford Hall in Suffolk remain, including an

octagonal two-storeyed pavilion with, however, modernised windows.)

Magnificent though these enterprising and occasionally palatial country houses are, it is undeniable that they are often ostentatious to the point of vulgarity, and crude in detail. Possibly this is because Renaissance motifs were only half understood by the unsophisticated English craftsmen, and therefore tended to be misapplied.

Sir William Brereton travelling in Scotland during 1635 comments on the poverty and roughness of life then, though he records that from Dunbar to Edinburgh he 'passed very many stately seats of the nobles'. Apart from inevitable crudity, Scottish architecture at this period was, and had long been, different from that south of the border. The Renaissance had scarcely penetrated the country; a rare example of its influence can be seen at Falkland Palace.

The most distinctive early phase came when Mary, after the death of her husband, Francis II of France, returned to take her troubled place as Queen of the Scots in 1561. Her pronounced taste for things French is reflected in those tall castle-like structures, often heavily and fancifully be-towered and be-turretted, quite unlike anything outside Scotland.

The Renaissance

The beginning of the Renaissance in Italy is conveniently if not very soundly dated 1453. In this

Melford Hall: the Early Renaissance porch.

year the remains of the classical Empire at Constantinople were dispersed after the destruction of the city by the Turks. Those that escaped sought refuge in Italy. But it is obvious that this event alone could not have revitalised intellectual and aesthetic life in Italy, although, with the invention of the printing press, information could be disseminated with a new and dramatic ease.

During the intervening years, the Gothic style of architecture, so very different from that described by Vitruvius, had become dominant. An early Italian Renaissance study, largely looking back to classical times, was Leone Battista Alberti's of 1485. The next important publication was Andrea Palladio's *I Quattro Libri dell' Architettura* of 1570. As well as looking back to Vitruvius, and describing the writer's own work, it was a study of the remains of Roman buildings. While, as we have seen, certain superficial elements from this classical repertoire had been taken up by our elaborate Elizabethans, the style's calmness and simplicity and very strict attention to rules of proportion was lost upon them.

The first English architect fully to understand the classical orders was Inigo Jones, who travelled and studied in Europe at a time when such journeys were still unusual and even dangerous. (It is interesting to note that he was born in 1573 and might be classed as belonging to the Elizabethan period from which his work differs so fundamentally.)

Jones successfully adapted Italian Renaissance architecture to English requirements and was concerned to make his buildings works of art independent of their function: he was to go down in history as the first of our Palladians. An essential characteristic of Palladianism is the correct relationship of the proportions of the component parts of a building one to another (as in classical architecture). To achieve this, he ignored the principles of earlier houses, however grand, whose design was largely conditioned by the lengths of timber available.

To describe his methods in simple terms, he therefore designed his buildings as rectangles – so different from the prevailing 'E' and 'H' shapes. His roofs were flat-topped, usually lit by a lantern in a cupola; this was an anglicised version of the low-pitched Italian roof. The chimneys no longer straggled over the roof, but were grouped together in blocks as part of the design. Internally, the hall was no longer a living room, but an entrance room and a means of access to passageways and other rooms; its height reached to the top of the house and in it was the stairway, now promoted to a magnificent feature. It is worth noting that his windows consisted of a single stone mullion and transom. These were later replaced (since their proportions were suitable) by the sash window, which came into use about 1685. He also used the Venetian window.

23

A good deal of doubt exists about the correctness of attributing certain country houses to Jones. One of the finest country houses of this period, Coleshill in Berkshire (destroyed by fire), long attributed to Jones, was in fact by Sir Roger Pratt. He was concerned with Stoke Bruerne Park, which was intended to have a central block connected with pavilions by colonnades. The main building was never completed, but the pavilions remain, and provide the earliest example of this type of plan which later became widely used. His best known country house is Wilton, where he rebuilt the Tudor garden front and the rooms within it after a fire. His famous 'double-cube' room is also at Wilton. Associated with Jones was his pupil, assistant and relative by marriage, John Webb, who after his master's death, carried on in the same style.

During the Civil War, the increasing rate of country-house building abated considerably, but accelerated again after the Restoration. Charles II and his court returned from exile considerably influenced by their stay on the Continent. This was particularly true of several architects who had been in Holland and studied the Dutch form of Palladianism. Hugh May was the most prominent of these, though he carried out little work. The most

important feature of this movement was that it followed the Dutch example of using brick (instead of stone) which, as we can still see today, was particularly suited to English architecture. It was to set the general style of the moderate-sized English style for generations, traditionally known as 'Wren'. That great man, however, was scarcely concerned with building country houses; he worked on a vaster scale than any English architect before or probably since. He gave us St Paul's Cathedral, the magnificent additions to Hampton Court, university colleges, Greenwich, and the City churches. His great importance from the point of view of the develop-

ment of the country house was that he built up a team of superb craftsmen, that hints of Baroque magnificence appeared in his work, and that his assistant Nicholas Hawksmoor was later to make an important contribution in this field of architecture.

Among younger contemporaries of Wren to concern themselves with country houses, two are outstanding. The first, William Talman, was an original imaginative architect who worked in a grand manner; this is well displayed in the south front of Chatsworth (Derbyshire) and the east front of Dyrham (Gloucestershire). The other was William Winde, who was influenced by his Dutch

Ashdown House, Berkshire, and its pavilions from the east, c.1664.

upbringing. Soldier and designer of fortifications, he designed Combe Abbey (Warwickshire), possibly Belton (Lincolnshire), and very doubtfully, Ashdown House, which stands, tall and exciting, in isolation on the Berkshire Downs.

In Scotland and Ireland country house architecture was generally still undistinguished and still followed the traditional vernacular. After the Restoration, Sir Robert Bruce, in addition to official work, designed a number of country houses in the classical style, particularly his own, the hand-some Kinross House, beside Lochleven, begun in 1685. There was as yet no hint of the later importance of Scots architects, though before Kinross was finished, the first of the Adams (William) had been born. Soon Scottish houses rivalled the English.

It is possible at this stage to summarise the principal features in the design of our domestic architecture as it developed during the late 17th and well on into the 18th century:

1. The use of hipped roofs instead of gables.
2. The strongly marked horizontal cornice line

The entrance front of Belton House, Lincolnshire.

right round the building.

3. The reduction in the width of window openings and the general use of sash windows.

4. The use of dormer windows in the roof.

5. The considerable use of the classical orders, now carefully designed, not structurally but as applied decoration.

6. The refined form of mouldings, for example, on cornices and on the architraves of doors and windows.

7. A marked improvement in the quality, style and detail of plasterwork, carving, sculpture and other decorative work.

8. As water supplies and plumbing improved, houses were built more and more in elevated situations.

At this period, too, with the increasing number of books on architecture available, including some of the 'do it yourself' type, there was probably a growth in the number of houses designed and built by discerning amateurs making use of the skilled craftsmen then available.

Duncombe Park, Yorkshire: the west entrance front by
William Wakefield, c.1713.

It is important to consider the setting of the house
of this period. Even before the return of Charles II,
French gardeners were working here in the style
brought to such perfection in France by Le Nôtre
(1613-1700). Later, the partnership of George
London and Henry Wise from 1689 (probably
earlier) until the former's death in 1713, mono-
polised the design of noblemen's gardens. They
carried on the French manner of elaborate formality,
closely related to the house. Their gardens were
often of great size, and the area of canals, ornate
parterres and fountains provided a striking and
majestic setting for the houses. Within a few decades the English landscape movement swept all of

this away. Thus it is, alas, that we now see none of
the great mansions of the 17th and early 18th
centuries in their proper settings.

English Baroque

The straightforwardness of the houses associated
with the age of Wren was shortly to be shattered
when Sir John Vanbrugh, soldier and witty play-
wright, 'turned suddenly to architecture'. In 1699
he began work on Castle Howard, as massive and
heavily dramatic as his plays were airy. Baroque is
associated with the swirling vigour of Michelangelo
and the architects Giovanni Bernini (1589-1680)
and Francesco Borromini (1599-1667). Wren had
in fact met Bernini in Paris but learned little from

clearly demonstrated if we walk round the buildings and look at the west front from the point where a giant boar stands on a pedestal. This façade was designed by a member of the family, Sir Thomas Robinson, and begun in 1753. It was acknowledged to be 'correct' in its details, but today we see it as entirely devoid of genius. As Robert Adam said, Vanbrugh's work had 'movement, novelty and ingenuity.' To which might be added that it was on several occasions on a scale unusual in Britain.

The only other principal exponent of the Baroque in England was Thomas Archer. Like Vanbrugh he was a gentleman turned architect. He had, however, visited Italy and studied the style on the spot. His best known examples of country house work are the temple-like buildings with his typical curved dome. One is at Chatsworth sheltering the rise of the rushing waters of the cataract and another at Wrest Park, which faces a strongly contrasted calm canal.

This great and vigorous period of design did not last long. Vanbrugh and Archer had no successors though there are some smaller houses in a similar style by unnamed architects, particularly in the West of England. An example is Frampton Court.

Even today many still dislike the fertility of Vanbrugh's imagination and that of his for long underrated colleague Hawksmoor, recalling with reservation Abel Evan's satirical epitaph:

Under this stone, Reader, survey
Dead Sir John Vanbrugh's house of clay.
Lie heavy on him, Earth! for he
Laid many heavy loads on thee!
What glorious loads they were!

The New Palladians

The Vanbrugian era collapsed with surprising suddenness after Sir John's death. The pendulum swung to the other extreme, to the use and strict application of the Vitruvian rules and proportions as found in the works of Palladio, and originally sought out and brought to this country by Inigo Jones in the reign of Charles I. Since then, there had been a big social change. Whereas Jones's journeys had been exceptional and daring, when the rich young Earl

him, though he was interested in the new style. So was Nicholas Hawksmoor (1661–1736) who had studied earlier Italian architecture as well.

But the great inspirer of English Baroque was Vanbrugh at Castle Howard, with the help of the learned and imaginative Hawksmoor as his assistant. This great house is a work of immense imagination, both inside and out; like other Vanbrugh masterpieces, such as Blenheim Palace (rather more of a giant country house than a palace) and Seaton Delaval, it has little resemblance to other British buildings. The architectural elements are often incongruous, both designed and assembled so that they break the rules. At Castle Howard, this is of Burlington visited Italy in 1714-15, just before he was 21, it was as part of the Grand Tour now a routine among the aristocracy. It was largely because of this visit and others later (during which he met the English architect and designer William Kent, whom he brought home and established in England in 1719), that the doctrines of Palladio became *de rigeur* among British architects, or more importantly, among the leaders of taste and patronage. Of these, the powerful Burlington, a talented amateur architect himself, was predominant.

But Burlington did not originate this strangely reactionary yet progressive movement. He was influenced by the shadowy but important Scot, Colen Campbell, who studied in Italy and in 1714 produced the first volume of 100 engravings in his *Vitruvius Britannicus* devoted to British houses in the classical style. Campbell was actually employed by the Earl to alter Burlington House. At the same time a new translation of Palladio's works was published with engravings redrawn after the master by the Italian Leoni. Later, Burlington himself became a skilled architect—as did William Kent, who at first fancied himself a great painter, which he was not, rather than the master of design which he was.

It is amusing to note that this movement was well under way while Vanbrugh and Hawksmoor were still demonstrating their dramatic and lavish magnificance, of which the Burlingtonians icily disapproved. Indeed, if we try to analyse the success of the new style, well exemplified by Campbell's Mereworth and Kent's Holkham, we see in them the elements of the cool restraint—at least externally—that is allegedly a characteristic of the English. Both have typical but not invariable features of the period—for example, outbuildings placed symmetrically on either side of the main block, four at Holkham linked to it, two at Mereworth (added later) and separate from it. In many examples, colonnades join the outliers to the central unit. This dominating block is usually entered by a massive, pedimented portico. The windows, designed according to the rules, were placed with emphasised regularity. Inside all was different. The richness of the interiors in Mereworth, and the effect of the heavy sumptuousness of Kent's entrance hall inside the rather bleak exterior of Holkham can scarcely be appreciated except by experiencing them.

The Burlington Palladian (which is well represented by some good examples in Ireland) lasted in Scotland for two generations, but it did not entirely dominate our country houses. The Scot, James Gibbs, was working at the same time in an individual Baroque manner, whose style is exemplified well enough by his church of St Martin-in-the-Fields.

At about this time, the number of 'do it yourself' books increased. Batty Langley, a prolific writer of such works on gardening and fruit-growing, as well as architecture, published one in about 1740 which has the very descriptive title *The Builder's Director or Bench-Mate being a Pocket-Treasury of the Grecian, Roman and Gothic Orders of Architecture Made easy to the meanest Capacity by near 500 examples.*—engraved on 184 copper plates. In 1756 came the more consequential *A Complete Book of Architecture* by Isaac Ware, a practising architect.

The incongruity of English taste is particularly well illustrated at this period. The last of the great garden designers in the formal style of Le Nôtre, evolved in turn from the architectural gardens of the Italian Renaissance, was Henry Wise. The Classical architectural style in which he worked was more or less appropriate to the Palladian villa. But at the time of his death in 1738, the informal, naturalistic landscape gardens pioneered by William Kent had eclipsed formality. Within a few decades, garden designers such as 'Capability' Brown had largely obliterated the type of garden that was appropriate to any building in the Italian or French classical manner.

Barons, Greeks, Mandarins and Onwards

The reader will have noticed that since the days of Inigo Jones our architects have all sought inspiration in the past. The Burlingtonians looked behind them to Rome via Palladio, and it was in 1753, the year of his death, that Horace Walpole used the

Frampton Court, Gloucestershire: the arched chimneys may derive from Vanbrugh's at King's Weston.

below. Lord Burlington's *casino*: the portico and south front of Chiswick House, Middlesex.

Garden Gothick: the pavilion at Frampton Court,
possibly designed by William Halfpenny, *c*.1740.

often quoted phrase when writing to his friend, 'It has the true rust of the Barons' Wars'. The English had, however, always enjoyed taking a romantic retrospective look at the days of chivalry, even when they were relatively close, as when Spenser wrote his *Faerie Queene*. And at this point, a whimsical form of medievalism (today commonly called Gothick to distinguish it from the real thing) infected architecture. Walpole's Strawberry Hill and Sanderson Miller's Lacock Abbey and the sham ruin at Hagley are examples of this architectural diversion.

At this period, too, other novel influences were brought to bear on our architecture by students of antiquity, who travelling abroad off the beaten track came back with carefully studied drawings. Robert Wood and his colleagues went to Syria and in 1753 published *The Ruins of Palmyra* in 1751 and in 1757 *The Ruins of Balbec*. James Stuart and Nicholas Revett were in Greece from 1751-55 but their *Antiquitia of Athens* did not come out until 1762, by which time Stuart had built the first Greek Doric revival building at Hagley in Worcestershire. Other distinguished architects went travelling and studying, notably Robert Adam, William Chambers, and Robert Mylne.

In 1762 the philosopher Lord Kames wrote, 'judging by numbers, the Gothic taste of architecture must be preferred to that of Greece, and the Chinese taste before that of either'. Chinoiserie, never of great consequence in our architecture though long a feature of decoration, brings us back to Chambers whose pagoda in Kew Gardens, raising its angular form appropriately among strange, exotic trees, is our best known example of 'Chinese' architecture. He was the only English architect to have studied architecture in China, though his remarkable book on Chinese gardening was largely a leg-pull. He was an authoritative character, a founder of the Royal Academy and Royal Architect. In spite of his Chinese adventures, his architecture was classical in origins and displays his genius for faultless detail and masterly design of such important adjuncts of architecture as stairways.

He and his rival Robert Adam (assisted by James) dominated architecture during the 1750s and 60s. The Adam style was, above all, elegant. This applies particularly to the interiors, in which he used subtle colour schemes to pick out the delicate work of his craftsmen – something of a novelty. His enemies, however, described this practice as 'ginger-bread' and 'embroidery'. His use and adaptation of a wealth of classical detail was quite amazing, as was his fertile imagination in designing all sorts of furniture, musical instruments and a variety of domestic articles.

Typical of the generation following Chambers and the Adam brothers were Henry Holland and James Wyatt, both of whom lived into the 19th century. Both produced handsome, quite simple dignified buildings in styles developed from Greece and Rome. Both produced architectural fantasies; Holland the Chinese dairy at Woburn, Wyatt the crazy Gothick Fonthill for Beckford, whose enormous, absurd tower collapsed. Architecture was showing signs of coming adrift from the great classical traditions that had stabilised it for so long.

At this stage another entertaining symptom of the mixture of ideas and ideals that was afflicting architecture may be mentioned, though it did not come into full effect until the first half of the next century. In 1774 a rich and clever dilettante, Richard Payne Knight, began building a castle; Downtown Castle was not like the earlier castellated buildings in Gothick, but an imitation of the real thing – a massive fortress. Amusingly, the interior was decorated in a Grecian manner. It was the forerunner of many that were to weigh down the countryside for the next century – some, such as Penrhyn, Arundel and Cardiff, rising from genuine remains and many others newly built in the now peaceful countryside.

But before we advance into the varied and chaotic era of Queen Victoria, Sir John Soane, who appropriately died in the year of her coronation, must be fitted in. His calm and cool work is both distinctive and imaginative, with a pronounced emphasis on planes rather than masses.

Sir William Chambers' chinoiserie: the Pagoda in Kew Gardens.

Fonthill Abbey, Wiltshire, by James Wyatt, 1795-1807 (demolished).

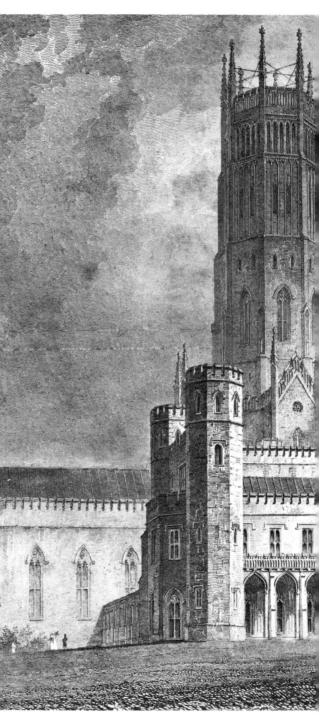

James Stuart: the Doric Temple at Hagley Hall, Worcestershire, 1758.

Sezincote, Gloucestershire, by S. P. Cockerell, 1803.

The Nineteenth Century

The origins of the movement known as Picturesque is conveniently attributed to Payne Knight with his castle, and to Uvedale Price his Herefordshire neighbour, the former dying in 1824 and the latter in 1829. This epithet may well apply to the making of landscapes, but it is an exaggeration so far as architecture is concerned. The beginning of the century saw the coming of a largely irresponsible eclecticism brought about by the profusion of architectural literature. You could now build your country mansion in any style that suited you – particularly if you were one of the many *nouveaux riches* who had done well out of the Napoleonic wars. The capable and industrious Sir Robert Smirke, for example, turned out the delightful more or less Grecian Haffield in 1818 within a

couple of miles of his Norman Castle at Eastnor begun in 1812. This wide range of styles was particularly applied to those smaller buildings associated with the country house, in which styles ranging from the Grecian through the thatched Elizabethan, Polish and Norwegian to the Hindoo, or even that of a Chinese mandarin might be employed. The most *outré* of the large houses still standing is the Indian Sezincote built by S. P. Cockerell at the beginning of the century. The maestro of this period, however, was John Nash, the architect of the Royal Pavilion at Brighton who was appointed Surveyor-General by the Prince

Regent in 1813 and became the planner of 'Regency' London.

We do not associate the Victorian age with the type of country house that we usually visit, but the prosperous manufacturers were now leaving the proximity of their satanic mills beside which they and their families had long dwelled, and were taking upon themselves the role of country gentlemen. Lady Mary Fox in 1843 published *The Country House* (with designs), which was clearly contrived to inform those who had not been brought up in one. For the benefit of the wives and daughters of such, Mrs Loudon was impelled to publish in 1845 *The Lady's Country Companion, or How to Enjoy a Country Life Rationally*.

Sir Charles Barry dropped the gothic style of his Houses of Parliament and made many a stately home statelier by re-fronting it and adding elaborate terracing in the Italian palazzo manner – of which there is no finer example than Harewood House near Leeds. Even more overwhelming was Anthony Salvin, whose massive buildings are so huge that most have inevitably become institutions, though we can pass through the still private portals of his Tudoresque Thoresby Hall of 1864. Even more remarkable is the Rothschild country house fantasy of Waddesdon Manor, begun in the late 1870s, in which Hippolyte Alexandre Destailleur incorporated, for example, towers based on Chambord and a staircase inspired by that at Blois.

A great deal more self-control and sensitivity returned towards the end of the century in the work of Norman Shaw. C. F. A. Voysey (1857-1941) brought a new simplicity and charm to a number of country houses that he designed. Among other architects who steered their way out of the gas-lit glories of Victorianism were M. H. Baillie Scott (1865-1945), Sir Guy Dawber (1869-1944) and the remarkable C. R. Mackintosh (1868-1928), the first British architect to influence, rather than draw inspiration from, the Continent. Finally, British country house architecture in the grand tradition blazed up for the last time in the work of Sir Edwin Lutyens (1869-1944).

The Royal Pavilion at Brighton by John Nash.

below. Thoresby Hall, Nottinghamshire, by Anthony Salvin.

Building Materials

Alec Clifton-Taylor

opposite. Cheshire 'Black and White':
Little Moreton Hall.

Until the Industrial Revolution the factor which determined a house's material was usually transport. Labour was cheap; materials too were relatively inexpensive, provided that one used those that were available locally. As soon as some material was wanted which had to be brought from a distance, up went the costs; for before the construction of the railways and the improvement of the roads the only easy method of transporting heavy materials was by water, and by no means everyone lived close to the coast or a navigable river.

The most common materials, not only in the Middle Ages but over much of England until the 17th century and in some places until even later, were unfired clay and wood. Mud was a normal material for cottage building in country districts, and many more mud houses survive than is generally realised. External rendering and often a $4\frac{1}{2}$ inch facing of brick, as well as internal plastering and sometimes wallpapering, disguise the material so effectively that even the inhabitants of mud-constructed buildings are sometimes unaware of the fact. Cob, the term current in the South West, especially in Dorset and Devon, sounds more respectable, but is really only another name for mud. Even so charming a place such as Milton Abbas in Dorset, a model village dating only from the second half of the 18th century, is built almost entirely of this material. The wet clay had to contain enough lime to ensure that, as it dried, it set firmly; chopped straw was commonly added as a binder, and sometimes cow-dung, or perhaps some gravel and sand; the mix varied according to the character of the clay. As long as a mud wall has a good plinth of stone or brick as a precaution against rising damp, and a broad coping to throw off the rainwater, it will last for centuries, and may even become harder with age.

Up to the time of the Tudors almost the whole country was so well wooded that timber was the other obvious material for house building. Entirely wooden houses would seem never to have been popular here; the usual practice was to use wood in conjunction with clay. The timber provided the strong skeleton of the house, including the rafters of the roof; wood, in the form first of wattles (preferably of willow, ash or hazel, for the sticks had to be pliable) and later of laths (for which rent oak or beech were the favourites), was also used as a base for the infilling between the beams or 'studs'. But these cannot normally be seen; the wattles were covered with mud ('daub'), the laths with lime-plaster (the modern replacements of which often contain too much cement to look pleasant). In the 17th century it became usual, at least in East Anglia, to render the entire building so that the timber frame also became invisible; thus some attention may now be required to recognise a timber-framed building in this part of England, except of course where the upper storey overhangs, which gives the game away at once.

Socially, timber-framing was always far more respectable than mud. In Worcestershire, Herefordshire, Shropshire, Cheshire and Lancashire very large houses, such as Speke and Bramall and Pitchford Halls, were often of this type, and it is evident that half-timbering was frequently the preferred material, because all these counties had plenty of stone. To use stone would certainly have cost more, but it seems doubtful whether this was the primary consideration; a building, such as Little Moreton Hall, Cheshire or Grange House at Leominster, lavishly adorned with crude but lively carvings, suggests that the attraction of wood in these least sophisticated counties of Elizabethan and early Stuart England was an expression of the natural preference of every society of *nouveaux riches* for unrestrained, exuberant display. In East Anglia and the South East, as is to be expected, wood was used with greater restraint and more refinement, both of taste and craftsmanship. Moreover, from about the middle of the 16th century, it was not quite so readily available everywhere as in the West; nevertheless many admirable timber-framed buildings of the Tudor period still survive in this part of the country, all the better, it may be felt, for not being 'black and white'. This, moreover, was the region where in the later 18th and early 19th centuries weather-boarding became so popular for cottages, farm-buildings and barns, and although by this time the wood itself was usually imported, these fully timbered buildings make a delightful and quite distinctive contribution to many country views in eastern and south-eastern counties.

But whereas in the country districts of, say, New England or Scandinavia one may travel for miles and scarcely see a single house not constructed of wood, England is today primarily a country of brick houses, with a powerful admixture of stone in a good many areas. Few if any countries possess a richer variety of good building stones, and the very complexity of the English geological pattern has brought immense benefits to the art of architecture. As we move about the country the colours and textures of the traditional building materials, brick as well as stone, are continually changing, sometimes quite abruptly even in the course of a journey of no more than five miles. And so distinctive is the vernacular architecture of the different regions that anyone who knows England well, given a bunch of architectural photographs, will have little difficulty in pinpointing them geographically as well as historically.

The king of English building materials is undoubtedly limestone. There are many limestones, of very different geological ages: the principal groups are the chalky limestones, the Jurassic (oolite and lias), the Magnesian, the Carboniferous and the Devonian. Of these it is the oolites that have made the supreme contribution. On the great ogee curve of oolitic limestone, stretching almost continuously from Portland Bill through the Cotswolds, Northamptonshire, Rutland and Lincolnshire to the Cleveland Hills, are situated many of England's most famous quarries: Portland, Doulting, Bath, Taynton, Weldon, Ketton, Barnack, Clipsham and Ancaster, to mention only some of them, with Purbeck and Chilmark as outliers. All these have yielded a magnificent inheritance, to be seen not only in splendid individual houses such as Dyrham Park and Daneway House but in whole towns like Chipping Camden and Burford and above all Bath

and Stamford. The colours range from the near-white of Portland stone, the best of all for use in combination with red brick, to the pale buffs and browns and honey yellows of many of the Cotswold stones; the textures vary from tweedy-looking rubblestone to the smoothest, most urbane ashlar.

The liassic limestones are often heavily impregnated with iron, which accounts for the deep golden browns that suffuse the Banbury district—where Broughton Castle is a specially lovely example—and much of the Somerset-Dorset border. In and around Sherborne, and west of Yeovil, the Ham Hill stone is captivating: Sandford Orcas or Montacute are gems among many. One of the special virtues of all these Jurassic limestones is that they lend themselves to a high degree of finish in the dressings. Cornices, copings, string-courses, buttress set-offs, door and window architraves, chimney-stacks, balustrades, finials, gate-piers: all are finely carved and usually excellently preserved even after several hundred years. Houses built of these stones were able to achieve a degree of refinement seldom possible elsewhere.

The other limestones tend mostly to be grey or white, and vary very much in durability. The Cretaceous group includes buildings such as Ashdown House in Berkshire which are actually built of chalk, but the chief limestone is that brittle, coarse-textured, long used yet decidedly treacherous stone Kentish Rag, of which Knole provides an excellent example. Cretacious limestones belong to the South East; Magnesian, well represented by Howsham Hall in Yorkshire, to the North East. The Carboniferous group embraces the rough mountain limestones of the Derbyshire Peak District and the Pennines, which are not usually much associated with country house architecture but can be seen to excellent effect at Haddon Hall; the even more ancient Devonian limestone is much in evidence in south Devon.

The sandstones play a major part in the visual picture of England, with a still wider range of colours than the limestones. The most useful, and

Cotswold limestone: Talman's east front of Dyrham Park, Gloucestershire, 1700-03.

below. Broughton Castle, Oxfordshire: Elizabethan mansion of iron-impregnated liassic limestone.

Shropshire sandstone: Attingham Park by George Steuart.

the most widely used but by no means the most beautiful, belong to the Carboniferous series. In the industrial North millstone grit and the sandstones from the Coal Measures play a role of capital importance, for although under unfavourable conditions they may turn jet-black, no limestones, not even Portland, will stand up as well to a smoke-polluted atmosphere. They were often quarried in enormous blocks, which produce effects of monumental strength and dignity. Old Red sandstones are virtually confined to Herefordshire, Devonian to the South West. New Red (Triassic) sandstones, often not red, are widely distributed but are specially characteristic of the west and north-west Midlands; some have weathered badly and given a great deal of trouble, but the best, such as the Hollington stone of Staffordshire or the Grinshill stone of Shropshire well seen at Attingham Park, are excellent. Both these have 'red' and 'white' quarries within a few hundred yards of each other; the 'red' varies from purplish pink to chocolate brown, the 'white' from pale buff to light grey, here and there with a distinctly greenish tinge. The subtle colour variations, sometimes within the compass of a single wall, are a recurrent delight in the sandstone areas.

Of the geologically younger sandstones, the Jurassic is mainly to be found in Yorkshire; Castle Howard, built like so many great houses with stone found on its own estate, is a fine example. The Cretaceous sandstones appear prominently among the country houses of the South East; they include the greensand stones formerly quarried on the fringes of the Lincolnshire Wolds, at the base of the North Downs and along the south coast of the Isle of Wight, the 'gingerbread stone' (carstone) of north-west Norfolk and, best of this group, the beautiful Wealden stone of Sussex and Kent, well represented at Wakehurst Place, Ardingly.

Some of these limestones and sandstones are fissile enough to be split into comparatively thin pieces, which were once widely in demand for roofs. New stone roofing slates are now difficult, although still not impossible, to obtain, but happily

millions have survived in the stone districts, and these roofs, the sizes of the slates graduated with much artistry from eaves to ridge, are a source of never-ending pleasure. (The terminology is unfortunate, for stone slates have of course no geological connection with slate.)

England has no true marbles, and this is no cause for regret, as churchyards and cemeteries filled with the products of Italian quarries imported since the Victorian period amply demonstrate. Such staring whites, not always enjoyable even in Italy, are quite out of tone with our native stones and demand much brighter light than prevails here. Coloured marbles would be equally inappropriate. The semi-marbles, as limestones are sometimes called when they can be given a polish, are only suitable for internal use: out of doors the polish speedily disappears.

Apart from the limestones and sandstones, the principal stones used for English buildings are granite, slate and flint. Slate, much of it coming from Wales, has been used on a very wide scale for roofs, for which it is specially suitable where a low pitch is required, as it often was during the Georgian period. But roofs apart, granite and slate are only to be seen in a few areas where other less intractable materials are absent. Granite has been used extensively in Devon and especially Cornwall; it dictates its own forms—gritty, grainy, sparing in ornamentation but magnificently durable. Occasional granite houses may also be found on the fringes of the Lake District and of the Charnwood Forest in Leicestershire. Slate-stone occurs in much the same areas; Lake District slate, ranging from green to bluish-grey, is still an important and beautiful building stone.

Flint, which is always found in association with chalk, is a product of East Anglia and the South East, where it long remained a normal material not only for cottages but also for churches; large houses built of flint, like Goodwood, can be seen too, here and there, but for major buildings it was aesthetically more satisfactory to use it in combination with limestone. Stockton House in Wiltshire provides an attractive instance of dressed stone (Chilmark oolite) and knapped flints arranged both in bands and in chequer patterns.

With such splendid resources in stone and wood, it seems hardly fair that England should have reeds that make the best thatch of any, and clays that provide the raw materials for some of the world's most beautiful bricks: yet it is indeed so. Brick-making until the Tudor period was virtually confined to East Anglia and the region around the Humber, but with its use on a lavish scale for the royal palace of Richmond after the fire of 1497, and soon afterwards for Hampton Court, brick became fashionable. During the following hundred years or so some of England's grandest houses, from Nonsuch and Hengrave to Burton Agnes, Hatfield, Bramshill and Blickling were mainly constructed of this material. The bricks were small ($9 \times 4\frac{1}{2} \times 2\frac{1}{4}$ inches on an average) and somewhat roughly made, with wide mortar joints, but although opportunities for ornamentation were naturally much more restricted than in stone, effects of considerable virtuosity were sometimes achieved, especially in the design and construction of chimney-stacks. Bricks at this time were almost always red (the 'white' bricks of Hengrave are a notable but rare exception), and few materials are more enjoyable than the mellow brickwork of a Tudor or a Jacobean house.

After the Restoration the arrival of more classical ideals brought with it a demand for bricks that were slightly thicker ($2\frac{1}{2}$ inches), more carefully fashioned and more uniform in colour. These requirements the brickmakers appear to have met with ease, to be followed before long by the manufacture of specially soft, rich red bricks that could be rubbed smooth to yield a very fine joint, or even be carved into swags of fruit and flowers, masks and putti. English brickwork in the first half of the 18th century is perhaps the finest known; not only many individual houses but whole towns, like Farnham or Blandford, still bear witness to its quality.

Despite these triumphs of craftsmanship the Georgian aristocrat usually yearned for stone, a material in which one can undeniably be grander.

Even quite a small house in ashlared stone has 'presence', whereas the essential quality of brickwork, with its small mesh and avoidance, as a rule, of elaborate ornamentation, is intimacy. Thus many Georgian brick houses were carefully faced, at great expense, with stone; and if stone cost too much hard stucco could be employed as a substitute. In the reign of George III red brick was specially out of favour with the aristocracy; browns and yellows were more acceptable, and best of all were the silver-greys, as at Donnington Grove near Newbury. But lower down the social scale red brick was becoming far more widely used than any other building material, and in the 19th century it was even to invade and conquer some of the stone areas.

The arrival of cheap transport encouraged the use of mass-produced materials wherever one might be building. The result was that a large part of the population was better housed, in material terms, than ever before. Nevertheless these social improvements were only attained at appalling cost artistically. Brick, often of miserable colour and quality, thrust its way into stone towns, while in the countryside stone slates and thatch all too often yielded place to bright red tiles and corrugated iron. Higher up the social scale architects liked to incorporate a pot-pourri of materials on the elevations of a single building, usually with distressing results. The principle of the *genius loci*, to which for generations the English scene had owed so much, was rudely cast aside.

Very large country houses are now seldom built; but in recent years some of medium size, like Eridge Park in Sussex and Buckminster Hall in Leicestershire, have been erected on the sites of big impracticable houses, often of no great merit, which have been demolished. In other places, such as Arundel and Goodwood, new houses adapted to modern requirements have arisen on estates where the former mansion is now only a show-place for visitors. As for small houses, every year they submerge more country in an ever-spreading flood.

Today the spread of concrete, steel and glass poses new problems. Sited in isolation, provided

Jacobean brickwork: the gatehouse at Burton Agnes, Yorkshire.

only that it does not go too high, a house can virtually make its own rules, and my impression is that some of the most progressive designs are among the best. In a closely built community, however, a house, like any other building, has a responsibility to its neighbours. There are signs that architects are now rather more conscious of the vital aesthetic importance of using the right materials than they were two or three generations ago. The employ-ment of natural materials for cladding is almost always a good move, and some excellent results have been achieved. Westmorland slate in the South has admittedly nothing to do with the *genius loci*, but how greatly preferable it is to naked, rapidly dirtying concrete. Nor need concrete be offensive, for in recent years new aggregates have been evolved that are a pleasure to see. They cost more, but no worthy architecture has ever been born out of cheese-paring. If we cannot build worthily, let us not build at all.

Interior Decoration

Geoffrey Beard

opposite. The entrance hall at Burton Agnes.

When Sir Balthazar Gerbier wrote his book on *The Three Chief Principles of Magnificent Building* in 1662 he was careful to define on his crisp title-page that 'Solidity, Conveniency and Ornament' were what he had in mind. The pursuit of ornament was to lead him, his noble predecessors and successors, into a wild extravagant chase after the great Goddess of Taste, the results of which are to be seen, revered (and in some cases reviled) across the length of the British Isles.

When Henry VIII erected his temporary Banqueting Hall at the Field of the Cloth of Gold in 1520 he was seeking to dazzle Francis I and the French court with a strange, extravagant building soon destined for ruin. What it did, apart from expressing the distilled essence of rivalry and one-upmanship, was to enable a bridge-point to be erected over which foreign decorative influences in all their attractive variety could enter England. The Gothic domination of the medieval church still persisted but both the King and Cardinal Wolsey welcomed the heralds of the Renaissance in the person of sculptors and stuccoists from Italy to work at Westminster Abbey, Hampton Court and Henry's great palace of Nonsuch. Planned by the King and the officers of the King's Works, Nonsuch was described by Camden as 'magnificent to so high a pitch of ostentation, as one would think the whole art of architects were crowded into this simple work'. Its jumble of towers painted the sky in a romantic silhouette, a medley of uncontrolled and exuberant ornament that in truth was far from 'simple'.

Henry started to build Nonsuch in 1538; yet two years earlier he had authorised the destruction of the priceless accumulations of an age of monasticism. Ruin was spread to the great libraries and rich ornaments, and many of the commissioners appointed to survey the process made extensive fortunes. With them they built great houses, such as Longleat, but in an assessment of the building and decoration of this time the vanished houses succeed in leaving the period without precise outline. Severed from Rome by Henry's conduct, England boasted few large houses with all the opportunities their decoration gave to artists. While the external mannerisms of Wollaton and the interior riches in wood, tapestry and plaster of Hardwick pay court to an age which set its fancies on fire and lived in paradises of pleasure, the house was the centre of the family's existence. It indicated wealth and status, it was bargained for in mortgage and marriage settlement, altered and realigned at a patron and surveyor's whim, and painted, carved, and bedecked in a thousand strange and curious ways.

The Jacobean style of the early 17th century was still largely derived from Elizabethan techniques and the influence of the Low Countries. Strapwork and arabesque, cartouche and mythological panel vied for attention with the great wooden screens and carved staircases. This was the time when the great tradition of English connoisseurship was beginning to form. Thomas Howard, Earl of Arundel, was with Inigo Jones pursuing Italianate interests, while the Duke of Buckingham, his rival, and the Earl of Somerset were avidly collecting pictures. Many envoys applied themselves assiduously to enriching their patrons' collections. Pattern and instruction books made their appearance and no gentleman could afford to ignore these and the many new decorative trends. But as with so many movements the emphasis was soon in the hands of the distinguished few. Hatfield House, which Robert Cecil, 1st Earl of Salisbury built between 1608-12, shows the extent to which the patron extended a welcome to foreign, particularly Dutch, artists.

In 1618 Sir Thomas Holte started the building of Aston Hall, Birmingham and four years later Sir Arthur Ingram, Secretary of the Council of the North, created the vast pile of Temple Newsam House, Leeds. In the former there was the interesting departure from a hall with entrance passages and screens to a doorway opening into the centre of the hall. The early 17th-century interior may be seen at its most typical arrangement at Burton Agnes in East Yorkshire. Here the screens, the elaborate carved allegories on the 1610 (dated) overmantel in the state bedroom and a south stair-

47

Elizabethan strapwork: a fireplace at Hardwick Hall.

case with its continuous newel-posts are perhaps more impressive than those at Audley End. The timbered ceilings, possibly the chief glory of medieval England, have surrendered pride of place to the newcomers in plaster, ribbed and compartmented and full of motifs and patterns derived from the emblem books, Bible stories or tales of travel. The long galleries ran their nervous length across one complete front, and entrance porches with their double-clustered Corinthian columns, elaborate pediments and deeply incised stonework tried to emulate the engraved title-pages of folio books. But in London the Surveyor to the Crown, Inigo Jones, was supervising the erection of the new Banqueting House in Whitehall with its close adherence to the proportions set down by Palladio. Here was something entirely imaginative and bold, which was finished eventually in splendid style by the rich ceiling paintings of Rubens. These set the style for decorative painting in England as the building itself was to do a hundred years later for the Palladian architects in the days of George I.

The glories of the reigns of James and Charles I however came tumbling at the Civil Wars, and Charles himself went to the scaffold in 1649. Three years later Jones, who had supported the King at Oxford, died and the Royal Works were reorganised. Styles and moods could hardly ferment into activity at such a time and there is little architecture to speak of in this period. The inscription over the west door of Staunton Harold Church in Leicestershire is indicative of the deep despair that gripped not only the Church but all men of vision and intellect:

'when all things sacred throughout
the nation were either demolished or
prophaned Sir Robert Shirley, Bart.
founded this church whose singular
praise it is, to have done the best
things in the worst time.'

The resilience and brevity of memory blurred this 'worst time' and the urgent pace of building and decoration was resumed at the restoration of Charles II. In the same year, 1660, Sir Roger Pratt was

writing about the methods of working with a builder and books of instruction, with the advice of knowledgeable friends. 'First resolve' he wrote 'with yourself what house will be answerable to your purse and estate, and after you have pitched upon the number of the rooms, and the dimensions of each, and desire in some measure to make use of whatsoever you have either observed, or heard to be excellent elsewhere, then if you are not able to handsomely contrive it yourself, get some ingenious gentleman who has seen much of that kind abroad and been somewhat versed in the best authors of Architecture: viz. Palladio, Scamozzi, Serlio etc. to do it for you . . .' Towards the end of the 17th century this period of amateur competence had played itself in, but the splendours of interior decoration had changed little since the days of Inigo Jones and there were frequent mistakes and misunderstanding of instructions.

In building a large country house in these years there came a time when a talented army of craftsmen, many of them foreign, were assembled by the patron and his advisors. Grinling Gibbons, Jonathan Maine and Edward Pearce were busy at wood and stone carving, Antonio Verrio, Louis Laguerre and Sir James Thornhill were embellishing almost every ceiling of note, and the skilled French decorative smith Jean Tijou was creating filigree patterns in wrought iron. George London and Henry Wise were transforming or making gardens and bringing order and pattern with parterres and long vistas of canals and fountains; Leonard Knyff and Johannes Kip busied themselves with their perspective engravings, fulsome dedications and elevations of the 'great fine houses'. John Vanderbank inherited the traditions of the long-established tapestry manufacturers, and soon his exciting and colourful Soho chinoiseries were hanging over the sombre wainscoting. Dufresnoy and Francis Lapierre stretched their damasks and velvets over skilfully-wrought wood and papier-mâché and erected the great 'state beds', which still adorn houses like Belton and Chatsworth. Edward Goudge was the leading plasterer and, as the architect Captain William

Winde told his cousin Lady Mary Bridgeman, 'is looked on as the beste master in England in his profession'. John Wilkes of Birmingham provided delicately wrought locks with elaborate mechanisms and Thomas Tompion and Joseph Knibb clocks stood on ornate overmantels, surmounted by portraits of arrogant patrons by Kneller, Riley, Closterman and Van Dyck.

Into this scene came the youthful Christopher Wren, writer, scientist, Professor of Astronomy and, seemingly by accident, architect. He was able to witness and assist the process whereby in house and City church the settings were created to display all talents. Cedar and oak wainscoting were overlaid with soft fruit-wood carving of incredible dexterity (Burghley House); great compartmented ceilings of ovals and squares had ribs encrusted with plasterwork fruit and flowers (Belton); marble floors and marble monuments in embellished private chapels (Petworth, Belton). They vied with the leather-hangings and simulated marble in paint (Dyrham), and richly carved foliage in wood to contain the staircase as it led upwards to the swirling mythological paintings far overhead (Sudbury).

The eager respect for decoration tumbled its way towards the 18th century and was then swept into a whirlpool of activity by at least five moods–Palladianism, Rococo, Gothick, Chinese and Neo-

classicism. The houses of this time were more than arrays of ordered precise columns, Crusader-like castles with tumbled battlements, rooms full of frivolous and gay wood and stucco or painted versions of ancient Rome with fresco and gilded martial trophy. They were more because their

rooms embodied the distilled essence of patronage and discernment and the best of craftsmanship even if it was sometimes outmoded and outdated by London or European standards. And then there came the looking back to the precise buildings of Palladio, which could be remembered against hot Italian skies, and those of Inigo Jones which were thrown into cold isolation by the cessation of building in the Civil War. The impetus came with the publication of two important pattern-books and the ambitions of a group of influential patrons.

The architectural movement in England in the early 18th century, which tried to perpetuate the ideas of the 16th-century Italian architect of Vicenza, Andrea Palladio, had already had a forerunner in the work of Inigo Jones (1573-1652). He visited Italy at least twice and acquired about two hundred and fifty 'Palladio' designs. These he added to his own collection, and the designs now survive at Chatsworth, Oxford and London.

These important drawings were to be the inspiration of the early 18th-century devotees, who, spurred on by Leoni's edition of Palladio in 1714 and the publication of the first volume of Colen Campbell's pattern-book *Vitruvius Britannicus* in 1715, were also eager to look at the original buildings and then come back to show their own abilities. Particularly involved were the third Earl of Burlington and the Scottish-born Campbell himself. Burlington's villa at Chiswick and his Burlington House in Piccadilly were to show all the world what a man of taste he was. As a patron he was praised for excelling the ancients and rescuing the arts from decay and oblivion. But he was an amateur compared to Campbell, whose recently discovered drawings have reinforced the strongly held opinion that he was the most important figure in early 18th-century architecture.

Precise and polished as the great stone Palladian houses were, with their pediments and ordered array of doors and windows, there is enough evidence to show that the Italian original could not be faithfully observed in England if one wanted comfort. High walls that screened the villas of

Chinoiserie decoration in the Tea Parlour, Claydon
House, Buckinghamshire.

Late 18th-century Gothick: the vaulted saloon at Arbury Hall, Warwickshire.

Palladio from the heat of the sun were unsuitable to a land where the portals had to be planted on 'the bosom of a sunless vale'. And such was the swift change in fashion that while Baroque was yielding to Palladianism the gay, asymmetrical Rococo style originating in the France of Louis XIV was ready for its introduction to England. Its heady style influenced architects and decorators, who had hitherto shown unswerving allegiance to Palladian ideals.

The Rococo style owed its character to asymmetry and its plastic, ever-changing form was most suited to the enrichment of the already grand interiors of houses. Its sinuous S- and C-shaped curves combined with an exquisite sense of balance and tension were purveyed by means of engravings. These were the sources that provided the stimulus to copy and adapt, and in consequence they were very welcome to the craftsmen of the time as workshop patterns.

The impulses of patrons to decorate their houses was not however entirely satisfied by Palladian strictures and Rococo gaiety. The Gothic style was available to tempt those with antiquarian enthusiasms. Most people now connect this mood for tumbled folly castles and weed-cracked battlements with Horace Walpole and his house of Strawberry Hill. It can however be traced back to Wren, Vanbrugh and Hawksmoor, and in the strictest sense may be held never to have quite died away at all from its medieval origins. It survived to await its eager revival. But it took time to wind up the clock of time, and during ten years it was necessary to find an exotic alternative in the form of Chinese taste. Here was a complete escape to a frivolous world which forgot 'that the very end of all buildings' is to have some 'relation of one proportion to another, of the thing supporting to the thing supported, of the accessory to the principal, and of the parts to the whole'. Indeed James Cawthorn in his *Of Taste*, written in 1756, was specific about the spirit of curiosity abroad:

'Of late, 'tis true, quite sick of Rome and Greece,
We fetch our models from the wise Chinese.'

This style persisted in competition with Wal-

pole's beloved Gothic until the intellectual mood, ever swinging to novelty and invention, could choose from a vogue for Greek architecture, launched by Stuart and Revett's *Antiquities of Athens,* or the classical revival inspired by Robert Adam. Adam introduced a 'beautiful variety of light mouldings gracefully formed and delicately enriched'. Rule and order had come again to enforce the disciplines demanded by an imitation of the arts of classical times. The 'littleness and ugliness of the Chinese, and the barbarity of the Goths' were dispersed 'that we may see no more useless and expensive trifles . . .' The fact that we are now mesmerised by the crumbling beauty of Gothick arches, and inspired to frivolous thought by the sensuous display of Rococo stucco makes it difficult to feel anything but bewilderment at the rapid dispersal of these trappings that took place after 1760.

The principal exponents of the new movement were William Chambers and Robert Adam. While they disagreed with each other and Chambers flattered himself that he interpreted the mood of the ancients more accurately, they were to act as joint Architects of His Majesty's Works. They had the ability to design room settings, to control the assembled craftsmen, and to carry out the many demands laid on them by tiresome but knowledgeable patrons. What emerged – and the 9000 or so drawings by Adam at Sir John Soane's Museum are impressive witness – were interiors filled with colourful paintings, Gobelins tapestries, marble and ormulu mantelpieces, carpets by Thomas Moore and walls embellished with classical stuccoes by Joseph Rose. A whole 'regiment of artificers' were to hand to provide the copper skylights, Etruscan style paintings, wrought-iron balusters and elaborate door furniture. One mind – the architect's – controlled all.

When Robert Adam died in 1792, however, the strongholds of classical architecture had at last been stormed and the eye had to condition and reconcile itself to a revival of Gothic. Sir John Soane, Henry Holland and John Nash were to be the leaders who crossed the threshold of the century into that vague period (say 1811 to 1830) of the Regency. They tried to go on matching the achievements of the 18th century which had included their years of training and greatest activity but a new patronage wedded to commerce was emerging. The great castles of Sir Robert Smirke – Eastnor of 1812-20 is a good example – were more in the mood of the

The drawing room in Red House, Bexley Heath, designed by Philip Webb for William Morris in 1859.

moment. The burning in 1834 and the subsequent rebuilding and decoration of the Houses of Parliament set Gothic as the official style, but one that was far removed from the fantasy Gothick of Horace Walpole and Sanderson Miller eighty years before.

Across the long years of Queen Victoria's reign the eccentric houses of Anthony Salvin and William Burges provided many aggressive and turretted silhouettes on the skyline. The thin spires of Street and Butterfield churches filled with marble, glazed brick and Minton tiles tried in all their polychromatic splendour to outdo one another against the backcloth of a return to the medieval hand-craft system proposed by William Morris and the Pre-Raphaelites. And incredibly the Queen was still alive when in the 1890s the ferment of active minds in Glasgow produced the Art Nouveau movement, with its writhing insistent lines snaking across walls and ceilings. Voysey, Norman Shaw, Philip Webb all helped to create out of those years that amorphous version of Baroque in Edwardian England. This produced a mood for the noble structures of Edwin Lutyens, surrounded by dreaming gardens created by Gertrude Jekyll. They stood in sharp contrast to the work of the German Bauhaus, and the cloying environment of the Garden Cities. But the stuff of that story must be woven on other pages if and when the time comes for us to venerate the houses and interior decoration of a modern school as we now revere those of centuries before.

The Picture in Country Houses

St John Gore

opposite. Pompeo Batoni (1708-87):
Portrait of Sir H. Fetherstonhaugh. Uppark, Sussex.

The two greatest tragedies in the history of English collecting were the dispersal by the Commonwealth of the collection of Charles I in 1649 and the sale of Sir Robert Walpole's pictures by his nephew, the 3rd Lord Orford, to Queen Catherine of Russia in 1779. With certain exceptions–the Raphael and Mantegna cartoons were considered inviolable and other pictures were recovered at the Restoration– the Continent of Europe is still the beneficiary of England's royal patron and collector. As for the Houghton pictures, the sale of which aroused opposition at the time and influenced Wilkes to demand their retention as the basis of a national gallery, they are today in the Hermitage Museum at Leningrad. Yet these examples are no more than the reverse of the procedure that until recently has ensured the position of Britain as the most lavish of all importers of works of art.

The process of accumulating pictures from abroad and their dispersal within this country lasted for nearly three hundred years. When, during the 19th century with its more advanced sociological views, museums and galleries found a place in public life, a new market was to appear which as time went by became increasingly importunate. It is true that museums in this country resort on occasions to international buying, but on the whole their contents are derived, by sale or gift, from the private collections of England. In other words, it is hardly an exaggeration to say that almost the total sum of pictures to be seen in this country today, come from the private collector's almost limitless stock. This vast wealth of pictures of all schools is the lasting memorial to his enthusiasm and catholic taste.

During the present century gaps have appeared in the great horde. As long ago as 1838 Passavant, the studious German artist who wrote an account of paintings in English collections, deplored the loss of works of art from these shores. He did not live to see the age of the voracious transatlantic industrialist who became to Britain what the insatiable English aristocrat had formerly been to Europe. The 20th century opened as the century of thought-less dispersal. That this dispersal has to some extent been checked today is partly the result of the Government's tardy awareness of the situation but, as often happens, it is a private body that has done most to counteract the situation. Support for the National Art Collections Fund has always been limited, but its influence and assistance to museums have been out of all proportion to the number of its subscribers.

It is however the centuries of acquisition that concern us here: the 17th century, which saw the emergence of classical collecting; the 18th century, in which this taste was intensified; and the 19th century, which was the period of expanding sympathies and comprehension. Just as the age of a rock is implicit in its structure, so with certain reservations should the pattern of a collection be discernible from its different strata, seen as the accretions of successive epochs. To illustrate this development, let us take the hypothetical case of a family whose riches accrued in the 16th century, whose Elizabethan mansion was undisturbed in the 17th century, classicised in the 18th, Gothicised in the 19th, and in the 20th century, institutionalised.

The original formation of this particular collection followed a similar pattern to others of the period: that is, in its origins it was little more than a collection of portraits. Members of the family or related notabilities, elaborately attired and stiffly posed, looked down from the walls of the long gallery in increasing numbers. Primarily they were there for purposes of record. The need for decoration was met by tapestries. The picture frames were no more than lengths of prepared moulding, stored in the house and cut up as the occasion demanded.

During the first half of the following century the same approach prevailed and Jacobean and Caroline portraits were added to the Elizabethan ones. In the late 1630s, however, the head of the family, whose position on the fringe of the court led to his choice of the King's painter, sat to Van Dyck. Although he could not have been unaware of the difference between the beautiful and sophisticated work of art that he had just acquired and the pedes-

Claude Lorraine (1600-82): *Ascanius shooting the stag.* Ashmolean Museum, Oxford.

Sir Anthony van Dyck (1599-1641): *Portrait of Henry, Lord Percy* (detail). Petworth House, Sussex.

trian likenesses that had hitherto surrounded him, he remained oblivious it seems to the change in collecting and patronage, which, as a result of the influence of Charles I and of the second Lord Arundel, had spread to a select circle of Whitehall courtiers. The head of this hypothetical family was not alone in failing to perceive that the King's discernment and breadth of sympathy, and the magnitude of his accumulations, would ever afterwards entitle him to be regarded as the greatest of all English collectors. Of the few contemporary collections which remain intact today, that of the 10th Earl of Northumberland, now divided between Petworth and Alnwick, and that of the Earl of Pembroke at Wilton are the two most notable.

It was at the Restoration that the family acquired their peerage. The first Earl commemorated the creation by commissioning Lely to paint portraits of himself and his wife, and of their young son, who appears in a chilly and anomalous Roman costume. Two decades later the 2nd Earl, as he had by then become, was painted by Kneller, at that moment on the threshold of his fashionable career. Little else was added during the remainder of the century. In this the family merely conformed with the general desuetude into which the arts had fallen. The 3rd Earl, preoccupied with his political activities and Hanoverian sympathies, paid little attention, apart from giving further employment to Kneller and to

various subsidiary artists, to the contents of the house. It was left to the 4th Earl, born in the year of George I's succession, to follow the example of Walpole, Marlborough and others and to become the founder of a great classical collection.

The 18th century is ideologically so compact that it encourages generalisation. There were of course underlying trends in picture collecting just as there were in architecture and decoration. By and large however the composition of a collection of pictures was unequivocally prescribed. The 4th Earl showed no signs of deviating from these accepted canons of taste. He bought Classical and Baroque works of art by the greatest masters.

The 4th Earl returned from the two years, which as a young man he had inevitably spent in Rome and Venice, with two hundred packing cases filled with paintings: by the artists of the High Renaissance and by the Bolognese and Roman eclectics of the early 17th century; by Claude, whose sylvan landscapes recalled to him the still evenings of the Campagna; and by Salvator Rosa, whose rocks and swirling torrents reminded him of his hazardous crossing of the Alps. (Both these artists idealised nature in different ways and both appealed to the 18th century educated man's subjective approach to nature.) The great mythological scenes by Rubens and Poussin, reconciling the tedious arguments between on the one hand the upholders of colour and

Arthur Devis (1711-87): *Richard Vernon Atherton and his family in the grounds of his house* (Atherton Hall, Lancs., by William Wakefield, 1722). Paul Mellon Coll.

on the other of design, were his purchase, as were the large still-lifes by Snyders. The existing rooms were found to be inadequate to contain these treasures and Flintcroft was called in to modernise them.

In the course of the century the house underwent a further modification. The 5th Earl, who during his Grand Tour had fully indulged his taste for classical sculpture, remodelled a series of rooms to form a gallery for his newly acquired statues and reliefs. Less interested in pictures than his father, his lifetime coincided with the greatest age of English portraiture. He had already as a matter of course been painted in Rome by Batoni. Now he and his family sat to Reynolds, Gainsborough and Romney. His horses were painted by Stubbs. He died in the early years of the 19th century at a moment when the rigid precepts formulated by the Augustans were on the point of losing their compelling power.

If the contents of a collection of pictures in the 18th century can be seen in terms of architecture as a synthesis of the Classical, Baroque and Rococo styles, it is perhaps possible to continue the analogy and to find a similar parallel with the greater diversity of styles in 19th-century architecture. It is true the centry possessed certain ponderous characteristics—Sir Osbert Sitwell, comparing the

Thomas Gainsborough (1722-88): *Mr and Mrs Robert Andrews, c.*1748. National Gallery, London.

Grand Tour collectors with the historians and professors that followed, observed that those 'untoiling butterflies accomplished more for English art than all the labouring stage elephants of the next century' – but this should not blind us to the fact that because of its diverse interests the 19th century is our supreme age of picture collecting. When in 1857 the first comprehensive exhibition of privately owned works of art was held at Manchester, it comprised, as well as classical works of art, pictures of the French 18th century, the Dutch 17th century and the early Italian schools on a scale that would have been quite unthinkable fifty years earlier.

The 6th Earl, who succeeded the title in the year of Austerlitz, ignored the new opportunities for acquiring classical paintings which European collectors had, before the advance of Napoleon's armies, been sending for dispersal in England. He was a friend of the Prince Regent and he shared the latter's tastes. Like the Prince and like the 3rd Lord Hertford he bought Dutch and Flemish 17th-century pictures; and just as these two men are res-

ponsible for the superb examples of these schools in the Royal Collection and in the Wallace collection, so it is the achievement of the 6th Earl that they are so eloquently represented, albeit on a lesser scale, in his own family collection.

The Earl's patronage of British artists can be seen as complementary, with certain reservations, to his love of Dutch paintings. In the previous century, despite the bitter satires of Hogarth and the weighty prose of Reynolds, the patronage extended to British artists was limited. They were considered sufficiently accomplished to produce likenesses of members of a family or their animals, but subject pictures, then regarded as the highest form of art, were only acceptable if they came from abroad. In the 19th century these prejudices began to disappear; and partly as a result of the increasing appreciation of Dutch art and partly because of the emergence of a newly rich class of industrialist, to whom the grand classical paintings of the Whig aristocracy were alien and whose sympathies lay more readily with qualities such as the verisimilitude pur-

Sir Joshua Reynolds (1723-92): *Portrait of Mrs John Parker,* Saltram House, Devon. (The National Trust).

veyed by Dutch artists, the approach to British art underwent a change. By the end of the first quarter of the century the exhibitions at the Royal Academy, which had previously consisted mainly of portraits, now contained a preponderance of subject pictures. It was neither Turner nor Constable who were the most highly admired British artists: it was Wilkie, and one of the reasons for his popularity was his resemblance to Jan Steen.

In comparison with the Dutch pictures bought by the 6th Earl, which are of a consistently high standard and declare the passion of a true connoisseur, the English pictures, a heterogeneous assortment by living painters, suggest that the Earl was more con-

cerned with supporting these artists than in acquiring significant objects. One may assume that he esteemed the two romantic Turners; and one may surmise that he would not have bought the vast Haydon had he not admired it. But he possessed no painting by Constable and on the whole it is the work of the popular academician in a story-telling vein which he has chosen to represent.

At the death of the 6th Earl in 1840 the collection may be said to have reached its end. Had his successor displayed any interest in extending it he would have realised that by subscribing at this moment to the awakening response to French 18th-century painting and to the early Italian schools, he would have conformed with the traditions of his ancestors. He did not watch the astronomical rise in the prices of the *dix-huitième* artists when the great banking families such as the Rothschilds entered the market; nor did he take account of the waning popularity of the artists of the *seicento*. He only neglected his ministerial duties during his long life in order to sell the Raphael to America and to build the Gothick addition that today encloses the house on the fourth side. He died before the first World War in the unshaken belief that the fortunes of his family would for ever prosper.

His convictions were soon to be dispelled. The death of the 9th Earl in 1945 forced his successor to open negotiations with local councils. The family moved; the building was saved. Today, tidy and characterless, the house welcomes the public. The ghosts have been driven from their haunts in the galleries and chambers. Smartly uniformed attendants stand in the doorways; the clean scent of floor polish has superseded the musty smell of potpourri and the unsatisfactory old flagstones have been replaced by improved modern ones of a non-skid variety. Bright flowers planted in the architect-designed, geometrically patterned beds make an interesting contrast with the Elizabethan brickwork. The pictures and furniture however still line the walls of the state rooms; and there they remain, in cold storage, as an example of three centuries of fashion and of a family's taste and prodigal spending.

The Grand Tour

Kenneth Garlick

opposite. Carlo Maratta (1625-1713): *Robert Spencer, 2nd Earl of Sunderland.* Althorp, Northamptonshire.

'The Grand Tour' was the name given to the tour or journey through France and Italy undertaken by young Englishmen of good birth and fortune in order to complete their education. It is not really possible to say exactly when the phrase was first used, but the concept came into being in the 17th century. By the middle of the 18th century the Tour was established and fashionable. A hundred years later it was almost a thing of the past. To the Grand Tour the English country house owed its collections of paintings, statuary and *objets d'art* of all kinds, and sometimes even its architectural style and plan, and therefore any book which takes the country house as its theme, must devote some pages to this subject.

If you read the plays of Shakespeare you will find frequent references to Italy. Shakespeare's knowledge came from books. He could not have met many persons who had been so far afield, for in his time travel in Italy was dangerous, partly for political reasons and partly because England was no longer a Catholic country. It was only towards the end of his life, at the beginning of the 17th century, that conditions began to ease. In 1604 King James I sent Sir Henry Wootton as Ambassador to Venice, and from 1615 there was also an English envoy in Turin. Even so, travelling abroad was very largely reserved for those who had official business. It was exceptional that Inigo Jones should make a journey to Venice early in his career, and that later, in 1613, the Earl of Arundel should take him in his suite when he travelled through Italy after escorting the Princess Elizabeth, Electress Palatine, to her home in Heidelberg. Jones returned to England with an informed enthusiasm for the architecture of Palladio. The Banqueting House, Whitehall, and the Queen's House, Greenwich were among the splendid fruits of it. However, his journey was the result of chance and good fortune. It was not a Grand Tour. It was only after about 1630 that some sort of planned and lengthy, independent tour through France and the whole of the Italian peninsula became possible. One must, of course, remember that at this time Italy was a collection of separate states whose political relationships were often changing, and that the whole business of going abroad was complicated, risky and adventurous to a degree that is difficult for the modern traveller to appreciate. It was quite possible to get oneself imprisoned for no justifiable reason, and it was positively easy to contract a fatal disease.

As time went on a kind of itinerary was worked out which became known as the *giro d'Italia* (the 'round of Italy'). This involved making one's way to Florence in the late autumn, either by one of the Alpine passes or by boat from Marseilles to Genoa, going down from Florence to Rome and from Rome to Naples, returning to Rome for Easter, travelling North by way of Loreto, Ancona and Bologna to Venice, and coming home through France with a lengthy stay in Paris on the way. The number of Englishmen who made this journey in some form or other increased as the century progressed.

When the Earl of Arundel journeyed through Italy taking Inigo Jones with him, he made a collection of antique (that is Greek and Roman) sculpture, which he ultimately placed in a special gallery in his London house. He was perhaps the first Englishman to travel on the Continent with the purpose in mind of acquiring works of art; and he had no immediate successor. In the middle of the century however, Robert, 2nd Earl of Sunderland, who was in Rome about the year 1644, had himself painted in classical costume by Carlo Maratta – you may see the portrait at Althorp, his home in Northamptonshire, today – and although he did not purchase many other paintings on that journey, he acquired a taste for collecting, which he indulged when he came home. Like his contemporary, the 5th Earl of Exeter, who went to Italy three times, he thought of his collection as a proud adornment of his house, and at Althorp, as at Burghley House, Lord Exeter's home, one may sense the scale and the style of collecting that very soon became a fashion and an industry.

The journeys of many Grand Tourists are recorded in letters and journals, far too many to mention here. One will suffice, that of Thomas

Coke, later Earl of Leicester, who set out in 1712 when he was only fifteen, in the company of his tutor Mr Ferrari, his 'governor' Mr Hobart, two grooms, a valet and a 'superior servant' whose business was to pay the bills and keep the accounts. They travelled in a coach with four horses, and when they left the family seat, Holkham in Norfolk, the church bells were rung and ships fired their guns offshore. This was an exceptionally long journey because Coke did not return until 1718, but in its pattern and achievement it epitomises all Grand Tours. On the way to Italy the party dallied six weeks in Paris and six months in Angers (to perfect such arts as fencing and dancing and to study classics and civil law). They passed in a very leisurely way across the South of France, over the Mont Cenis pass, and down to Florence, and by May, 1714, they were in Rome. Here young Coke first felt the urge to collect. 'I am become since my stay in Rome' he wrote 'a perfect virtuoso, and a great lover of pictures.' He met and became friendly with William Kent, the painter architect, and without his expressing it in so many words, Europe had begun to thrill him. He did not come straight home but went from Italy to Switzerland and Germany, to France again, and then again to Italy. The result of it all was that he became an enthusiastic collector of books as well as pictures, and that some years later he employed Kent to build the great Palladian mansion at Holkham where his descendants still live. There, in a setting that has Roman grandeur, you may see many of his Grand Tour purchases and others that he bought through agents after his return.

Not all Grand Tourists were as perceptive as Coke. They were nearly all rich, they were nearly all young, and although in the majority of cases there was a tutor to keep an eye on them, they were 'milords' aware of their consequence and independence. So it is not surprising that some of them were duped by unscrupulous dealers or middlemen and that a quantity of spurious 'antique sculpture' and 'Old Masters' came home along with much that was superb. This was inevitable. When one reads that the young Duke of Beaufort who went on the Tour in 1726 sent home a ship-load of marbles, 96 cases 'great and small', one is astonished that the average quality of the works of art that poured into England at this time was so high. For the English connoisseur, or, as he was then often called, the dilettante, this was a marvellous time to live. It was not only the Tourists themselves who benefited. A number of artists went out to Italy, sometimes in the company or the employ of a Tourist, sometimes alone but hoping for the patronage of fellow-Englishmen when they got there. Richard Wilson spent much of the 1750s in Venice, Rome and Naples where his patrons were English travellers, notably the Earl of Dartmouth. Nathaniel Dance was in Rome in the sixties and painted portraits such as that of the young Duke of Northumberland sitting moodily in front of the Colosseum with his tutor. John Robert Cozens accompanied William Beckford as his watercolour painter in the 'eighties. One of the favourite painters of the English was however the Italian portraitist Pompeo Batoni, who portrayed them elegant and alert in settings which indicate their admiration for all things classical. There are examples of his work in such well-known houses as Castle Ashby, Uppark and Charlecote.

Rome, Florence and Naples were the cities where the Grand Tourists steeped themselves in the history and literature of the Roman Empire, where they formed their collections, and where they contemplated the romance of ruins crumbling in scenes of great natural beauty. Venice was where they had fun. The fantasy of Venice, the music and the masquerades, was quite another world. Here they did not buy Old Masters. They bought Moderns. That is to say they bought views of the city, the canals and the lagoons. There was no camera to make things easy, but there was, very fortunately, Canaletto and his active studio. There were view-painters (*vedutisti*) all over Italy, but Canaletto and Guardi who recorded the life and face of Venice, were superior to almost all. For some reason it was Canaletto rather than Guardi whom the English admired and whose work

Antonio Canaletto (1697-1768): *View of the Grand Canal*. Uppark, Sussex.

they bought in quantity and to this day, if you wish to see Canalettos you do not go to Italy, but to England or America (where the Canalettos have mostly come from England). There is a room of his views of Venice at Woburn Abbey.

The Grand Tour was no extravagance. No doubt many of the young men spent more than they should have done, and while they filled the Italian purse they impoverished Italy of treasure, and that was hardly commendable. But they enormously enriched England. It was not only the collections they formed, but the houses, the galleries, the libraries they built in a noble 'Italian' style, which added beauty to the English scene and quality to English life. On the Grand Tour the intelligent 'milord' or squire must have acquired a new and larger conception of what his station in life implied, its obligations and its potentialities. His experience was a contribution to that indefinable word, culture, and all classes of society gained from it.

Two things killed the Grand Tour. One was the railway engine. The other was Mr Cook's tours. Cheaper, quicker travel opened up Europe to the middle classes and Mr Cook helped them to make their arrangements. Then came the motor-car. One day, when Henry James was wandering in the hills above Florence he sniffed the air and wrote down wistfully, 'the operation left me no doubts. The odour was that of petroleum'. It was the beginning of the end. Now has come the aeroplane and everyone goes everywhere all the time. Ease of travel has largely defeated the traveller's aim, for the mechanical age has brought destruction to the beauties and the values which the Grand Tourist enjoyed and understood.

Furniture in English Houses

Christopher Gilbert

opposite. Berkeley Castle, Gloucestershire: state bed, 1605.

Oak Furniture

Comparatively little is known about the development of domestic furniture in England before the reign of Elizabeth because of the rarity of surviving pieces. Useful information can, however, be derived from contemporary inventories and pictorial sources. It is clear that by modern standards of comfort living conditions, even in great houses, were primitive and furnishings scanty. By the late medieval period three-legged stools, plain benches, simple trestle tables and stout chests (which served as both receptacles and seats) were in common use, while wealthy households might possess in addition a cupboard with open shelves for the display of plate, several presses or aumbries enclosed by double doors for storing food or apparel, fixed wall settles, a ceremonial chair for the master and generally a great canopied bed. The most costly furnishings recorded in ancient inventories were often fine tapestries and gorgeous fabrics used variously for hangings, cushions and table carpets, which doubtless created an impression of great splendour.

Although furniture tended to be roughly made, surfaces were often elaborately decorated in the style of Gothic church architecture, and brightly gilded or painted. Carved roundels, tracery, linenfold panels and pictorial subjects were widely popular. Furniture in the Gothic manner continued to be made well into the 16th century, but during the reign of Henry VIII contact with Italian craftsmen employed to decorate the royal palaces, for example Nonsuch, led to the adoption of Renaissance motifs characterised by lozenge panels, scrolled foliage, vine trails, guilloche bands, acanthus, egg-and-dart mouldings and portrait medallions. By about 1550 the native Gothic style became absorbed into a provincial version of the Renaissance decorative idiom. Because English pieces lacked the refinement of continental prototypes the nobility often acquired furniture abroad.

The Reformation disrupted cultural ties with Italy and thereafter England received a northern European, predominantly Flemish interpretation of Renaissance design and ornament, typified by bulbous supports, a profuse employment of low-relief strapwork often accompanied by floral or geometric inlay, masks and an assortment of pseudo-classical details amalgamated with traditional Gothic elements.

Although furniture in all but the grandest houses remained simple, a definite advance occurred during Elizabeth's reign. Chests of panelled construction superseded those formed of broad planks nailed together and several lighter classes of chair appeared, namely the type known as *caqueteuse*, richly upholstered cross-framed chairs, turned chairs, sometimes with leather seats and backs, and the so-called farthingale stools. These were usually placed in parlours and bedrooms, since the great hall, still the social centre of the threshold, was supplied with benches and stools and an armchair for the master. Large draw-leaf tables of framed construction gradually replaced the trestle form, while gate-leg tables and small occasional tables, often adapted for games, became more plentiful. Elaborately carved cupboards incorporating inlaid panels and possibly a drawer in the frieze supplemented chests as storage receptacles, but luxurious beds and great tapestries remained the most costly items in most aristocratic establishments.

During the first half of the 17th century furniture design remained almost static; the most important innovations were an increased use of upholstery on chairs and the evolution of the chest of drawers. A fairly large number of pieces from this period have survived, illustrating the prevalent taste for floral inlay, ornamental turning and overall low-relief carving in the Flemish manner. As a rule oak was used by English joiners, although after about 1570 walnut and to a lesser extent cedar, yew, chestnut and other woods enjoyed a limited vogue. Most innovations stemmed from London; the provinces were more conservative, although interesting regional characteristics developed, notably in chair design. The Commonwealth period witnessed a temporary reaction against florid ornament, furniture of this date being severe and plain, apart from an attractive use of bobbin-turning on chairs.

67

Haddon Hall, Derbyshire: the dais of the hall, tapestry c.1460, oak table c.1600.

Crathes Castle, Kincardineshire: the chairs of Alexander Burnet and Katherine Gordon, c.1597.

Early Walnut

The return of Charles II and his court from exile in Holland in 1660 ushered in 'a politer way of living' as John Evelyn put it, for their experience of continental fashions had engendered a taste for luxury. The new social standards inspired a revolution in the design and arrangement of furnishings; the ponderous oak tables, benches, chairs, chests and cupboards that sufficed during the reigns of the first two Stuart kings were considered unacceptable and were soon replaced by lighter, more compact pieces, generally of walnut. These changes were made possible by improvements in craftsmanship promoted by Huguenot workmen who settled in England; the most significant development was the emergence of cabinet-makers, skilled in the art of veneering and decorating surfaces with intricate curvilinear designs in woods of contrasting colour – a technique known as marquetry. This represented an important advance on the traditional methods of the joiner, who worked with solid timber and depended on mortice and tenon joints and panelled construction.

During the second half of the 17th century many new, conveniently designed types of furniture were made. There was a steady demand for drawer-fitted furniture such as bureaux, writing-tables of various forms, commodes, tallboys and cabinets on stands incorporating tiers of drawers. Such pieces were generally veneered with figured walnut or laburnum, while sumptuous examples might be decorated with floral marquetry or olivewood 'oystershell' parquetry, a treatment sometimes extended to tabletops, clock cases and mirror frames.

Small, easily portable occasional tables with folding tops for cards and on tripod stands for tea became fashionable, and since it was now customary to take meals in small parties instead of seated round a large table, oval gate-leg tables of oak or walnut were required. Another innovation was the introduction of splendid side tables with marble or carved and gilt gesso tops in the continental Baroque style. Tall mirrors, usually imported, but made in small numbers in England, also became a feature of reception rooms and large frames, skilfully carved with naturalistic compositions by Grinling Gibbons and his school, adorned the walls of many great houses.

The design of seat furniture was completely transformed after the Restoration. Sets of chairs in walnut or beech with high backs, spiral turned members and cane panels, generally lavishly carved with stylised foliage and scrolls, replaced the heavy oak and leather covered types of the previous age (although stools and benches were retained in homes where etiquette was strictly observed). Towards the end of the century, richly upholstered day-beds, settees and winged armchairs based on

Late Stuart, early walnut furniture in the Great
Chamber at Castle Ashby, Northamptonshire.

opulent contin
remain today.
magnificently
taste for luxur
   The love of
ved in the us
quetry (comb
and mother-(
frames and ch
sive use of gil
tables and chạ
ted on carved
chinoiserie sc
were import(
native craftsı
examples of
Knole, indica
cult of luxur
of the 17th (

al models appeared, although few
h pieces, together with towering,
oed beds emphasise the prevailing
d display.
ace embellishment already obser-
figured veneer, colourful mar-
d on occasion with stained ivory
earl) and the lavish carving of
packs is also apparent in the exten-
; on tripod stands, mirror frames,
Exotic japanned cabinets, moun-
gilt stands, enriched with fanciful
on glossy black or red grounds
large quantities and copied by
   The vogue for silver furniture,
h are preserved at Windsor and
ie astonishing length to which the
s carried during the closing years
ıry. However, when considering

Restoration furniture it must not be forgotten that joiners in the provinces continued to make solid oak pieces of traditional Jacobean character displaying little awareness of foreign influences or new-fangled fashions promoted in London.

Later Walnut

By the early years of the 18th century the finest English cabinet-work was comparable with anything produced on the Continent; the improvement was largely brought about by the stimulus of Huguenot craftsmen who settled here after the revocation of the Edict of Nantes in 1685. During the reign of Queen Anne a striking contrast developed between everyday domestic furniture and magnificent pieces in Venetian Baroque style commissioned for the great Palladian houses of the ruling Whig oligarchy. William Kent, the author of Holkham and Houghton, has given his name to this grandiose furniture of architectural character. Massive side tables with marble tops, scrolled supports and aprons decorated with a scallop shell, masks or weighty swags epitomise this class of furniture. Pedestals and brackets of elaborate sculptural form suggestive of stone or plaster were placed in reception rooms together with gilt 'dolphin' or 'eagle' console tables, while walls were hung with large mirrors having broken pediments and floral pendants similar to doorways and overmantels. These monumental pieces reflect the ideas of Inigo Jones, Andrea Palladio and the furnishings of French and Italian palaces. A less ostentatious version of the style was widely adopted by the lesser gentry to give dignity and grandeur to their reception rooms.

   Returning to ordinary domestic furniture, there was, during the reign of Queen Anne, a movement away from the exuberant Baroque manner in favour of finely veneered walnut furniture displaying modest proportions and restrained but effective ornament. Chair backs became lower, stretchers disappeared, rectangular design was replaced by a graceful curvilinear style in which the flowing line of the cabriole leg was echoed in the smooth contours of the back and seat rail; carving was generally confined to an unobtrusive shell or frond on the cresting or knee. Lightly constructed bureaux bookcases, tallboys, commodes, cabinets, card and writing tables in figured walnut with cross-banding and simple mouldings were made in large numbers for small town houses where monumental Baroque pieces would seem out of place. Conversation pictures show that the average room was fairly sparsely furnished at this period.

There was a steady demand for neat lookingglasses on stands fitted with drawers, and handsome mirrors in walnut and gesso-gilt frames with classical mouldings and pedimented tops. However, in remote country districts such as Wales the taste for traditional oak furniture lingered on well into the reign of George II.

Rococo Furniture

The sober 'Queen Anne' style walnut furniture and bold versions of continental Baroque, which had dominated English taste for a generation, began to wane in popularity about 1740 owing to the introduction of mahogany and the influence of the Rococo style. In contrast to the formal architectural qualities of Palladian design, Rococo furniture displays a restless curvilinear system of ornament in which C-scrolls, plants, animals, contorted rockwork and fanciful naturalistic motifs combine in an asymmetrical yet balanced composition. Mirror frames, console tables, sconces and stands were among the first pieces to reflect the new rhythms.

This frivolous idiom was admirably suited to the art of wood-carving and many flamboyant Rococo designs were produced by Matthias Lock and Thomas Johnson. However, the most accomplished series of designs was published by Thomas Chippendale in 1754 under the title *The Gentleman and Cabinet-Maker's Director*, which contained 277 engravings illustrating the entire range of domestic furniture in which varied Rococo motifs became fully integrated into the English tradition. Serpentine lines and extravagant ornament were employed with rather more restraint in England than on the Continent. (In fact, the more conservative furniture makers such as William Vile, who executed com-

missions for the Crown, displayed little awareness of the latest smart vogue and continued to work in the tradition established by William Kent.) Although relatively few pieces from Chippendale's workshop can now be identified with certainty, his name is habitually used to describe English mid-18th century furniture in the Rococo manner.

Chippendale, in common with his contemporaries, often combined Rococo ornament with pseudo-Gothic and Chinese details. The vogue for chinoiserie which emerged at the close of the previous century enjoyed a revival during the 1750s, since picturesque mandarins, ho-ho birds, dragons, pagoda-like structures, lattice work, imitation bamboo and so forth could be easily amalgamated with stock Rococo ingredients. The pattern of Chinese paling was extensively used for chairbacks and glazing bars, while Oriental frets appeared on legs and pierced galleries. The style was particularly favoured for bedroom furnishings.

The mid-18th century Gothic revival, which was confined solely to this country, forms a delightful episode in the history of taste. No attempt was made to copy ancient furniture; late-medieval ornaments such as finials, tracery, clustered columns, roundels, cusps and bosses were merely grafted onto traditional forms. The pseudo-Gothic manner was

Neo-classical furniture designed by Robert Adam, in Osterley Park House, London.

below. The Regency North Drawing Room in the Royal Pavilion at Brighton.

considered especially appropriate for library tables, bookcases and chairs.

The Neo-Classical Period

During the 1760s there was a reaction against the Rococo taste. This stemmed from the work of Robert Adam, who evolved a new style as a result of his study of classical remains, in particular the newly discovered sites at Herculaneum and Pompeii. In contrast to the naturalistic curvilinear idiom of Rococo, Adam's style was based on a repertoire of ornament derived from the interior decoration of ancient Roman villas. Classical motifs such as urns, *paterae*, husk-chains, running scrolls of foliage, ram's heads and stylised honeysuckle (*anthemion*) were used in formal arrangements to create an effect of 'delicacy, gaiety, grace and beauty'. In contrast to Kent's use of large scale architectural features for furniture and the serpentine rhythms of Rococo, he favoured straight lines, simple curves and forms based on classical tripods, altars and so on, enriched with delicate Neo-classical devices in marquetry or carved in low relief.

The revolutionary new style speedily influenced every branch of the decorative arts and by 1770 the leading furniture makers were embodying his ideals in their work. Although Adam has left an important series of designs for furnishings supplied to the great houses that he built, the best remembered disseminator of Neo-classical fashion is George Hepplewhite, who produced a comprehensive series of furniture designs issued in 1788 under the title of *The Cabinet-Maker and Upholsterer's Guide*. The volume, illustrating a wide range of ordinary domestic furniture in the new mode, popularised the style throughout the provinces. Although conservative, the *Guide* contains many elegant and refined designs for shield-back chairs, small tables with slender, tapering legs, bookcases, secretaire cabinets and neat, compact bedroom furniture. Most were intended to be executed in light mahogany or satinwood.

Between 1791 and 1794 Thomas Sheraton published *The Cabinet-Maker and Upholsterer's Drawing Book* in four parts containing 113 plates illustrating lightly constructed furniture representative of the 1790s in which the Neo-classical element is less obtrusive. He includes many square-backed chairs and tastefully decorated cabinet pieces reminiscent of the late Louis XVI period. Sheraton is noted for his discreet use of painted ornament and a number of ingenious multipurpose designs which, 'unite elegance with utility and blend the useful with the agreeable'.

Regency Furniture

It is difficult to define the so-called 'Regency' style, but this term is generally used to describe fashions current during the first three decades of the 19th century. There was a movement towards historical exactitude in furniture designs; purists of the new generation such as Thomas Hope copied ancient Greek and Roman furniture closely, whereas Adam attempted only to capture 'the beautiful spirit of antiquity' without aiming at archaeological accuracy. Grecian couches, sabre-legged chairs, tables with lyre-shaped supports or monopodial legs, cross-framed stools and stands modelled on Roman tripods became widely popular.

The fashion for Egyptian ornament (sphinx, mummy case, lotus flowers etc.), introduced into France as a result of Napoleon's Egyptian campaign, spread to England after Nelson's success at the battle of the Nile in 1798, and his victory at Trafalgar in 1805 promoted a taste for marine emblems. There was also a revival of interest in Gothic and Chinese styles, both of which feature in George Smith's *Designs for Household Furniture* 1808. The severe rectangular forms of French Empire furniture were adopted by many cabinet-makers and other features typical of the period are reeded legs, lion-paw feet and brass inlay.

Long before the accession of Queen Victoria the 18th century tradition of design had coarsened and disintegrated through the pursuit of novelty; the furniture industry became geared to the requirements of a commercial middle-class who were satisfied with a succession of revivals of past styles and although the quality of craftsmanship remained high there was a sad decline in taste.

A Country House Guide

Charles Lines

opposite. Claydon House, Bucks.: the inlaid staircase.

The list that follows is selective and aims to describe no more than representatives of the principal types of country house discussed in this book, together with good instances of the work of architects and craftsmen named in the earlier sections.

Thus the visitor of an enquiring mind can use it to select houses with those particular features that he or she wishes to see from amongst the great number now available for inspection.

Those named have been chosen because they are generally accessible to the public at stated times. And here it is important to give a warning that, before making a visit, it is essential to check the times of opening in up-to-date publications, such as those issued by the National Trust, the National Trust for Scotland, the Ministry of Public Building and Works or the Index Guides, for they are not infrequently changed.

BEDFORD
Luton Hoo

Successive fires and successive architects (Robert Adam, Sir Robert Smirke and G. E. Street among them), have helped to produce the present Luton Hoo, but there has been a house here for centuries and a great transformation in the French taste took place under Sir Julius Wernher early this century. To this extremely wealthy man is owed much of the quite fantastic collection of works of art ranging from magnificent tapestries and paintings to enamels, German silver-gilt and ivories. His wife (later Lady Ludlow) collected fine English porcelain, his son, Sir Harold, added English furniture and his daughter-in-law (daughter of the Grand Duke Michael) works by Fabergé. To give some indication of the splendour, the Blue Hall contains superb Gobelins tapestries, part of a dressing-set by David Willaume and a collection of Sèvres ware; the great dining room extremely important Beauvais tapestries, Paul de Lamerie silver-gilt and Bohemian crystal, while Italian, Spanish, German and Flemish pictures are found in the former chapel, as well as dazzling Renaissance jewellery. Brown landscaped the park.

Woburn Abbey

The huge house of the Dukes of Bedford has been reduced in size since the Second World War, but is still very large and imposing. Part of a 17th-century house of the Russells still exists; there is much work by Flitcroft for the fourth Duke, and not a little by Henry Holland. The principal rooms are sumptuously furnished and decorated – some very good French furniture, and a multitude of pictures including a room full of Canalettos and an Armada portrait of Elizabeth I. Porcelain, too, and a Chinese Room, as well as Mortlake tapestries with designs from Raphael's 'Acts of the Apostles'. Holland's delightful Chinese Dairy is reflected in a lake. Vast Flitcroft stables. Bison, wallabies and varieties of deer in an enormous park.

BERKSHIRE
Buscot Park

Built about 1780 by Townsend Loveden, who appears to have been his own architect, Buscot was afterwards greatly enlarged and altered. Fortunately, tasteless Victorian accretions have been removed, thanks, in the main, to the present Lord Faringdon who is now a tenant of the National Trust. The exquisitely decorated rooms contain much furniture of importance and paintings of the French, Italian and English schools, including examples of Murillo, Rembrandt and Reynolds, as well as the Briar Rose paintings by Burne-Jones. The fine gardens were laid out by Harold Peto, but have been altered and extended. There are lakeside walks, vistas, statuary, avenues and a formal canal. A small private theatre and squash court adjoin the mansion, balanced on the far side of the house by a pavilion to house domestic staff.

BUCKINGHAMSHIRE
Ascott

An early 17th-century farmhouse is the nucleus of Ascott which was greatly enlarged last century for Leopold de Rothschild. The interior was transformed by Mr and Mrs Anthony de Rothschild and in 1949 the former (who had inherited in 1937) gave the house, grounds and a very large collection of works of art to the National Trust with an endowment. There is a grand collection of Chinese porcelain, English paintings by Hogarth, Reynolds, Romney, Gainsborough and Stubbs, and important Italian, Dutch and French pictures. French furniture includes a kingwood table with the stamp of Montigny, a splendid lacquered Louis XV commode and a *bonheur-du-jour* by Riesener. There is also impressive English furniture of the mid-Georgian period. The lovely thirty-acre garden, famous for autumn colour, contains statuary by the American, Julian Story.

Claydon House

The home of the Buckinghamshire Verneys was once much larger, and some of the existing, and by no means tiny, house is older than it looks. The second Earl Verney, a Whig, ruined himself in attempting to rival the Tory Lord Grenville at Stowe. Two thirds of his west front have gone. What still exists is a series of rooms worth a long journey to see. The carved woodwork in the Rococo manner by a certain Lightfoot in the North Parlour, the Rose plasterwork and the inlaid staircase with waving ears-of-corn in the balustrade are enchanting. Upstairs is a fantastic Chinese Room (actually Rococo and Chinese), and a museum with family costumes and relics of 'The Lady with the Lamp'. The parish church is in the garden. Claydon belongs to the National Trust.

Hughenden Manor

Benjamin Disraeli bought Hughenden in 1848 and later reconstructed the pleasing, white house, using red and blue bricks and lavishly embellishing the parapet. His architect was Edward Buckton Lamb and the result has been described as 'a romantic version of Tudor' and 'a typical example of a Victorian gentleman's country seat.' The statesman's statues and urns remain in the gardens once renowned for their peacocks. His personal belongings are in the study. This, like the present library, which has Sir Francis Grant's portrait of Disraeli, retains its Georgian decoration; not so the dining-room which is in dubious taste. The drawing-room, once the library, is very pretty and has chairs with needlework by Lady Beaconsfield. There are some of the manuscripts of the novels, letters from Queen Victoria and the 'Gallery of Friendship' with portraits of Benjamin's friends.

Waddesdon Manor

On his death in 1957, James de Rothschild left Waddesdon (built late last century by Baron Ferdinand de Rothschild) and his great collections to the National Trust, with a very large endowment. He inherited the house with many of the present contents from his aunt, Miss Alice de Rothschild – Ferdinand's sister – and added furniture, pictures and other treasures left to him by his father, Baron Edmond. The house, designed by Destailleur and like a château, is enriched with panelling from old French houses, paintings by Guardi, Watteau, Reynolds, Romney, Gainsborough and Rubens, Aubusson and Savonnerie carpets, Dresden and Sèvres china, Beauvais tapestries, French furniture (including Riesener's marquetry and ormulu table made for Marie Antoinette), fans, gold snuff-boxes, arms and armour, Venetian, German and Bohemian glass and Limoges enamels. Richly wooded grounds with fountains and statuary.

West Wycombe Park

The estate was bought by the merchant Dashwoods at the end of the 17th century. A house existed and was retained and considerably altered by Sir Francis Dashwood early in the following century. Sir Francis's son of the same name (founder of the Hell Fire Club, Chancellor of the Exchequer and eventually Lord le Despencer) transformed the building with Robert Adam among his architects. Features include a Neo-Grecian west portico, an east portico copied from Mereworth and the remarkable two-storeyed colonnade to the south. Two generations of the Italian Borgnis family, and a Scotsman, William Hanna, painted walls and ceilings. A man of great taste, Dashwood furnished his house extremely well, but the pictures are not exciting. Brown and Humphry Repton worked on the grounds which include temples. West Wycombe Church, with its famous globe and mausoleum in front, stands on a hill and is part of the brilliantly-contrived landscape setting.

Claydon House, Bucks.: Lightfoot's carved woodwork
around a niche in the North Hall.

CAMBRIDGESHIRE
Anglesey Abbey

There was an Augustinian priory here (never an abbey), and among post-Dissolution owners was Hobson of 'Hobson's Choice' fame. A mansion incorporating remains of the priory was enlarged and much altered by the first Baron Fairhaven, a very wealthy patron of the arts who filled it with a superb collection of English, French, Italian, Chinese and other furniture, tapestries, clocks, porcelain, silver, bronzes, paintings and finely bound books. (There are more than 100 paintings, 150 watercolours, and 500 prints of Windsor Castle). Lord Fairhaven also extended and transformed the existing garden, 'which', says Sir Arthur Bryant, 'can compare with the great masterpieces of the Georgian era.' Its vistas, avenues and vast lawns are of great beauty and the statuary includes figures from Stowe. There are herbaceous borders, roses and a water-mill.

Sawston Hall

The ancestral home of the recusant Huddlestons was begun in 1557, incorporating part of an older house with Mary Tudor associations. The Great Hall has oak panelling painted to imitate walnut. Much other panelling, Mortlake and Flemish tapestries, long gallery and private chapel are to be seen, as well as royal and family portraits (including Queen Mary by Scrots), good furniture and two hiding-places. Father Huddleston, who assisted Charles II in his escape after Worcester, was of this family, and the house has a copy of the proclamation exempting him from the order banishing Roman Catholic priests from this country. The gardens have yew hedges and form a peaceful setting to the romantic house.

CHESHIRE
Adlington Hall

The name of Legh has been interwoven for centuries with Adlington's history; ever since, in fact, Thomas de Corona gave the estate to his sister and her husband, John Legh of Booths, in 1315. Once moated, the present house surrounds a quadrangle and is a striking mixture of styles, although it was reduced in size in 1929. 16th-century timbering neighbours 17th and 18th-century brick; the south front is dominated by a lofty stone portico. In the Great Hall are supporting oak trees with their roots still in the ground, which are remnants of a hunting-lodge once on the site. The Great Hall is also notable for its heraldic canopy, murals and 'Father Smith' organ. A finely panelled dining room of 1749 has fluted pilasters and carved overdoors, and there are family portraits and some good furniture.

Capesthorne

Incredibly, this great house of the Bromley-Davenports, which presents an enormous turreted façade to park and lake, goes back to the early 18th century and John Wood the elder. It was extensively altered by Blore, and Salvin reconstructed the centre block after the 1861 fire. The spacious rooms, some with moulded ceilings, are chiefly notable for their contents, though the saloon, drawing room and the staircase hall are handsome in themselves. There are important Italian pictures, works by Knapton and Kneller, an Allan Ramsay of Rousseau and Dahl portraits of Queen Anne and Speaker Bromley, whose robes and silver are here. Unfortunately the famous Romney of Mrs Davies Davenport III is now in Washington. Greek and Roman sculpture, votive heads and ancient vases, English, French, German and American furnishings are shown. Dorothy Davenport spent twenty-six years working the hangings on the bed in the room bearing her name. There is a private theatre and, in the gardens, a chapel originally by Wood.

Lyme Park

In 1946 Richard Legh, third Baron Newton, made over Lyme Park and an estate of some 1,300 acres to the National Trust. The property had belonged to

Lyme Park, Cheshire: the 1720 front by Leoni.

Tatton Park, Cheshire: Lewis Wyatt's entrance hall,
*c.*1807-13.

Tatton Park, Cheshire: Lewis Wyatt's library, 1809.

below. Lanhydrock House, Cornwall: the east front
(1635-50; partly rebuilt after 1881).

the Leghs for exactly 600 years and part of the present house goes back to Sir Piers Legh who succeeded in 1541. Alterations were made after the Restoration (such as the removal of gables and insertion of sash windows), and in 1720 Leoni was engaged to carry out major work which involved recasing the sides and remodelling the central courtyard. Lewis Wyatt made further alterations, adding an odd, balustraded 'box' for servants over Leoni's portico. The drawing room retains inlaid Elizabethan panelling, magnificent plasterwork and heraldic glass. The saloon (with Leoni's Rococo ceiling), has early 18th-century pearwood carvings of great elaboration. Leoni's 'Grand Staircase' and the Elizabethan gallery must be noted. There is a formal garden and red and fallow deer roam the park.

Tatton Park

William Egerton began the present Tatton with Samuel Wyatt as architect; the work was carried on by his son assisted by Samuel's nephew, Lewis Wyatt. Victorian and later additions have been made, including the remarkable Tenant's Hall. After the death of the fourth and last Baron Egerton of Tatton, the house and its magnificent contents went, as he wished, to the National Trust. Among the rooms the Music Room and Drawing Room, with decorated ceilings and cherry-coloured silk and the Yellow Drawing Room in turquoise and yellow are particularly fine. Very many pictures of different schools; English, French and Italian furniture (some Gillow), and much silver, glass and porcelain. The extensive and very beautiful gardens contain a Lewis Wyatt orangery, a Japanese garden, a pinetum and many rhododendrons and azaleas planted by the last Lord Egerton. The park, partly landscaped by Repton, contains red and fallow deer, goats, Soay and St Kilda sheep.

CORNWALL

Antony House

Antony is early 18th century, austere but noble, with silvery stone and excellent proportions in the main structure allied to brick forecourt buildings and arcades. The interior is especially notable for its original wainscoting and staircase, and has a range of family portraits, china, needlework and good furniture. Terraced gardens descend from the house. There are yew hedges and fine iron gates and views to the River Lynher and beyond. The estate became the property of the Carews about 1450, passing to the Poles in 1799. The stable block dates from 1694, and like the early 17th-century building beside it, is a relic of the previous house, the home of Richard Carew, author of 'The Survey of Cornwall' (1602). Sir John Carew Pole made over the house to the National Trust in 1961.

Cotehele

Sometimes called the 'Knole of the West', Cotehele belonged for many generations to the very ancient family of Edgcumbe, but was only rarely occupied by them in recent times. A remarkably little altered granite house on older foundations, it dates mainly from between 1485 and 1539 and has a gatehouse, courtyards and a striking Great Hall. House and land were acquired by the Treasury in 1947 from the sixth Earl of Mount Edgcumbe in lieu of death duties, Cotehele being the first of historic houses to be taken over in this way. They now belong to the National Trust. The furniture, tapestries and needlework (mainly 17th and early 18th century), and armour, in which Cotehele is so rich, are, however, loaned by Lord Mount Edgcumbe. The chapel has notable woodwork and a clock retaining the original foliot balance, 'a device in use prior to the introduction of the pendulum'. The gardens, with ponds, rills, rhododendrons, terraces and dovecote are of great charm, as is the wooded setting by the Tamar.

Lanhydrock

Lanhydrock was built in the 17th century by two members of the Robartes family, but the east wing was removed in 1780 and in 1881 a fire did very serious damage. Careful rebuilding followed and fortunately the long gallery, with its barrel-vaulted ceiling depicting Old Testament scenes, entirely escaped, though bookcases have replaced much of its panelling. The house contains Brussels and Mortlake tapestries, portraits by Kneller, Romney and Thomas Hudson, and some excellent giltwood George II furniture from Wimpole Hall, Cambridgeshire, as well as Louis XIV writing-tables. The charming pinnacled gatehouse of two storeys was begun in 1636, but not finished until 1651. The gardens are of outstanding interest and beauty. Lanhydrock was given to the National Trust by the seventh Viscount Clifden (Francis Gerald Agar-Robartes) in 1953.

St Michael's Mount

Rising romantically on its island (accessible by causeway or ferry, according to tide) St Michael's Mount is of great historical interest. Edward the Confessor founded a monastery here which was attached to the Abbey of Mont St Michel in Normandy. At the close of the 12th century a royal castle was built and this underwent the ignominy in 1473 of being captured by Lancastrians disguised as pilgrims! St Michael's Mount was also captured by Perkin Warbeck and in the Civil War served as a Royalist stronghold. Sir John St Aubyn bought it in 1660 and it descended to the third Lord St Levan who gave the property to the National Trust in 1954. There has been a great deal of alteration through the centuries and the buildings are a mixture of medieval, 17th, 18th and 19th-century work. Particularly interesting is the Chevy Chase Hall with its plaster frieze of the battle. Painting, furniture, arms and armour. Notable planting in the gardens.

Trerice

The present house, built by Sir John Arundell about 1570, includes something of an earlier structure, and stands on land long in the possession of Sir John's family. External features include the very beautiful scrolled gables, the huge window of the Great Hall with 576 panes, some being of the original glass, and the semi-circular window of the drawing room or solar. Inside, one particularly notes the magnificent plasterwork in the attractively furnished hall with the initials of John, his wife and his sister, the even more elaborate ceiling of the drawing room and its heraldic overmantel with the curious date: ANNO:DOMINI:MCCCCCLX3! The plasterwork at Trerice bears striking similarity to that in certain other West Country houses, including Buckland Abbey. The house passed from the Arundells to the Wentworths and Aclands and was bought by the National Trust in 1953 from Mr Somerset de Chair with funds from the will of Mrs Annie Woodward.

DERBYSHIRE
Chatsworth

The Elizabethan mansion, built by 'Bess of Hard-wick' and her second husband, Sir William Cavendish, was completely demolished by their descendant, the first Duke of Devonshire. William Talman and Thomas Archer were employed on the magnificent house completed before the Duke's death in 1707. Interior decoration by Samuel Watson (and his assistants), Laguerre, Verrio, Thorn-hill, Tijou, Gardom and Cibber is all of great splendour. The paintings, tapestries, furniture, books, manuscripts and old master drawings defy description in a small space. Wyatville added a large wing with a theatre for the sixth Duke. The grand setting of a vast park with climbing woods, cascade, fountains and statuary, is of varying dates. The estate village of Edensor has a Gilbert Scott church.

Haddon Hall

This very lovely hillside house dates from Norman to Jacobean times, and is set around two courtyards with the 14th century Great Hall in the middle range. A private chapel contains medieval murals (St Christopher is depicted) and 17th-century wood-work, and there is more of the latter in the gallery which has windows on both sides. Most of the work at Haddon is either by the Vernon or Manners family, Sir John Manners, as is often related, having married the Vernon heiress under (allegedly) romantic circumstances. Their descendant, the ninth Duke of Rutland, restored and most carefully modernised Haddon after a very long period during which it was an unoccupied showplace. There are fine tapestries and the terraced gardens are celebrated.

Hardwick Hall

Traditionally 'more glass than wall', Hardwick was built by Elizabeth, Dowager Countess of Shrews-bury, on land which had long belonged to a branch of her family. She married four times, each time in-creasing her riches so that eventually, though of comparatively humble origins, she became prob-ably the richest woman in the country after the Queen. She displayed her power and wealth in her insatiable passion for building, Hardwick being her supreme achievement. With its original plan and enormous windows it was in its day a novelty. The High Great Chamber was described by Sacheverell Sitwell as 'the most beautiful room, not in England alone, but in the whole of Europe'. The contents are of equal quality; references to some in an ac-count book of 1587 show that certain of the rooms were specially designed to house them, while the purchase of many others are found dated in sub-sequent records. Long the property of the Caven-dish family, Hardwick passed to the National Trust in 1959.

Kedleston

Although Horace Walpole and Dr Samuel Johnson were critical of Kedleston, this 18th-century 'palace' of the Curzons is an outstanding building with central block and flanking wings. Replacing a mansion which was almost certainly by Smith of Warwick, it had no less than four architects—James Paine, Matthew Brettingham, Robert Adam and, as Geoffrey Beard has shown, Samuel Wyatt. The Marble Hall, 'Roman in magnificence' (Sacheve-rell Sitwell), boasts immense alabaster columns, classical statues and plasterwork by George Rich-ardson. Joseph Rose (1746-1799) was responsible for other stucco-work, that in the dining room frames ceiling paintings by Zucchi and Kauffmann, and on the walls paintings by Snyders, Zuccarelli and other artists. The famous palm-tree bed and dolphin furniture must be mentioned, and also the bridge in the park (Adam again) and the church, with family monuments, which has survived the village.

Melbourne Hall

In Jacobean times, Sir John Coke leased Melbourne from the Bishop of Carlisle. Thomas Coke, Vice-Chamberlain to Queen Anne and George I, added handsomely to the house (the east façade is by William Smith the younger) and laid out magnifi-cent formal gardens which survive in somewhat modified form with lead figures, fountains, vistas, yew hedges and Robert Bakewell's 'birdcage'

Chatsworth, Derbs.: the Cascade House
by Thomas Archer.

Haddon Hall, Derbs.: a distant view.

below. Haddon Hall: the long gallery, *c.*1550-1607.

Haddon Hall: the great hall and the 15th-century
panelled screen.

Hardwick Hall, Derbs.: the great presence chamber with its painted plaster frieze modelled by Abraham Smith.

Hardwick Hall: the main staircase.   *below*. Hardwick Hall: the tapestry-hung long gallery.

Kedleston, Derbs.: the Roman hall, with columns of
Derbyshire alabaster.

arbour. Through a daughter, the house passed to the Lambs, one of whom was Queen Victoria's Lord Melbourne. His sister Emily (first Countess Cowper, then Lady Palmerston), took Melbourne to the Cowpers, from whom it passed to the present Lord Lothian's family. The interior is of exceptional charm, with royal and family paintings, Rembrandt and Gainsborough drawings, Charles II chairs, Chippendale mirrors, a Tompion clock and good glass and china.

DEVON
Arlington Court
In the 14th century John Chichester married the heiress of Sir John Raleigh who brought him the Arlington estate which was to descend to the late, much-travelled and remarkable Miss Rosaline Chichester. She gave the house, contents and nearly 3,500 acres to the National Trust in 1946-47. It is thought that a Tudor house survived until 1790, when John Palmer Chichester built a new mansion to be seen in old pictures. This went in 1820 and Thomas Lee of Barnstaple designed the present building (later extended), of severe exterior save for giant pilasters and a Doric porch. A good deal of original decoration remains internally and the suite along the south front, divided by pillars and pilasters into three 'rooms', is imposing. The house contains 18th and 19th-century furniture, French, Chinese and English porcelain, snuff boxes, ship models, shells, gauache drawings of Neapolitan scenes, but the most important feature is Blake's 'Vision of the Cycle of Man's Life' found on top of a cupboard after a century.

Saltram
Work of different dates between 1720 and 1820 masks the remains of a Tudor house, but the most important architectural features are rooms designed after 1768 by Robert Adam. His dining room has exquisite plasterwork, which provides a setting for wall and ceiling paintings by Zucchi, and contains a sideboard with accompanying urns and pedestals from his design. He was also responsible for the magnificent saloon, the sofas and armchairs in which are undoubtedly his, and were presumably made by Chippendale who received over £200 for work at Saltram in 1771-1772. Both rooms have carpets of Adam design. The house contains fourteen portraits by Reynolds whose father was a local schoolmaster. Other English, as well as continental, furniture is to be seen, together with Chelsea, Meissen and Chinese porcelain, a fine library, an Adam orangery and a landscaped park overlooking Plymouth Sound. Saltram has passed from the Parkers, Earls of Morley, to the National Trust.

Saltram House, Devon: the saloon, with plasterwork
by J. Rose jnr. and ceiling paintings by Zucchi,
c.1769.

DORSET

Creech Grange

A grange of Bindon Abbey stood at Creech. Shortly after the Dissolution, Oliver Lawrence built a mansion which survives in lovely surroundings, though in an altered and reconstructed condition. Denis Bond, whose family acquired the estate at the close of the 17th century (and still retains it) classicised the south front in 1740, and gave the library an effective Ionic screen. The gabled entrance front is a remarkably good Victorian rebuilding. Kentian mirrors and Louis XV pieces are among the furniture and there are family portraits. Lawns, clipped yews, formal beds and a 'canal' make a suitable background for the peacocks.

Forde Abbey

The mansion incorporates many remains of the large Cistercian abbey, including refectories, monks' dormitory, chapter house and cloisters, and in this way is of unique interest. Edmund Prideaux, M.P. for Lyme Regis in the Long Parliament, converted the buildings into a residence, with magnificent ceilings and wainscoting and a superb and elaborate staircase. Despite a great sale in 1846, and changes of ownership, Forde Abbey still retains Mortlake tapestries given to Sir Francis Gwyn (Prideaux's son-in-law) by Queen Anne. Other furnishings were bought back by Herbert Evans who planted many noble conifers in the last century. Some years after his death the estate passed by inheritance to Mrs Freeman Roper who, with her husband, successfully altered the extensive gardens.

Sandford Orcas

This old stone house with its gables, pinnacles, gatehouse, lawns and yews makes a lovely picture in conjunction with the nearby church. Various dates have been assigned to it, but it was most probably built just before the accession of Elizabeth I. The Knoyles and Hutchings families lived here and for a long while it was a farmhouse. Surprisingly well restored in Victorian times, it passed from a Hutchings to Sir Hubert Medlycott, Bart., of Ven in 1914, and it still remains with his family. Features within include a Jacobean hall screen with elaborate pierced parapet, a chimneypiece incorporating a coat-of-arms of James I brought from the Joiners' Hall, Salisbury, as well as restored 'draught' porches in the former great chamber. Medlycott portraits, a fine Wilton carpet with the family arms, pewter, porcelain, armour and coins are among the contents.

Sherborne Castle

An architectural conceit in a magnificent landscape (by Lancelot Brown whose only other Dorset commission was at Milton Abbey), Sherborne was begun by Sir Walter Raleigh, whose arms are on the Green Drawing Room ceiling, at the time when restoration of the ancient castle was abandoned. Sherborne Lodge, as it was once known, was originally a tall house with four corner towers. It was enlarged in the Jacobean period after its acquisition by the Digbys; wings and more towers were added, and the plan is now H-shaped. There are 18th-century ceilings, armorial fireplaces of considerable grandeur, a 'Strawberry Hill' library, and Victorian restoration and enlargements that could have been much worse. The collection includes family pictures, French and English furniture, and a famous painting showing Elizabeth I going in procession to a 'Society' wedding. The Digbys' heraldic ostrich (about to consume a horseshoe) is prominent at Sherborne.

Forde Abbey, Dorset: the south front.

below. Forde Abbey: the dining room, mid 17th-century.

DURHAM
Washington Old Hall

Parts of a very ancient house owned and occupied by the Washington family, including direct ancestors of George Washington, are incorporated in the stone-built 17th-century building rescued at the last moment from demolition in 1936, and now the property of the National Trust. In addition to appropriate 17th-century furniture, the Great Hall now contains busts of the first President by the sculptor Houdon who visited him at Mount Vernon, and a portrait of Washington (on a parchment drumhead) by Joshua Trumbull of Salem. The withdrawing room has very good Jacobean panelling from Abbots Langley and Elizabethan and Jacobean furniture. A good deal of restoration was needed and the staircase comes from the White Hart Inn at Guildford. There are prints and other pictures connected with George Washington, some original fireplaces and 18th-century iron gates from elsewhere.

ESSEX
Audley End

At vast expense, Thomas Howard, Earl of Suffolk built a palace here at the beginning of James I's reign, in a style which was described by Evelyn as being 'twixt antiq and modern'. Much of the building (at one time a residence of Charles II) has gone and much has been altered or rebuilt, but it is still a magnificent and remarkably harmonious structure. Vanbrugh worked on the house, and later the first Lord Braybrooke employed Robert Adam on a series of rooms and also built a chapel in 'Strawberry Hill' Gothick style. The original hall screen is quite outstanding. There are Dutch, Flemish and English pictures and an important Venetian scene by Canaletto; some very fine furniture includes tables by Adam, and Chippendale pieces. The Capability Brown landscape is kept as it should be, with mown grass. The property of the Ministry of Public Building and Works.

Bradwell Lodge

Late in the 18th century John Johnson added a classical house, of delightful detail, to a Tudor rectory for that extraordinary character, Henry Bate Dudley, who presented himself to the living from which he was eventually, and uncharitably ejected by the Bishop of London. As well as being an early editor of the 'Morning Post' and an agriculturist of note, Bate Dudley was a friend of Thomas Gainsborough who, we are told, sketched Mrs Siddons here. The 'elegant cheateau', to use one description, has an octagon room, a belvedere overlooking the Blackwater and concealing the chimneys, and grisaille paintings by Robert Smirke the elder in the drawing room.

GLOUCESTERSHIRE
Badminton

This truly ducal mansion was begun by Henry Somerset, first Duke of Beaufort, in the reign of Charles II. More work was carried out by the third Duke with the help of William Kent although the documentation is by no means all one would desire. One room contains panelling from Raglan Castle where the Somersets formerly lived, and there is a dining room with decorations by Grinling Gibbons. The 18th-century hall has large paintings by John Wootton. The state rooms house a truly magnificent collection of portraits and the famous Canalettos (the artist's first works in England). One of the latter includes a distant glimpse of Kent's delightful Worcester Lodge across the vast park, a building 'intended for supper on summer evenings when the view led across the Bristol Channel to the Welsh hills', to quote Sacheverell Sitwell. The parish church of Badminton is attached to the house and is in the Gibbs style, but later. The monument to the first Duke was formerly at Windsor and there is a 'drawing room' pew for 'the family'. Queen Mary made her home here in the Second World War.

Berkeley Castle

A building of great beauty and historic importance above terraced gardens and park, Berkeley has been the home of one family – with only short breaks in possession – for about 800 years, though the original FitzHarding name has become Berkeley. Some 12th-century work remains, including a steep mound. The 14th-century hall has an heraldic screen and minstrels' gallery imported by the last Earl of Berkeley from Wales. The chamber where Edward II was traditionally imprisoned before his murder in 1327 still exists. A series of noble rooms about an inner bailey contains magnificent tapestries, pictures by Hoppner, Gainsborough and others, superb mirrors, silver and 18th-century needlework on gilt furniture.

Blaise Castle

This classical mansion of the late 18th and early 19th centuries still retains a magnificent, wooded 'backcloth' despite nearby urban development. The estate is graced by a small, mock-medieval castle; the house itself was begun by John Harford to William Paty's design. The grand landscape is by Humphry Repton, and John Nash was responsible for an orangery and charming thatched dairy. Nash also designed the 'story-book' Blaise Hamlet for estate pensioners which now belongs to the National Trust. The mansion, which has a good staircase-hall and was once noted for its paintings, was enlarged to C. R. Cockerell's designs in William IV's reign. It remained in the Harford family until 1926 when it was acquired by the Corporation of Bristol. It is now used as a folk museum of great interest, though the 'family' atmosphere has, of course, departed.

Dodington House

Christopher Bethell Codrington employed James Wyatt to design the present outwardly austere but impressive house on an estate which had been family property since 1578. There is a huge portico, and a graceful carving conservatory connects a contemporary church to the mansion. The entrance hall has scagliola columns with gilded capitals, coving and the original chandeliers. The internal glory of the Codringtons' home, however, is the immense central hall where much of the noble branching staircase came from Fonthill Abbey. There are good pieces of Sheraton and Chippendale furniture, busts, portraits and interesting relics of the slave trade. A Capability Brown landscape with lakes and a Gothic cascade survives; delightful classical lodges terminate the drives.

Dyrham Park

This very beautifully situated mansion of Bath stone was built by William Blathwayt, Secretary of State to William III, who employed more than one architect and incorporated parts of an earlier house. Hauduroy, a Frenchman, was responsible for one front, while the other is by William Talman of Chatsworth fame. The spacious and eminently habitable interior has two noble staircases, and other fine woodwork, including the wainscoting of the Balcony Room, as well as tapestries, Dutch paintings and good furniture, some by Gillow. A mag-

Berkeley Castle, Glos.: the stairway dated 1637.

Dodington House, Glos.: the west front. The quadrant greenhouse screened the service court and connects with the domed church.

below. Dodington: the entrance hall with porphyry columns, coloured marble floor and terra-cotta and gilded ceiling.

Dyrham Park: Talman's east front.

nificent state bed, long at the Lady Lever Art Gallery, has been returned on loan. An orangery flanks the house; the famous formal gardens have almost entirely vanished, but the church on its terrace forms a delightful adjunct. Dyrham belongs to the National Trust.

Owlpen Old Manor

This house, in its setting amongst church, hillside and terraced garden, has great romantic charm. Gabled and stone-built, and with medieval remains, it was rebuilt in the 16th-century by a Daunt(e), his family having acquired the estate by marriage with an Olepenne about 1464. A partial rebuilding was undertaken by Thomas Daunt in 1616; the east wing was altered for a descendant in George I's reign. Thus Owlpen exhibits both mullioned and sash windows, Tudor fireplaces and such features as a good Georgian doorway leading from hall to drawing room and a shell-headed alcove. Rare painted cloth and the arms of Daunt and Olepenne survive. In 1803 an heiress conveyed the property to a Stoughton. After neglect and sale, a conservative restoration was carried out between the Wars by Norman Jewson.

Snowshill Manor

Restored by the late Charles Paget Wade, who found it in a state of sad neglect, Snowshill (standing in an attractive village), goes back to the 16th century and has had many owners including the Sanbachs whose arms can still be seen. 17th and early 18th-century additions were made to the original gabled building of Cotswold stone and the pleasing entrance front, with high-pitched roof and both sash and mullioned and transomed windows, gives no hint of the rambling structure behind. The rooms, with their curious names, contain a highly individual collection of furniture, toys, clocks, antique bicycles, Japanese armour, model farm wagons, musical instruments, spinners' and weavers' tools, and other curios. Charming terraced gardens descend from the house and were laid out by the late owner who cleverly incorporated existing buildings into the scheme. Mr Wade made over the property to the National Trust in 1951.

HAMPSHIRE
Mottisfont Abbey

The house is on the west bank of the River Test, surrounded by beech, chestnut, cedar and spacious lawns. There was actually no abbey – only a small priory of Augustinian Canons whose property passed after the Dissolution to Lord Sandys of The Vyne. Monastic work and alterations by Sandys are incorporated in the mansion which owes much of its present character to Sir Richard Mill, Sandys' descendant, who remodelled the south front and much of the interior in the early 1740s. A lovely room, painted in *tromp l'oeil*, is the last decorative work of Rex Whistler. Important monastic remains are the 'pulpitum' with heraldic shields and the 'cellarium'. The house and estate were given to the National Trust in 1957 by Mrs Gilbert Russell whose husband was of the ducal house of Bedford.

The Vyne

This very beautiful and unusual house, the diapered red brickwork of which is mirrored in a lake, goes back to the days of Lord Sandys, Henry VIII's Lord Chancellor and there is still a chapel, with important glass and a long gallery with linenfold panelling, of this date. In the mid-17th century, however, extensive alterations were made and John Webb designed the earliest classical portico possessed by any English country house. The Vyne was sold after the Civil War to Chaloner Chute, Speaker of the House of Commons, in 1659. A grand Palladian staircase was inserted in the 1760s and Rococo rooms of much charm date from about this time. The house contains good furniture and pictures, and a room papered with prints, as at Castletown and elsewhere. Sir Charles Chute, Baronet, left The Vyne to the National Trust in 1956.

The Vyne, Hampshire: the north front, with the
Tudor chapel on the left and Webb's portico in the
centre.

HEREFORD

Berrington Hall

This splendid stone house, with its portico and lovely setting amid gardens and Herefordshire countryside, was designed for Thomas Harley by Henry Holland. It was begun in 1778 and Lancelot Brown remodelled the surrounding landscape between 1775 and 1781. The original interior decoration of plasterwork and colouring is wonderfully graceful: the library ceiling has painted medallions of authors from Chaucer onwards; that in the drawing room has moulded figures of cupids leading sea-horses–evidently to commemorate the marriage of Harley's daughter to Admiral Lord Rodney's son in 1781. There is an outstanding staircase-hall and the boudoir boasts handsome scagliola columns. Paintings of Admiral Rodney's victories remain in the house, although it was sold in 1900 to the future Lord Cawley. Berrington is now a property of the National Trust, together with some of its contents.

Croft Castle

The Crofts apparently held land and houses here from before the Conquest until about 1746. The estate was repurchased in 1923 by the trustees of the 11th baronet who bequeathed it to the first Lord Croft. Complicated history after the Second World War left it a National Trust property with resident members of the family. The 14th or 15th-century structure has corner towers and 'Gothick' and mock-Jacobean windows, and inside there is a good 'Gothick' staircase and the Blue Room with Jacobean wainscoting from Radnorshire. Pictures by Gainsborough, Beechey and Lemuel Abbot decorate rooms with 17th and 18th-century ceilings and fireplaces. The park contains some famous chestnuts and beeches and in the charming church are tomb effigies of both Sir Richard Croft (d. 1509) and his wife.

Eastnor Castle

Eastnor was begun in 1812 by John, Second Baron (later first Earl) Somers, to the design of Sir Robert Smirke and no less than about 250 people appear to have been employed on the structure over a period of years. Owing to the scarcity of suitable timber, cast-iron roof trusses were employed. In the time of the second Earl, A. W. N. Pugin and G. E. Fox were engaged on extensive internal decoration and the third Earl adorned the great rooms with treasures, and the grounds with trees and shrubs, from abroad. The gatehouse, soaring corner towers, battlements and the Great Hall with its clerestory give an impressive 'baronial' effect, which is strengthened by the collection of Italian, German and English armour. Pugin's Gothic drawing room has French tapestries of the 'Seasons'; magnificent woodwork in the main library is of walnut inlaid with box, and much of that in a smaller library came from the Academy of the Intronati in Siena. The pictures include Italian works and examples of Van Dyck, Kneller, Romney and G. F. Watts. There are Indian and French carpets and Italian, Flemish and French furniture.

Eye Manor

Standing close to the medieval church and looking like the vicarage–a purpose which, in fact, it did serve for a time–Eye Manor was built by a rich slave-trader and sugar-planter called Ferdinando Gorges. It dates from the late 17th century, but the exterior was afterwards given sash-windows and a new porch. Ferdinando's fine rooms, however, were left virtually untouched and are quite remarkable for their elaborate ceilings in a naturalistic style. In the Great Parlour, for instance, flowers, fruit and leaves appear together with Diana, Hercules and the Hydra, boys with a lion, and a spaniel which has just flushed a wild duck. There is good contemporary wainscoting and a pleasing staircase, as well as Dutch paintings and marquetry, needlework pictures, Nankin and Staffordshire ware, colour-prints and costumes. Eye once belonged to Thomas Harley who also built the nearby mansion of Berrington.

below. Berrington Hall:
the first floor of the staircase hall.

Berrington Hall, Hereford: the entrance portico.

Berrington: the drawing room ceiling that celebrates the Harley-Rodney wedding in 1781.

below. Eastnor Castle, Hereford, seen from across the lake.

HERTFORDSHIRE
Hatfield House

Robert Cecil, Earl of Salisbury, second son of Lord Treasurer Burghley (and ancestor of the present Marquess of Salisbury) originally built this great Jacobean pile of brick and Caen stone, though there has been a great deal of careful restoration. Set in a huge park and elaborate formal gardens, with the interesting remains of a royal palace at hand, Hatfield has a splendid and richly carved staircase – one of the very best of its period – moulded ceilings, wainscoting, great library, private chapel and an exceptional gallery 150 feet long. The collection contains much 17th and 18th-century furniture, royal relics, manuscripts and a great range of paintings including the celebrated 'Rainbow' portrait (ascribed to Zucchero) and the 'Ermine' portrait (Nicholas Hilliard) of Elizabeth I.

Knebworth House

Although a curious and often fascinating house with interesting literary associations, Knebworth is but a small part of its ancient self. Much of the great house of the Lyttons was demolished, for financial reasons, by that formidable character Mrs William Bulwer (Elizabeth Lytton), who incidentally deprived the village parson of his congregations by holding her own service in the drawing room and forbidding her dependents to attend his! The west side of the once quadrangular mansion remains and this was extravagantly embellished by her son, the novelist, with turrets, weathervanes and battlements in 1843. Queen Elizabeth's room, and that used by leaders of the Long Parliament, survive. There are family portraits, elaborate chimneypieces and extensive gardens. The Lytton connection goes back to Henry VII's time, when Sir Robert Lytton, Under-Treasurer and Keeper of the Great Wardrobe, bought the estate from Sir Thomas Bourchier.

KENT
Hever Castle

The Boleyn family built a Tudor house inside a late 13th-century castle. In 1903, the moated home of Anne Boleyn (which had become a farmhouse) was purchased by William Waldorf Astor, first Viscount Astor of Hever Castle, who restored and extended it at enormous cost, adding a 'Tudor village' to house guests, servants, etc. Although much magnificent new woodwork was introduced, panelling in the Boleyns' gallery, and Henry VIII's and the Rochford Room is original. Pictures include examples of Holbein, Titian and Antonio Moro. There are Flemish and Burgundian tapestries, French royal armour, and Italian, French, Spanish and English furniture. Like the castle, the modern maze, the lake, the rhododendron walk and the Italian Garden, with its great assembly of statuary, draw very large crowds.

Knole

Knole has been successively an archbishop's palace, a royal possession and the home of the Sackvilles, Dukes of Dorset. Dating from medieval to Jacobean times it is of great size and built of Kentish 'rag', with reputedly 365 rooms, 7 courtyards and 52 staircases. The galleries and (often small) rooms contain a great collection of family pictures, furniture, tapestries and rugs, dating from the early 17th to the late 18th centuries. The ballroom retains Elizabethan panelling painted white, with an elaborate frieze. The Royal Bedroom contains the famous silver furniture. There are acres of garden and a great deer park. Knole, of course, is the 'Chevron' of Miss V. Sackville-West's novel 'The Edwardians'. It is a National Trust property though still occupied by Sackville-Wests.

Mereworth Castle

Though originally reflected in a medieval moat, Mereworth Castle is not a castle at all, but one of four English houses (Chiswick House and the now vanished Footscray Place and Nuthall Temple were the others) built in the style of Palladio's Villa Rotonda at Vicenza. Designed by Colen Campbell for the Hon John Fane, Mereworth is, in fact, an

Hatfield House, Herts.: the south front, dated 1611.   *below.* Knole House, Kent: the south front.

Knole House: the central gatehouse in the west front.

almost exact copy of the Italian building, but the two detached pavilions, providing extra bedroom space, were built after Campbell's time. The house has a portico to each front and the rooms are grouped around a domed octagonal hall. Twenty-four flues ascend to the cupola. Italian artists and craftsmen were employed on the grand interior. There are formal gardens, cedars and a landscaped park. Mereworth Church, in the style of Inigo Jones's St Paul's, Covent Garden, was built to replace an edifice pulled down when one of the castle pavilions was built.

Penshurst Place

The home of Viscount De L'Isle, V.C. goes back to the 14th century and the time of the de Poultneys who built the Great Hall with its superb oak roof and other surviving work. In 1552 Penshurst was granted by the King to Sir William Sidney whose son, Lord President of the Marches and father of Sir Philip Sidney (who was born here), built the President's Tower and probably the gatehouse. Robert Sidney, Philip's brother, who was made Earl of Leicester, also added to it. The descent is too complex to be followed here, but Penshurst eventually passed to Sir John Shelley who took the additional name of Sidney. His son and grandson, the first and second Lords De L'Isle and Dudley, did much to restore the house and the latter made a notable garden. The contents – family portraits, tapestries, 17th and 18th-century and earlier furniture, silver, glass, arms and armour – are fabulous. The setting of church, park and village is a joy.

Squerryes Court

Sir Nicholas Crisp, or Crispe, built the present elegant house, with typical high-pitched roof and dormers, in or about 1681. The property was bought in 1731 by John Warde and has thereafter continued with his descendants; since that date various additions to the Charles II structure have been demolished. Some original features exist internally, but the dignified rooms (one with an 'Adam' ceiling) are more remarkable for their contents, among them a Wootton group of the Warde family in 1735, Dutch paintings, Van Dyck's 'St Sebastian', heraldic mirrors, good china, oriental cabinets and Joshua Morris tapestries. Squerryes has associations with General Wolfe whose home, Quebec House, is near. His portrait may be seen and in the charming gardens a cenotaph marks the spot where he received his first commission.

Squerryes Court, Kent: the garden front, 1681.

Mereworth Castle, Kent: a doorway in the gallery,
*c.*1723.

LANCASHIRE
Astley Hall

This extraordinary house—more strictly, extraordinary in its decoration—deserves to be better known. Given to Chorley by Mr R. A. Tatton soon after the First World War, it is a mixture of styles and materials and owes its origin to a family called Charnock. In 1665, Richard, son of Sir Peter Brooke of Mere, Cheshire, married the Charnock heiress and he replaced much of the old timbering with balustraded brick walls (later stuccoed) and large windows that include handsome bays. To him is due the quite fantastic (French?) plaster-work with its most elaborate designs of wreaths, putti, scallop-shells and festoons. Richard's staircase and long gallery are noteworthy and there are earlier wall-paintings depicting such diverse characters as Elizabeth I, Philip II of Spain, Tamerlane, Columbus, Drake and Spinola, as well as tapestries, pictures and furniture.

Leighton Hall

Set, with wonderful views, on the fringe of the Lake District, Leighton wears a Gothic disguise. In 1765 Thomas Towneley began building a classical house attached to medieval remains. A nephew sold the estate to Alexander Worswick and either he, or his son, Thomas, carried out the Gothic transformation, probably to the design of Thomas Atkinson of Chester. In 1822 Leighton Hall was sold by the nephew to his cousin, Richard Gillow of the famous furnishing family, and a Victorian wing was added. There are attractive interiors, much interesting furniture of the Gillow regime and family portraits, but it is the setting which visitors particularly remember.

LEICESTERSHIRE
Belvoir Castle

The first Belvoir castle was built in Norman times by the Conqueror's standard bearer at Hastings. The fifth Duke of Rutland, whose family had owned the estate for generations, employed James Wyatt in 1800 to design a vast, baronial edifice which was partly destroyed by fire sixteen years later. Rebuilding was carried out under the direction of the Duke's chaplain. Matthew Wyatt was responsible for the sumptuous Elizabeth Saloon in Louis XIV style, with panelling from a château belonging to Madame de Maintenon. Equally splendid is the Regent's Gallery with Gobelins tapestries and a series of busts by Nollekens. There is Chinese wallpaper in the King's Rooms, a dining room fit only for banquets, and a mass of arms—arranged decoratively—in the guardroom. Pictures include works by Poussin, Claude Lorraine, Teniers the younger, Hoppner, Reynolds, Gainsborough and Dame Laura Knight. The castle commands wide views.

Prestwold Hall

Prestwold, which was once described as 'the palace of the Wolds', is a house of mid-18th century, if not earlier, origin. It was extensively remodelled and encased in stone for Charles William Packe in about 1843. The architect of this transformation was William Burn and the result is most successful. The fine hall ceiling was inspired by some of Raphael's work and the whole interior, in fact, is notable for its Italian Renaissance decoration. It was attractively redecorated in parts in 1875. There are Chippendale mirrors and chairs, sculpture, Aubusson carpets, and family portraits. The conservatory is by Burn and the extensive grounds have cedars, yew hedges and many roses. A 'family' church is close to the mansion; its many monuments include that to Charles Hussey Packe (who died at Eton when fifteen), by the younger Westmacott.

Stanford Hall

The home of Lord Braye is in Leicestershire, although the exceptionally interesting church of Stanford-upon-Avon (tombs, medieval glass and

Belvoir Castle, Leicestershire: James Wyatt's south-
east and south-west fronts.

Belvoir Castle: the Elizabethan Saloon, 1825.

organ case of distinction) is just over the border of Northamptonshire. The William and Mary mansion was commissioned by Sir Roger Cave, second baronet, from William Smith the elder, but the interior was not completed at Cave's death in 1703. The grand staircase is by Francis Smith; the ballroom, with a coved ceiling, is by the younger William and incorporates remarkably good Victorian features. Many pictures include Stuart portraits bought in Rome, after the death of Cardinal York, by Sarah, Baroness Braye, sister of the seventh baronet. Francis Smith was probably also the designer of the elegant stable block which houses an aviation and motor vehicle museum. On the estate is a monument to Percy Pilcher, the flying pioneer who crashed fatally here in 1899.

LINCOLNSHIRE
Belton House
A stone house of exceptional beauty and dignity, Belton is sadly undocumented. Wren is reputed to have designed it, but it was probably Winde. The interior is decorated with carvings in the manner of Gibbons, original wainscoting and plasterwork, many fine family and other pictures, including works by Titian, Rembrandt and Reynolds. There are tapestries, excellent furniture and clocks by Vulliamy and Tompion; a Chinese Room has painted wallpaper and woodwork simulating bamboo. The garden, with Irish yews, fountain and statuary is delightful; so is the orangery. A parish church, reached from the grounds through wrought-iron gates, is encrusted with family monuments. Belton is the home of Lord Brownlow, descended in the female line from its builder, Sir John Brownlow.

Gunby Hall
Said to be Tennyson's 'haunt of ancient peace', Gunby Hall dates from 1700 and the time of Sir William Massingberd. A 'town house in the country', it derives from the 'houses of the greater sort' specified in the London Building Act of 1667 and its mason-architect almost certainly came from the metropolis. Its beautiful brick (it is doubtful if any of this really came from Tattershall Castle as legend has it) contrasts pleasingly with stone angle-dressings and architraves and the whole has great dignity. The house was enlarged in 1873. There is good woodwork and the contents include portraits by Reynolds, fine furniture and interesting documents. A complicated descent ensued before the house was made over to the National Trust in 1944; one Victorian Massingberd went on an expedition up the Amazon and was never heard of again. The surroundings, with old garden walls, a pigeon house and yew hedges, are charming.

Belton House, Lincs.:
the centrepiece of the entrance front.

LONDON DISTRICT

Boston Manor House

Though surroundings have sadly changed, this early 17th-century house, now belonging to the London Borough of Hounslow, is not to be missed by the connoisseur. It was built by Lady Reade (her initials and the date 1622 appear on rainwater heads) and altered by James Clitherow who bought the property in 1670. The brick exterior is most attractive with gables and pedimented ground-floor windows, but the Jacobean plasterwork within is exceptional. That on the ceiling of the State Drawing Room has emblems of the Five Senses and the room also contains a very good chimney piece incorporating the Sacrifice of Isaac in relief. Another fine ceiling in the State Bedroom depicts Hope with her anchor, surrounded by much elaborate decoration. There is *trompe l'oeil* painting of balustrading on the Jacobean staircase and some interesting 18th-century wallpaper discovered during the restoration.

Ham House

Sir Thomas Vavasor began this noble brick house in 1610, giving it loggias, gables and simple mullioned and transomed windows in regular order. Great changes were to be made later in the century, culminating in the work undertaken by William Murray, Duke of Lauderdale, and his wife. A hipped roof now replaces the gables; there are bays with sash-windows and external roundels for busts between the ground and first floor. The Duke and Duchess did much sumptuous redecoration and furnishing. The Duchess's descendants (she was Countess of Dysart by a previous marriage), Sir Lyonel Tollemache and Mr C. L. N. Tollemache gave the house and grounds to the National Trust in 1948, while the contents, including some of the best late Stuart furniture in England, were bought by the Government. The house is in the care of the Victoria and Albert Museum.

Hampton Court Palace

The palace was originally built by Cardinal Wolsey. He presented the huge building, with its splendid contents, to Henry VIII in a vain endeavour to regain the royal favour. The king enlarged the palace (where Edward VI was born), and there was extensive rebuilding to Wren's designs under William and Mary, rich decoration being completed in the time of Queen Anne and the earlier Georges. Tudor turrets and battlements contrast with the stately classicism of Wren. Henry VIII's Great Hall and Wolsey's (altered) chapel survive, as well as a Tudor kitchen. In the Wren buildings is work by Verrio, Honthorst, Kent and Tijou, state beds and pictures by Titian, Veronese, Corregio, Lely, Kneller and other artists. The Mantegna cartoons, which survive from Charles I's great collection, are here. There are grand formal gardens with Tijou gates, the great vine and the celebrated maze. The palace has not been a royal residence since George II's reign. Queen Victoria opened it to the public, and many rooms are used as 'grace and favour' apartments.

Kenwood (The Iveagh Bequest)

Transformed by the first Earl of Mansfield, the famous Georgian lawyer, with Robert Adam's assistance, Kenwood has been described as 'the product not of one but of many generations', and certainly goes back to the late 17th century. Lord Mansfield's nephew and heir soon enlarged the house with remarkable success, employing George Saunders as his architect. Adam's long library, with stucco work by Rose and panels by Zucchi, has apsidal ends with elegant columns and pilasters and is rightly regarded as one of his masterpieces. The house and over seventy acres (more land has also been preserved) were acquired for the nation by the first Earl of Iveagh who died in 1927. He also gave a fine collection of pictures, but most unfortunately the original Adam furnishings and some notable French furniture were sold before this time.

Osterley Park

Cedars, parkland, water and stables form the setting for Osterley, although it is now ensconced in London suburbia. The impressive house if far older in origin than might be imagined at first sight and was begun by Sir Thomas Gresham, founder of the Royal Exchange. Sir Francis Child bought the

Ham House, Richmond: the gallery, panelled in 1639.

Osterley Park House, Middlesex: the staircase.

Osterley Park: the entrance front with Adam's
portico.

below. Syon House, Middlesex: Adam's entrance hall.

property in 1711 and his grandson employed Sir William Chambers and Robert Adam to transform the turreted house into a splendid Georgian mansion. Osterley passed by marriage to the Earls of Jersey and the ninth Earl made it over to the National Trust in 1949. The house surrounds a central courtyard, raised in height in the 18th century and entered through a striking double portico with Ionic columns. The entrance hall is in blue and white with trophies in stucco; fine rooms sport beautifully moulded and coloured ceilings by Rose, fine carpets, Boucher/Gobelins tapestries, and, among other furniture designed by Adam, a fantastic state bed.

Syon House

Syon's history is a long one, and there was a monastery here, but we need not probe further than the time of Sir Hugh Smithson who assumed the Percy name through his heiress wife and became Earl, and then Duke, of Northumberland. He employed Robert Adam to carry out sweeping and magnificent changes within this embattled and turreted Thames-side house from 1752 onwards. The Great Hall, the State Dining Room, the Red Drawing Room (Spitalfields silk and an Adam carpet by Thomas Moore), the Ante Room (with columns of verd antique dredged from the Tiber), and the Gallery with its sunken bookcases and lovely colouring–to say naught of the Rose plasterwork and Adam furniture–all combine to create one of England's finest domestic interiors. Capability Brown was employed out-of-doors; the great conservatory was built later to Charles Fowler's design.

NORFOLK
Blickling Hall

The present mansion, the very epitome of the English country house, was built by Sir Henry Hobart, to Robert Lyminge's design, to replace an old seat of the Boleyns. The fifth Hobart baronet became Earl of Buckinghamshire in 1746, and the house (much altered by the second Earl who employed the Ivorys of Norwich) descended to the eighth Marquess of Lothian. The 11th Marquess left the property to the National Trust, having engaged Mrs Norah Lindsay to redesign the formal garden after 1930. The disposition of Lyminge's great staircase has been altered. Despite the attentions of J. Hungerford Pollen, the gallery with its rich ceiling is still impressive. Peter the Great appears on a tapestry presented by Catherine the Great to the second Earl and the collection includes pictures after Van Dyck and by Kneller and Gainsborough, and from Allan Ramsay's studio. There is some fine 17th and 18th-century furniture, an important library, an orangery, a park in the manner of 'Capability' Brown and a mausoleum by Joseph Bonomi.

Holkham Hall

The vast brick house of the Earls of Leicester is one of England's grandest Palladian mansions and is closely associated with the names of Lord Burlington, William Kent, Matthew Brettingham and Thomas Coke, first Earl of Leicester (died 1759). The last 'supervised every detail of the structure and the decoration' (Laver), and filled it with treasures brought back from his continental travels. The Great Hall, modelled on a Roman basilica, has been called 'a superb temple of dazzling alabaster', and all the principal rooms are magnificent, even sumptuous. Ceilings and chimney-pieces taken from designs by Inigo Jones and John Webb. Kent furniture, tapestries, sculpture and books are in abundance, as well as Gainsborough's 'Coke of Norfolk', and works by Rubens, Van Dyck and Batoni. Sir Charles Barry laid out the terraces and fountains and Humphry Repton altered the park.

Blickling Hall, Norfolk: the main façade.

NORTHAMPTONSHIRE

Althorp

Thanks to Henry Holland one is not immediately aware of the antiquity of this magnificent house. A 16th-century mansion was altered in Charles II's time, twice in the 18th century, and again last century and later. The gallery was panelled by Robert Spencer, second Earl of Sunderland; the extremely impressive staircase in a former courtyard was begun in 1666. A private chapel has woodwork from the great Duke of Marlborough's pew at St Albans (the senior Spencer line succeeded to the dukedom and personal possessions of Duchess Sarah are here), and there are doorcases and chimney pieces from Spencer House in London, and features from the family manor house at Wormleighton, Warwickshire. The particularly fine entrance hall contains pictures by Wootton, while the wealth of paintings in the house includes Italian and Dutch masters, and examples of Van Dyck, Lely, Kneller, Gainsborough and Reynolds. The furniture and china, the magnificent stables and extensive park are further delights. Mention, too, must be made of the family monuments in superb array at Great Brington.

Burghley House

Outwardly, this vast and noble pile is very much as it was left by Lord Treasurer Burghley, whose imposing monument is in St Martin's, Stamford, where other Cecils are commemorated. Much of the interior–the Great Hall and vaulted kitchen are exceptions–was transformed in the late Stuart era. Antonio Verrio worked here for many years, and his Heaven Room, the walls and ceiling completely from his brush, is probably the finest painted room in the British Isles. Magnificent state beds, Mortlake and Gobelins tapestries, Vauxhall mirrors, Chippendale commodes, marquetry tables, crimson damask vie with a mass of pictures. Waagen said of the last: 'There is no other seat which afford so completely, and on so grand a scale, a view of the taste in the arts which prevailed among the English nobility from the middle of the 17th till about the 18th century.' A formal garden with fountains, 'Capability'

Brown stables and a conservatory are set in the expansive landscape.

Castle Ashby

An ancestral home of the Marquess of Northampton, who also owns Compton Wynyates, Castle Ashby is an important 16th and 17th-century mansion originally enclosing three sides of a quadrangle, with an entrance 'screen' on the fourth which is ascribed to Inigo Jones. Wording from the 127th Psalm forms the parapet around the house, and the interior has fine moulded ceilings, richly carved chimney pieces and staircases. Fabulous contents comprise works by Bellini, Mantegna, Antonio More (Mary Tudor), Kneller, Raeburn, Lawrence, Dutch paintings, Brussels and Mortlake tapestry, and a collection of Greek vases called 'the richest private collection in Great Britain and one of the richest in the world'. Terraced and Italian gardens and a 3-mile avenue.

Deene Park

Pevsner devotes nearly three pages to this very large and rather extraordinary house where he notes some medieval work. Most of the much altered and extended building dates from after 1514 and the advent of the Brudenells who are still here. Their work extends from Tudor times to mid-19th-century when Lord Cardigan (Charge of the Light Brigade) built the ballroom. Features are the Elizabethan porch, the Great Hall with heraldic glass and open roof, the Tapestry Room, which 'has one of the finest and most elaborate Jacobean ceilings that can be found in the country' (Gotch) and the Georgian work. Crimean relics include the head and tail of the famous charger, Ronald. A much restored and rebuilt parish church (Matthew Digby Wyatt) contains Brudenell tombs and an important 17th-century reredos.

Rockingham Castle

Strikingly situated above Rockingham church and village, and with widespread views, the castle was once a royal hunting lodge, but after being given by Edward IV to Elizabeth Woodville it fell into decay. Restoration and rebuilding were begun about 1530 by Edward Watson, and it has ever since

Althorp, Northants.: the frontispiece designed by
Henry Holland, 1790.

Althorp: the entrance hall, c.1733, with paintings by
John Wootton.

Burghley House, Northants.: the west and south fronts from across 'Capability' Brown's lake.

below. Burghley House: the Heaven Room, Verrio's masterpiece.

Stoke Park Pavilions, Northants., by Inigo Jones, *c.* 1630.

remained with his descendants. The present owner is Sir Edward Culme-Seymour, Bart. Features include Norman drum towers, the heraldry in the Panel Room, the Great Hall and the gallery where Dickens produced plays. (The castle is the 'Chesney Wold' of *Bleak House*). Van Dyck, Reynolds and Zoffany portraits are matched by a collection of modern paintings.

Stoke Park Pavilions

These two delightful buildings, approached by a long drive, were almost certainly designed by Inigo Jones. They were the flanking pavilions (the earliest of their kind in the country) of a house which belonged to Sir Francis Crane, of Mortlake tapestry fame, who died in 1636. The house was burnt in 1886 and replaced by an elaborate 'Jacobean' effort absurdly attached to one pavilion! Fortunately this has now gone and the twin structures of stone with their charming detail have been carefully restored and are used residentially. The connecting colonnades survive fairly well and a Victorian pool reflects the pavilions. There is balustrading, also Victorian, and a statue which Pevsner thinks may be by Sir Henry Cheere. Peacocks parade in the garden which has a remarkable feeling of peace.

Sulgrave Manor

This small stone manor house has seen many changes since the ancestors of George Washington lived here, but there are still some notable features dating from the time of Lawrence Washington who died in 1584. The projecting porch to the south bears the remains of the Elizabethan royal arms as well as the family arms (that in plaster is modern) and the Great Hall survives with open fireplace and screens passage. The panelling in the Oak Parlour is probably of about 1700 when Sulgrave had passed from the Makepeaces, Lawrence's descendants, and there is a Charles II staircase. The appropriate contents include some delightful children's furniture, a lacquered clock by Thomas Utting of Yarmouth, tapestry, needlework, canopied beds, Washington relics and a Gilbert Stuart portrait of the first President. The kitchen, with its old equipment, is of much interest.

NORTHUMBERLAND
Callaly Castle

This huge house, which was so long in the hands of the Claverings, and bears scant resemblance to a castle, is far older in origin than might be thought for it is in part a 14th-century pele tower. Perhaps its most important feature architecturally, however, is the work designed about 1675 by Robert Trollope, the Newcastle architect, which incorporates very decorative pediments over the windows, but there is a grand saloon of mid-18th-century date which was most probably the work of James Paine. Very possibly some of its enchanting plasterwork was carried out by Italians who were responsible for decoration at Wallington. Much enlargement took place last century to house the Foreman collection of sculpture, afterwards most unfortunately sold. Among the pictures are examples of the work of Francis Hayman which once decorated supper boxes at Vauxhall Gardens in London. Nearby wooded hills add much to the charm of the setting.

Seaton Delaval

This extraordinary pile, magnificent, dramatic, and in some ways Sir John Vanbrugh's masterpiece, was badly damaged by fire in 1814, shortly after it had passed from the 'mad' Delavals to the Astleys. Fortunately the two vast wings – the courtyard between them is 180 feet deep – were undamaged and much restoration has now taken place on the central block. Huge, ringed Tuscan columns beneath a Doric entablature, clerestory, urns, pediments, balustrades, a splendid south portico and the fire-damaged statues within, all help to build up exciting and theatrical pictures. One wing has perhaps the finest stables in England, the other (kitchen) wing is used residentially and contains Delaval portraits, original furniture and relevant documents. There is a modern formal garden and a Norman church. The partly rural/partly industrial setting and the proximity of the sea add to the strange, romantic charm of the place.

Wallington

The house was begun in 1688 by Sir William Blackett, being intended probably, to quote the late Sir Charles Trevelyan, as 'a glorified shooting lodge'. It was left to his grandson, a Calverley who took the Blackett name, to transform 'the interior . . . from a comfortless barrack to a villa worthy of standing on the Pincian Hill . . .' He also made the great stable court, as well as gardens some distance from the house, and he planted extensively on the estate. Sir Walter, whose portrait by Reynolds adorns the saloon which has very lovely plasterwork, was succeeded by a Trevelyan nephew, and the estate remained with the Trevelyans until Sir Charles made it over to the Trust in 1941. In 1855 a central hall was formed and decorated with historical paintings by William Bell Scott. Among the portraits in the house are those of Susanna Trevelyan by both Reynolds and Gainsborough, and there is Chinese, Japanese and Meissen porcelain, important needlework and furniture and the library of Sir George Otto Trevelyan.

NOTTINGHAMSHIRE
Serlby Hall

Built of brick about 1740 for the first Viscount Galway (with whose family it has since remained) to the design of James Paine, Serlby was much altered after 1812, and further changes took place in the early part of this century. The handsome dining room still has its original moulded ceiling, with painting by Zucchi, and there is a delightful pillared drawing room. Serlby contains Chelsea and continental porcelain and much good continental glass. Among the many paintings are examples of Mytens, Lely, Pannini, Kneller, Wootton, Stubbs, Cotes, and there are pastels by John Russell and Daniel Gardner; a portrait of a Medici child is ascribed to Bronzino. The furniture includes notable English and French pieces, and there are mirrors which belonged to Madame de Sévigné. Fine trees are matched by the rather beautiful gardens.

Thoresby Hall

Built just over 100 years ago, Thoresby is the last great house of the 'Dukeries' to be privately occupied. Salvin's design is Neo-Tudor; turrets, gables and mullioned windows in a 'baronial' setting of deer park and elaborate grounds. The Great Hall is fifty feet high and lavishly decorated with arms, armour and many pictures including an equestrian portrait of the first Duc de Coigny (an ancestral connection) by La Cretelle. Chandeliers from the Château de Coigny hang in the sumptuous Blue Drawing Room, which has maple and walnut woodwork, a Savonnerie carpet and much blue silk damask. A surprisingly charming suite was occupied by Queen Victoria. The Pierreponts, who have owned Thoresby for centuries, held the Earldom and Dukedom of Kingston prior to a break in the male line.

OXFORDSHIRE
Aynho Park

Until recent years this great house was the home of the Cartwrights and the setting for a galaxy of treasures – Chinese and Worcester porcelain, Silesian glass, many pictures, fine rugs, French clocks and much more. By no means all the riches have gone, despite the sale and conversion of the house (it now consists of residential suites with the principal rooms as common rooms), and the building itself is well worth seeing. An Elizabethan or Jacobean house suffered badly in the Civil War. What was left was used after the Restoration for John Cartwright's new seat on which Edward Marshall, the King's Master Mason, seems to have been employed. Thomas Archer almost certainly carried out the extensive changes made by Thomas Cartwright, who had succeeded his grandfather in 1676, but much of this work was undone in alterations wrought by Sir John Soane. Soane's rooms are of dignified simplicity, and he linked the house to its flanking wings and made the orangery into a picture gallery. A delightful village and a Georgian church attached to an older tower are hard by.

Blenheim Palace

Built, with much dispute and fuss, to commemorate the military genius of John Churchill, Duke of Marlborough (with whose descendants in the female line it continues), Blenheim is one of the great Baroque palaces of Europe. Designed by Vanbrugh and Hawksmoor, it displays later embellishments by Sir William Chambers. The entrance hall, with a Thornhill ceiling, is sixty-seven feet high. The saloon was painted by Laguerre and one of its huge marble doorcases is by Gibbons who worked extensively here, though he did little work in wood. Brussels tapestries illustrate the famous victories, but an organ has displaced Van Dyck's great 'Charles I', now in the National Gallery. The Rysbrack/Kent tomb of the first Duke and Duchess is in the chapel. The modern gardens are striking; the 'Capability' Brown lake is spanned by Vanbrugh's earlier and gargantuan bridge. Blenheim was the birthplace of Sir Winston Churchill.

Aynho Park, Oxon.: the north front and forecourt flanked by Archer's wings.

below. Aynho Park: the Soane library.

im Palace, Oxon.: the entrance front, 1705-24.

Ditchley, Oxon.: the entrance front and pavilions

below. Rousham, Oxon.: the Jacobean entrance front as altered by Kent.

Broughton Castle

The late Sir Charles Oman called Broughton 'about the most beautiful castle in all England'. Enchantingly set within moated gardens and deprived of almost all its defences, it is really a highly successful marriage of medieval castle and later manor house. There are great mullioned and transomed windows, a hall with bare stone walls and an Elizabethan ceiling with pendants, armour, rows of gables and a private chapel which has a stone altar. The handsomely panelled drawing room contains an interior porch, and in a Gothic Revival gallery is a good assembly of family portraits. A vaulted dining room (with linenfold panelling probably from the hall screen), a bedroom with Chinese wallpaper and a superb fireplace are also distinctive features. The castle belonged to William of Wykeham and descended to the Fiennes and Twistleton families: the Viscounty of Saye and Sele is extinct, but the barony survives. A parish church, near the gatehouse, completes the picture, and has family tombs.

Chastleton House

Structurally a perfect example of a very early 17th-century house, Chastleton contains a barrel vaulted gallery, a Great Hall with screen and good plasterwork. Built by Walter Jones of Witney, this Cotswold stone house has never been sold, but has unfortunately lost its Sheldon tapestries, some of the best furniture and a set of Jacobite glass, though the family possessions are still of much interest. A parish church – rather overwhelmed by the mansion – adjoins the forecourt and a formal garden of about 1700.

Ditchley Park

James Gibbs was the architect of this very important early 18th-century mansion built by Francis Smith of Warwick. Kent and Flitcroft and the Italians, Vassalli, Artari and Serena all worked on the fine interior decoration. Large pavilions with cupolas flank the main house which suffers somewhat from the lack of a pediment on the entrance front (Gibbs did prepare a design), though one's gaze is drawn to the figures of Fame and Loyalty at roof-level.

Ditchley was built for George Lee, second Earl of Litchfield. Portraits of his grandparents, Charles II and Barbara Villiers, are still prominent features of the White Drawing Room, though, unfortunately, many of the pictures were dispersed after the death of Harold Lee-Dillon, 17th Viscount Dillon, in 1932. Genoa velvet remains in the Velvet Room and the stucco-work of the Saloon is excellent. There is a 'Capability' Brown landscape and a modern terrace and formal garden.

Edgcote House

Church, parsonage and the pedimented house with its stables make as delightful a group as any in Northamptonshire, and that is saying a good deal. In the church are beautiful Elizabethan tombs (as well as Rysbrack memorials) of the Chaunceys, the present house being built by Richard Chauncey who succeeded in 1742. William Jones has been described as the architect and certainly received fees of £250, but Pevsner considers that William Smith of Warwick may have been the designer, as he was of the stable block. The combination of iron-stone and dressings of fine grained grey stone is extremely effective. Abraham Swan was responsible for the interior woodwork, including an excellent staircase, Richard Newman made fireplaces and Jno. [Sic] Whitehead was paid £583-18-6d for 'plastering and stucco-work'. Much of the furniture is late 17th or early 18th-century. Edgcote passed by marriage to the Cartwrights and thence by purchase to the Courages.

Mapledurham House

Enchantingly situated beside the Thames, with attendant church and erstwhile almshouses, the former home of the Blounts, and now of the Eystons, is reached through narrow, wooded lanes. There is much older work, but the body of the house is Elizabethan with beautiful brickwork and projecting wings. Finely moulded and contemporary ceilings remain; a classical 'Adam' dining room and a 'Strawberry Hill' chapel of great distinction are also to be seen. A goodly series of family portraits include those of the Blount sisters associated with Alexander Pope. The carved heads of deer (of varying dates) in the hall are rare in England. The Bardolph aisle in the church (the Bardolphs were here before the Blounts) has notable monuments, including a particularly handsome brass.

Rousham

The view of Rousham, seat of the Cottrell-Dormers, from over the Cherwell is one of England's loveliest scenes, well-meriting Walpole's description of 'Daphne in little'. The house was begun by Sir Robert Dormer in time for it to be a Royalist garrison in the Civil War and bullet holes can still be seen in the main door. Subsequently much enlarged and altered, it contains handsome rooms by William Kent, who painted a ceiling, and Roberts of Oxford. There are some 150 pictures, including many family portraits, and some excellent furniture. Kent was responsible for the woodland gardens whose groves and glades are embellished with classical buildings, statuary and water, including a serpentine rill running through a stone channel and feeding the 'Cold Bath'. A dovecote and some formal bedding survive from an earlier garden. A small parish church, with family monuments, adjoins the grounds.

SHROPSHIRE
Attingham Park

Although incorporating older and later work, Attingham is chiefly by the Harley Street (London) architect, George Steuart, who designed a magnificent – if outwardly austere – mansion in neo-Grecian style for the first Lord Berwick. This was finished in 1785 and has a lofty portico and colonnades with large pavilions, the total width of the house extending to 400 feet. There are fine interiors, especially the red and gold dining room, and a small room in the style of Angelica Kauffmann, some of whose pictures are in the house. A picture gallery and staircase were added by John Nash. Many treasures assembled by the second Baron (who engaged Humphry Repton to landscape the park) had to be sold by him in 1827, but his successor collected paintings and important French and Italian furniture which are still to be seen. A portrait of Caroline Murat, Queen of Naples, Napoleon I's sister, is ascribed to F. P. S. Gerard, and a gilt daybed in the same room was probably made for the Queen.

Benthall Hall

Stone-faced, with prominent brick chimneys, Benthall was built towards the end of the 16th century despite a persistent tradition of earlier erection. The entrance front has five-faced bay windows of two storeys, a projecting porch and a series of gables and is particularly attractive. There are heraldic overmantels and Jacobean wainscoting. The rich 17th-century plasterwork of the West Drawing Room is exceptionally good, but the best feature of this charming house is the staircase resembling (but on a smaller scale) that at Aston Hall, Birmingham. The Great Chamber was restored in 1960. Welsh pewter and Jackfield pottery are among the contents. Mrs James Benthall gave the house to the National Trust in 1958. The pretty church by the gates is mainly 17th-century.

Mawley Hall

Romantically situated in a landscape park within sight of the crooked spire of Cleobury Mortimer, this very fine brick and stone, early Georgian, house of the Blounts narrowly escaped demolition in recent years. Mawley is sadly undocumented, but was probably the work of either Thomas White or Francis Smith. Unknown craftsmen of great skill gave the spacious interior magnificent plasterwork and wainscoting and an extraordinary staircase with a serpent-like monster as balustrading. The Inlaid Drawing Room sports the initials of Sir Edward Blount and his wife, Apollonia Throckmorton of Coughton; they built the house and placed their arms in a pediment, but these have been removed. The present owners have introduced appropriate furniture and pictures, as well as formal touches to the grounds.

Weston Park

Built mainly at the close of the 17th century for Sir Thomas and Lady Wilbraham, Weston has descended to the Bridgemans, Earls of Bradford. For years stucco hid the brickwork of the handsome, pedimented house but was removed by the fifth Earl. The gracious and wholly delightful interior (partly redecorated quite recently) contains Boucher-Neilson tapestries from the Gobelins factory, examples of Holbein, Jacopo Bassano, Van Dyck, Lely, Hoppner, Gainsborough and Stubbs, as well as Constable portraits. French and English furniture and a variety of porcelain. James Paine designed the Temple of Diana in the woodland garden, and 'Capability' Brown was responsible for the fine park landscape. A parish church adjoins house and orangery and contains family memorials.

SOMERSETSHIRE

Barrington Court

'In Barrington,' it has been said, 'English domestic architecture attains one of the 'peaks'.' The beautiful Renaissance house was built by the second Lord Daubeny about 1520. Subsequent owners were the Duke of Suffolk (Lady Jane Grey's father), Sir Thomas Phelips and the Strode family. It was bought by the National Trust in 1907 and rescued from ruin by Colonel A. A. Lyle who inserted much fine woodwork and turned the 17th-century brick stables of the Strodes into livingrooms. The strong French influence of the original stone house, with its twisted chimneys and finials, was probably dictated by Daubeny's long residence in France as Ambassador and Captain of Calais. Fine gardens.

Clevedon Court

Clevedon Court, which has close literary connections with W. M. Thackeray and the Hallams, was purchased by Sir Abraham Elton, first Baronet, in 1709, but the house goes back to the 14th century, being originally built, it is suggested, by Sir John de Clevedon. The chapel and porch are of that century, the former having a unique window in the form of a panel of quatrefoils. So is the much altered Great Hall which has a flat ceiling and Tudor windows and fireplace. For a period the house belonged to the Wakes of Northamptonshire, one of them selling the property in 1630 to John Digby, Earl of Bristol. The Elton ownership began after the death of the third Earl. Sir Edmund Elton, who died in 1920, started the Elton pottery and examples of the ware–no longer made–can be seen in the house. In its pleasing hillside situation, Clevedon Court– some extraneous features having been removed– now belongs to the National Trust, but a family connection is maintained.

Dunster Castle

The castle of the Mohuns came to the Luttrells in the first years of the 15th century. Dunster, 'guarding' a famous village, is Luttrell property today, though there has been one break in the male line. Sir Hugh Luttrell, Seneschal of Normandy, built the outer gatehouse and earlier work survives in

Attingham Park, Shropshire: the south front.

below. Barrington Court, Somerset: the original entrance front.

Clevedon Court, Somerset: the south front which includes the reticulated tracery window to the 14th-century chapel.

Montacute, Somerset: Jacobean bed, 1612.

below. Montacute: the hall with its Renaissance screen.

Montacute: another view of the hall.

Prior Park, Bath: the Palladian bridge, c.1755.

what has been called 'the greatest baronial survival of the West Country.' (Oman). Much belongs to the time of George Luttrell who succeeded in 1557, but a 'picturesque' restoration was effected last century by Salvin. The main staircase of 1681 is lavishly decorated with huntsmen, stags, hares, flowers and foliage. In the Leather Gallery are embossed, gilded and painted panels of leather depicting the story of Antony and Cleopatra. Portraits include works by Hans Eworth, Vanderbank, Dahl and Reynolds, and there is some excellent Chippendale furniture. Olives, lemons and mimosa grow out-of-doors.

Lytes Cary

The home for centuries of the Lyte family, this beautiful stone house dates from the 14th to the 20th century. It was bought, restored and enlarged by the late Sir Walter Jenner. He also made a charming topiary garden and left the estate to the National Trust in 1948 with a collection of furniture. There is a medieval chapel and a Great Hall with arch-braced roof. Jacobean panelling survives in the Great Parlour despite one-time misuse as a store. The Little Parlour may be that in which Henry Lyte, of herbal fame, and his son Thomas, pursued their horticultural and antiquarian studies. The important plasterwork of the Great Chamber dates from about 1533 and incorporates the arms of Henry VIII. The furnishings include Jacobean, Cromwellian, Charles II, Queen Anne and Georgian pieces.

Montacute

A late Elizabethan mansion of exceptional quality and charm, Montacute reputedly has the longest long gallery in England, where the Phelips children used to ride their ponies on wet days. Oriel windows, statues of the 'Nine Worthies', and the 'new' entrance front brought here from Clifton Maybanke are conspicuous aspects of the exterior. The delightful Great Hall still has its screen, and though, when the National Trusts took over the house, it was without ancestral contents, the atmosphere of a lived-in country house has been skilfully recreated. Pictures and furniture of much interest and the famous Stoke Edith hangings are among the contents. The garden, with balustraded terraces and pavilions, forms a beautiful setting.

Prior Park

Now a Roman Catholic college, Prior Park has an involved history and has long ceased to be a private residence. It was designed by John Wood the elder for Ralph Allen, who most successfully reorganised the postal service in the West with great financial advantage to himself. A special tramway conveyed masses of stone to the site of a house 'to see all Bath and for all Bath to see'. This was given a central block (with imposing portico) connected by curving arcades to wings for servants, horses and coaches. The buildings, much altered but still very impressive, extend for a quarter of a mile. Fire devastated the interior of the main structure in 1836 and many fine fittings from Hunstrete House were subsequently introduced. Allen's private chapel survives. The prospect over the city and down to the lakes and Palladian Bridge in a 'Capability' Brown landscape is superb.

Blithfield Hall: the great hall with plaster gothic
vault and decoration by Bernasconi (1822).

STAFFORDSHIRE
Blithfield Hall

This is a house in which many styles and periods mingle with remarkable success. The estate passed to the Bagots by a 14th-century marriage and the present mansion probably retains medieval work. 16th-century timbering, Elizabethan panelling, a mid-17th-century staircase of charming design, and architectural panelling of the early 18th century are a few of the most important features. The New Drawing Room was new in Georgian times and the Great Hall was decorated with Gothic plasterwork by Bernasconi in the early 19th century when the house received its 'baronial' front. Although many Bagot possessions have been dispersed, Blithfield contains family portraits, costumes and other objects of ancestral interest. Close to the house is a classical orangery and the parish church of Blithfield with family monuments. Family carriages are in the stables and from the park the great Blithfield reservoir is visible.

Chillington Hall

The Giffards have held the estate since 1178, and it is likely that part of a Tudor house is embedded in the 18th-century structure. Peter Giffard most probably employed William and Francis Smith on the south block. Most of the house, however, was rebuilt by his grandson, Thomas, to the designs of Soane who gave it the portico, pillared hall and stately top-lit saloon, though the architect's ideas were never fully realised. Peter's elegant staircase, adorned with heraldic panther heads, is accompanied by decorative (Italian?) stucco work. The ubiquitous panther motif, and that of a knight drawing a bow, appear in the saloon with its curious fireplace. The contents include portraits by Batoni and others, landscapes and pleasing Georgian furniture which includes a fabulous state bed. The large park has an exceptional 'Capability' Brown lake, a bridge by Paine and a temple very possibly by Soane. In a stone screen near the house are handsome gates which have been considered good enough to be by Robert Bakewell of Derby. Giffard's Cross marks the spot where Sir John Giffard of Henry VII's day shot an escaped panther (there were country house menageries long before Longleat, and hence the crests). There are good family tombs—displaying numerous progeny—in Brewood Church.

Moseley Old Hall

Like Boscobel, and the now vanished Bentley Hall and Whiteladies, Moseley is associated closely with the escape of King Charles II after the Battle of Worcester in 1651. Unfortunately, Victorian brickwork replaces the black and white exterior seen in old pictures, but the interior with its panelling, fine roof timbers and former chapel is of much interest. Appropriate furniture, portraits and relics have been placed on view and a small formal garden created. There is still the hiding-place adjacent to the royal bedroom, and the bed used by the King has been returned from Wightwick Manor. Descendants of Thomas Whitgreave, who was host to the King here, remained in possession until 1925. The house was later given to the National Trust by Mrs N. Wiggin whose husband started the work of restoration.

Shugborough

The present house was begun by William Anson in 1693, as a central block with connected pavilions. His elder son, Thomas (the younger was the famous admiral whose wealth helped to embellish the property), added to the mansion and erected the monuments by 'Athenian' Stuart and the Chinese House that are great features of park and grounds. The first Viscount Anson engaged Samuel Wyatt to carry out additions and alterations, the former including a grand portico. His son, the first Earl of Lichfield, had to sell many of the fine contents, but excellent French furniture was introduced by his successor. There are Reynolds and other portraits, and the principal rooms—some by Wyatt or Stuart—are most impressive. The property of the National Trust, Shugborough is leased to the Staffordshire County Council, and has a museum of county life in the kitchen and stable block.

Wightwick Manor

Wightwick, with its contents and grounds, has been

Shugborough, Staffs.: the east front
by Samuel Wyatt.

below. Shugborough: an *œil de bœuf.*

Shugborough: the Great Dining Room, probably by
James Stuart, 1764-70.

Wightwick Manor, Shropshire: the east end of the
garden front, 1893.

well described as 'an admirable specimen of the best artistic output of the mid- and late-Victorian era', and as 'representing the best of the Pre-Raphaelite and the Morris schools'. Begun by Theodore Mander in 1887, and enlarged a few years later, the timber-framed house with its embattled brick tower was chiefly designed by Edward Ould of Liverpool. The gardens are principally by Alfred Parsons and his partner, Partridge. There are moulded ceilings in English Renaissance style, de Morgan· tiles and pottery, Morris fabrics and wallpaper, plaster panels of Orpheus and Eurydice, Kempe glass, and that stange portrait of Mrs Morris with Mrs Rossetti's hair, the face by Rossetti, the rest by Ford Madox Brown. A National Trust property.

SUFFOLK
Heveningham Hall
A Queen Anne house is embodied in the present mansion which was begun by Sir Robert Taylor for Sir Gerard Vanneck. Imposing as the monumental exterior is, it is surpassed by James Wyatt's exquisite rooms. These include a hall nearly seventy feet long with a classical screen, elaborate paving and fan-vaulting. The lovely saloon has decorations by Biagio Rebecca and there is a delicately balustraded staircase and an Etruscan Room. Original furniture is to be seen, despite a great dispersal of contents at the end of the last century. Lancelot Brown was employed out-of-doors. 19th-century formal gardens include an exceptional orangery, and there is a pretty game-larder in a courtyard.

Ickworth
This is perhaps the strangest house in England, if not in the British Isles. A vast rotunda is flanked by long wings and terminal pavilions, giving a width of about 600 feet. Stuccoed and with external friezes from the Illiad and Odyssey by Flaxman, the mansion was begun in 1794 (Francis Sandys, architect) at the behest of Augustus Hervey, fourth Earl of Bristol, who was also Bishop of Derry and a great connoisseur and traveller. He died in Italy and never saw it, but the work was carried on by his heir. The chief rooms are of lofty grandeur and contain paintings by Gainsborough, Reynolds, Romney and Lawrence, and there are original Wilton carpets of about 1826, magnificent silver and English and French furniture of high quality. The gardens and immense park boast many fine trees which tend to obscure the buildings. A National Trust property.

Melford Hall
Standing on former monastic land, and in one of England's loveliest villages, Melford was built by Sir William Cordell, Master of the Rolls to Elizabeth I who visited him here. The gabled and turreted mansion of brick now displays sash as well as mullioned windows, and there has been much internal change. The Great Hall has armorial and portrait glass. The Hyde Parker Room (restored after a fire) contains Chippendale pieces and portraits by

Heveningham Hall, Suffolk: the hall by James Wyatt.

Ickworth, Suffolk: the north front.

below. Melford Hall, Suffolk: the Cordell room with mid-18th-century Rococo stuccowork.

Melford Hall: the four stately turrets of the west front.

Romney and Reynolds, of the Parker family which purchased Melford in the 18th century. An outstanding room is the Regency Library formed by Sir William Parker and retaining bookcases, tables and chairs of his time, as well as naval pictures by Serres of family interest. Also in the house is a painting of Countess Rivers of Melford, who suffered severely for her support of the Royalist cause when the house was looted and damaged.

SURREY
Clandon Park
Not the first great house on the site, and once utterly neglected, Clandon – of brick with some stone – was built by the second Baron Onslow to the design of Giacomo Leoni. It is suggested that Artari, 'gentleman plasterer', was responsible for the magnificent stucco decorations in the Hall, Palladio Room, Saloon and Red Drawing Room. Outstanding, too, are the chimneypieces, that of the hall being by Michael Rysbrack. Adam influence is also apparent. Furniture comprises a state bed of c. 1700, Kentian sidetables, Italian chairs and wall-lamps and Louis XV chairs, 18th-century wallpaper and brocatelle. There are also paintings by Knyff (of an earlier mansion), Michael Wright, Kneller, Daniel Gardner and Francis Barlow. Hogarth and Thornhill painted the House of Commons picture which includes Arthur Onslow as Speaker. There is now additional furniture bequeathed by Mrs Gubbay. Landscape and stables are by 'Capability' Brown.

Loseley House
Built in 1562 of ragstone from the ruins of Waverley Abbey, and of hard chalk, Loseley House owes its origin to Sir William More, a kinsman of Sir Thomas More. It still has its Great Hall with a deep bay window and there are fine ceilings, as well as family portraits, furniture, needlework and tapestries. One of the most important features of the house, however, is the series of carved, inlaid and painted panels from Henry VIII's palace of Nonsuch, so unfortunately destroyed after the Restoration. There is also a remarkable chimneypiece carved in chalk. Elizabeth I and James I and Anne of Denmark were here more than once. Margaret More married Sir Thomas Molyneux of the Sefton family; their son succeeded to the estate on his mother's death in 1704 and it has descended to the present owner with only one more break in the male line.

Clandon Park, Surrey: the garden front of the Palladian mansion designed by Leoni.

below. Clandon Park: details of the stuccowork in the great hall, attributed to Artari.

Clandon Park: the great hall.

SUSSEX

Bateman's

In 1903 Rudyard Kipling bought Bateman's and it was his home until he died in 1935, Mrs Kipling later leaving the house furnishings and small estate to the National Trust. Apart from its great literary associations, Bateman's is important in itself. It was built of local stone in Jacobean days by an unknown ironmaster and has a three-storied porch with graceful archway, mullions, dripstones and striking brick chimneys. Certain changes were made by a John Britan early in the 18th century and what had become a sadly neglected farmhouse was carefully restored in the 1890s. The interior had Jacobean wainscoting, Cordova leather (on the dining room walls), as well as a contemporary staircase. There are Kipling portraits (one by John Collier), 17th-century furniture, Persian carpets and Nankin ware. The study is exactly as Kipling left it with his writing materials, Indian rugs, books, bunting from Nelson's *Victory*, and his walnut chair raised on blocks. The garden is charming with yew hedges and water.

Firle Place

This beautiful house looks Georgian, but part of it goes back to the time of John Gage who married the heiress of Firle in Henry VI's reign. Handsome as the building is, however, its great interest lies in its pictures (many of which were inherited by the present Viscountess Gage from the celebrated Panshanger collection), including works by Fra Bartolommeo, Correggio, Marieschi, Rubens, Van Dyck, Gainsborough, Reynolds and Hoppner. There are also illuminated missals, Kent, Chippendale and French furniture and Sèvres and Chelsea porcelain. The alabaster effigies of Sir John and Lady Gage by Gerard Johnson, in Firle Church, should be seen.

Parham

In 1601, Thomas Bysshop bought Parham from a member of the Palmer family, the house having been built about a quarter of a century earlier. Much altered in the 18th and 19th centuries, it remained unsold until acquired from the 16th Baroness Zouche by the Hon Clive Pearson after the First World War. He carried out careful and extensive restoration. The Great Hall, richly hung with Elizabethan portraits, retains its fine Renaissance screen. The Great Parlour and Great Chamber are reconstructions; the former has a Mytens portrait of Charles I as Prince of Wales, as well as the painting of the Spanish Infanta which Charles gave to Buckingham ('take away the painted doll!'), when the marriage negotiations came to naught. The Saloon is Georgian in decoration; so is the Green Room containing two Romneys of Lady Hamilton and (from Mersham-le-Hatch) a Reynolds of Lady Beryl Gilbert. Various Bysshop portraits and much fine needlework and furniture are in the house. There is a long gallery and a park with deer.

Petworth House

The pompous Charles Seymour, sixth Duke of Somerset, came into the Petworth estate by marriage with the young heiress Elizabeth Percy, who had been twice widowed at fifteen. He built much of the present house, 'a cool and assured composition in grey stone with white Portland dressings', to quote Clough Williams-Ellis, in 1688-96. A medieval chapel survives and there is a staircase with walls probably by Laguerre and work by Salvin, but visitors go to see the state rooms which include the Beauty Room (Dahl portraits of beauties of Queen Anne's Court), the outstanding Grinling Gibbons carving and the great collection of pictures including many examples of Van Dyck and Turner. Turner enjoyed noble patronage here and had a studio in the house. The Seymours were succeeded at Petworth by the Wyndhams, Earls of Egremont and Lords Leconfield. The third Lord Leconfield made over the house and large park to the National Trust in 1947.

Uppark

Uppark, probably by William Talman, was built for the first Earl of Tankerville at the end of the 17th century and its brick has weathered into some of the loveliest in England. Sir Matthew Fetherstonhaugh acquired the estate in the mid-18th century and carried out extensive redecorating then and in

Firle Place, Sussex: the south front showing the early Tudor front on the left.

below. Petworth House, Sussex: the main façade.

Parham, Sussex: the hall seen through the screen.

the 1770s. Stucco, paint, textiles, wallpaper and furniture survive from his time; the Saloon still has its original Wilton carpet and the Little Parlour its green brocade curtains. Humphry Repton later was responsible for some redecoration. Sir Harry Fetherstonhaugh, painted by Reynolds and Batoni, married his young dairymaid when he was just over seventy. To her and her sister and successor (Miss Frances Fetherstonhaugh who died in 1895) is owed much of the credit for the preservation of this incredible house and its contents, though the labours of the Hon Lady Meade-Fetherstonhaugh in the present century must not be forgotten. There are associations with Lady Hamilton (before she achieved that name) and with H. G. Wells. The situation is superb.

WARWICKSHIRE
Arbury

The name of Newdigate, or Newdegate, has been associated with Arbury since Elizabethan times when the estate – then belonging to Sir Edmund Anderson – was exchanged for that of Harefield in Middlesex. Sir Roger Newdigate (George Eliot's 'Sir Christopher Cheverel') spent many years gothicising the house which possesses the elaborate stucco ceilings and other decorations of his day, a notable collection of royal and family portraits, good glass, needlework and porcelain, and Dutch, French and English furniture. The chapel has a Restoration ceiling and contemporary wainscoting bearing 'stringes of frute with cherumbims' heads', which cost ten shillings each. There are 17th-century stables, lakes, cedars, lawns, and the remains of Sir Roger's private canal system.

Aston Hall

One of England's grandest Jacobean houses today survives miraculously in the midst of industrial Birmingham, with a fragment of its former deer park. Built of brick, with stone dressings, handsome gables, turrets and chimneys, by Sir Thomas Holte between 1618 and 1635, it was repaired after considerable Civil War damage. Good, if restored, panelling and stucco and fine chimneypieces still exist, as do a few of its ancient treasures, notably 18th-century needlework hangings by a lady of the family, but most of the old contents have vanished like the Holtes. There is a Great Drawing Room, a Long Gallery, and a noble staircase ascending to the second floor. The house is admirably maintained from kitchen to attics by Birmingham Corporation, and has an authentic country house atmosphere – a great improvement on the stuffed giraffes and other incongruities of years ago.

Charlecote Park

This is not everybody's house and not, as was once said, 'a perfect example of an Elizabethan mansion!' Sir Thomas Lucy began it in 1558 and later entertained Elizabeth I here, but the brick and stone building has since undergone great alteration and extension. A delightful gatehouse is much as the

Arbury Hall, Warwicks: the south front, *c.* 1750-75.

Aston Hall, Warwicks: the entrance front flanked by the lodges of the forecourt.

below. Aston Hall: the long gallery.

Aston Hall: the entrance doorway placed in the
middle of the long side of the hall.

Charlecote Park, Warwicks: the Elizabethan house
from the air, showing the gatehouse and out-buildings.

Queen would have seen it, while connoisseurs of 19th-century wallpapers, needlework, fabrics and furniture will find much to charm them. There is a large and handsome collection of family pictures, including examples of Kneller, Gainsborough, Batoni and William Larkin, as well as a great family group (the 'third' Sir Thomas with wife, children, nurse and dogs), after Cornelius Johnson. Chippendale mirrors hang against faded marigold walls. Willement glass, a fine library, family carriages, red and fallow deer and Spanish sheep are also to be found, and 'Capability' Brown worked in the park which is watered by the Avon.

Compton Wynyates

This is one of England's most lovely and romantic houses, but has twice narrowly escaped destruction. It was the scene of Civil War fighting, when outbuildings and the parish church were destroyed, and 1774 saw the dispersal of the contents by order of the Earl of Northampton who temporarily ruined the family by gambling and great election expenses and ordered the demolition of Compton Wyngates. Thanks to the agent, this vandalism was avoided, and the house with its exquisite Tudor brick and elaborate chimneys still belongs to the descendants of Sir William Compton who built it in the reign of Henry VIII. The Great Hall screen has a panel thought to depict English and French knights at the Battle of Tournai, and the chapel screen includes remarkable carvings including 'seven frail humans . . . mounted on strange quadrupeds, each with a little devil seated behind him, driving him into hell'. Refurnished rooms contain good wainscoting and moulded ceilings, heraldic glass, family portraits, a Holy Family by Lorenzo Monaco, a Giorgione and a Crucifixion of the Umbrian School. Topiary, climbing parkland and water form a charming setting. The rebuilt church has hatchments, high pews and the mutilated remains of Compton monuments thrown into the moat by Roundhead soldiers.

Coughton Court

Though now National Trust property, Coughton is still the home of the Throckmortons whose associations with the estate goes back to 1409. A strange, romantic 'mixed-up' house, with everything from Tudor timbers to early 19th-century battlements replacing 17th-century gables, it is dominated by a splendid stone gatehouse almost certainly built by Sir George who figures prominently in A. L. Rowse's 'Raleigh and the Throckmortons'. Inside is an important family collection of pictures, tapestry, needlework, Jacobite relics and documents. Once moated, the Court adjoins the parish church which retains family tombs and was built by the Throckmortons.

Farnborough Hall

The ancestral home (now National Trust property) of the Holbech family still incorporates something of the house of their Raleigh predecessors. Stone built, and chiefly 18th-century, it has a superb setting of trees, water and lawn, with a half-mile terrace ascending past temples to an obelisk. Unfortunately, Canaletto and Pannini paintings were sold years ago and copies occupy the rich stucco 'framework' in the former dining room, but the general effect is still striking. The entrance hall, with paving 'reflecting' the patterned ceiling, keeps its 'Roman' busts. An attractive village is at hand.

Packwood House

Though much restored, and with no trace of its ancient timbering to be seen, Packwood remains a charming property of the National Trust to which it was given by Mr Graham Baron Ash. The house dates back to the 16th century, and was long the home of the Fetherstons, John Fetherston originally planting the famous yew garden in Restoration days, and also adding a delightful brick wing and stables with painted sundials. The interior, with a modern long gallery and a Great Hall converted from a byre, is far grander than it was in Fetherston days. There are notable tapestries, needlework and window glass, and good 17th and early 18th-century furniture.

Ragley Hall

The home of the Marquess of Hertford dates back to Charles II's reign, the original architect having been Robert Hooke. This grandly situated house, however, incorporates later work, including a wonderful hall of about 1750 (James Gibbs?) with Baroque and Rococo stucco, and a portico and interiors by, or ascribed to, James Wyatt. There was a Victorian restoration after much neglect when the Hertfords had other interests. Among the contents are Reynolds portraits (one of Horace Walpole who visited there), French furniture, much china and the gorgeous bed used by the Prince Regent. 'Capability' Brown destroyed the original formal layout, but there is a modified Victorian reconstruction.

Upton House

Probably designed by 'Smith of Warwick', Upton was built by Sir Rushout Cullen who died in 1730; later owners including the banker, Francis Child, and the Earls of Jersey. The stone house, which had suffered architecturally, was remodelled and extended by Morley Horder for the second Viscount Bearsted between the wars. Now a National Trust property, it has a large and important collection of pictures of the British, French, Dutch, Flemish and Netherlandish, German, Italian and Spanish schools, as well as tapestry, 18th-century furniture and Chelsea and Sèvres porcelain. Beyond a great lawn, gardens slope steeply to a lake, and there are cedars, long borders and another lake with a temple.

Warwick Castle

Warwick, by the Avon and seat of the Earls of Warwick, is of many periods, and retains the Norman mound of the de Newburghs and the magnificent 14th-century towers, gatehouse and barbican of the de Beauchamps. State rooms of the 17th, 18th and 19th centuries contain English, French and Italian furniture, and a superb collection of pictures, including works by Raphael, Rubens, and Van Dyck. There is important armour in the Great Hall and the Warwick Vase (ancient Greek) can be seen in the conservatory overlooking the Italian garden. There is landscaping by 'Capability' Brown and many peacocks decorate the grounds.

WESTMORLAND

Levens Hall

Levens began its existence as a medieval pele tower with hall attached. Late in the 15th century the property was acquired by one of the Bellinghams of Burneside in Lancashire, and his descendant, Sir James Bellingham (died 1641), made extensive alterations and additions, putting in much panelling and finely moulded ceilings. To this period also belongs the armorial frieze in the hall and a richly carved overmantel in the drawing room. In the late 17th century Levens passed to Sir James Grahme, and it was he who employed 'Monsieur Beaumont' to design the gardens with their unrivalled display of topiary. From Sir James, the estate has descended to the present owner. The contents include hangings of Cordova leather in the dining room, Elizabethan and Jacobean furniture, early glass, Italian, Flemish, Dutch and English pictures and fine needlework of different periods.

Sizergh Castle

The massive and outwardly austere home of the Stricklands and Hornyold-Stricklands has been greatly altered from time to time, but still keeps its pele tower of the 14th century. The Tudor Great Hall has been enlarged and remodelled, and there is an Elizabethan central block and wings. Features of the interior are the grandly carved overmantels and the wainscoting, although panelling from the famous Inlaid Room was unfortunately removed to the Victoria and Albert Museum years ago. Among the pictures is a series of the exiled Stuarts by Hyacinthe Rigaud with whom Sir Thomas and Lady Strickland lived at St Germain-en-Laye. Family portraits are by Huysmans, Wissing, Romney and J. E. Ferneley, and there are also 16th-century Gothic stools and Jacobean, Chippendale and Gillow furnishings, Stuart relics, porcelain, glass and Chinese needlework.

Sizergh Castle, Westmorland: a fine plaster ceiling in a bedroom.

WILTSHIRE

Corsham Court

It is not easy to do more than hint at the interest and charm of the great house now shared by Lord Methuen and the Bath Academy of Art. The mansion dates from 1582, but in the second half of the 18th century Paul Methuen employed Lancelot Brown to design a setting for the reception of pictures collected by his ambassador uncle of the same name. In 1844, when the architect Bellamy's enlargement took place, the marriage of Frederick Methuen to Anna Sanford brought a second collection to Corsham. Pictures include a triptych of the School of Bernardo Daddi, and examples of Guido Reni, Domenichino, Tintoretto, Rubens, Van Dyck, Poussin, Salvator Rosa, Reynolds, Gainsborough, Romney and Richard Wilson. One must also mention the putative Michaelangelo and such features as the picture gallery fireplace by Scheemakers, pier-glasses by Robert Adam, a commode and candlestands by James Cobb, and furniture ascribed to Chippendale comprising a state bed and a huge suite in the French style.

Lacock Abbey

Beautifully situated in its park and close to a famous village, Lacock Abbey exhibits an engaging variety of styles. An Augustinian convent was established here in 1229. Soon after the Dissolution, Sir William Sharington turned the convent into a handsome residence for himself, retaining the 13th and 15th-century cloisters and other important architectural features. There is rare Tudor work of his with moulded chimneys, an octagonal tower and stables. The hall was remodelled in the 18th century in the Gothick style by Sanderson Miller and is extremely effective. By that time Lacock had passed to the Talbots and further alterations took place early last century. The Abbey was the home of Fox Talbot, the photographic pioneer (one may rejoice that a daughter was not, after all, christened 'Photogenia'!) Both the house and the village now belong to the National Trust.

Littlecote

This romantic house in its peaceful park and gardens was built by the Darrells in the late 15th and early 16th centuries and after the death of 'Wild' Darrell (the story of the midwife and the murdered baby is well-known), passed to Sir John Popham, later Lord Chief Justice. Sir Ernest Wills, Bart., bought the property after the First World War, and it still contains many Popham treasures including an important collection of arms. Sir John's portrait is in the Great Hall and the long gallery has many more Popham pictures. A charming, galleried chapel is Cromwellian. There is painted Chinese wallpaper, and curious panels in the Dutch Parlour were the work of Dutch naval prisoners quartered at Littlecote in the 17th century. An Aubusson carpet has Louis XV's arms and came from Versailles via Hamilton Palace. Bow, Worcester, Chelsea and other porcelain, paperweights, French commodes and a needlework carpet of Queen Anne's day are a few of the treasures to be seen.

Longleat

Longleat was built by Sir John Thynne, ancestor of the Marquess of Bath. It still ranks as one of the grand Elizabethan houses of England, but was greatly altered internally last century when elaborate Italian ceilings and woodwork were introduced. A magnificent collection of pictures includes Italian masters, equestrian paintings by Wootton (in the Great Hall), a Lawrence of the first Marquess, a portrait of Arabella Stuart, ascribed to Paul van Somer, and a Siberechts prospect of Longleat. Flemish tapestries, French and English furniture, Sèvres and Chelsea porcelain, silver and costumes can be seen, as well as formal gardens and a 'Capability' Brown landscape, and lions, apes and other creatures for those who like them.

(continued on p.174)

Corsham Court, Wiltshire: the Elizabethan façade retained through 18th and 19th-century alterations.

below. Corsham Court: the great picture gallery, 1760-72.

Littlecote, Wiltshire: the Tudor entrance front.

below. Littlecote: the screen in the great hall with Sir John Popham's portrait and great chair.

Longleat, Wiltshire: the main façade of the first great house of the English Renaissance.

below left. Longleat: the decorated roof-line of the kitchen court.

below right. Longleat: a bay of the east front.

Longleat: the screen in the great hall, *c.*1603.

Wilton House, Wiltshire: the central gatehouse in the
east or old entrance façade, c.1550.

Wilton House: the Double Cube Room, *c*.1650,
decorated by Emmanuel de Critz and Edward Pierce.

Stourhead

In 1720 the wealthy banker, Henry Hoare, bought the estate from his brother Richard's trustees. Colen Campbell designed a Palladian house for him, to which Sir Richard Colt Hoare added flanking picture gallery and library wings about 1800. The central block was badly damaged by fire in 1902, but carefully restored. The pictures include works by Wootton, Gainsborough, Reynolds, Nicholas Poussin and William Owen (and many other artists), and there is outstanding furniture by the younger Chippendale. The grandeur of the house is equalled by the 18th-century gardens with temples, grotto and romantic cottage by a great lake. The sixth baronet and his wife gave Stourhead to the National Trust, their only son having been killed in the First World War.

Wilton House

The seat of the Herberts, Earls of Pembroke and Montgomery, is among England's most important houses, both architecturally and in content. It possesses a series of rooms by Inigo Jones and John Webb, of which the Double Cube is one of the world's outstanding rooms. In the Single Cube, scenes from Sidney's 'Arcadia' (written at Wilton) appear below the dado. Some work ascribed to Hans Holbein still remains and the Gothic cloisters and staircase are by James Wyatt. An immense wealth of pictures includes Van Dyck's largest family group, and examples of Tintoretto, Bloemart, the School of Fontainebleau, Rembrandt and Honthorst. There is also French, William Kent and Chippendale furniture and Cardinal Mazarin's collection of sculpture. The Palladian Bridge by Roger Morris and Lord Pembroke, enhances the very lovely grounds.

WORCESTERSHIRE

Dowles Manor

A small Elizabethan manor house – the residence of the bailiff rather than the lord of the manor – and incorporating earlier work in stone, Dowles is a delightful example of half-timbering in a wooded setting of much charm. It was purchased in 1902 by Jannion Steele Elliott from whom it passed to his daughter, Mrs M. C. Sheldon. Mr Elliott carefully restored and enlarged the house and was responsible for the discovery of an outstanding series of Elizabethan wall-paintings, to be seen in several rooms, and which show human figures, dragons and Grecian honeysuckle, vases and other motifs. Appropriate woodwork was introduced including panelling from the Angel, Bewdley and a chimney piece from the Saracen's Head. There is a large collection of brass, copper, pewter, 17th-century furniture, Liverpool and Staffordshire ware and needlework. The garden has terraces, topiary and a large tulip tree.

Hanbury Hall

Built for Thomas Vernon, a wealthy lawyer, by William Rudhall of Henley-in-Arden (of whom nothing else seems to be known), Hanbury is dated 1701. The elegant mansion is of red brick with stone angle-dressings, tall, white-painted sash windows, wooden cornice and high-pitched roof with dormers and cupola. The main staircase ceiling and walls were decorated allegorically by Sir James Thornhill and there are further paintings on the ceilings of the handsomely wainscoted hall and the Long Room which also has notable plasterwork and a fine modern Spanish carpet. Woodwork in the library reputedly came from the royal palace at Tickenhill. Some internal alteration seems to have been effected in the time of Henry Cecil, Tennyson's 'Lord of Burleigh', who married – and divorced – the Vernon heiress. The grounds contain a fine Georgian orangery and the parish church, visible from the forecourt, has important Vernon monuments, one by Roubiliac.

Hartlebury Castle

This ancient red sandstone seat of the Bishops of

Worcester was much rebuilt some time after the Restoration, having suffered great damage, but some medieval work survives. Still partly–and impressively–moated, it keeps its Great Hall hung with portraits of bishops. An adjoining drawing room has elaborate Rococo decoration and the later Hurd Library (the work of Bishop Hurd who entertained George III and his Queen here), contains 'Adam' plasterwork, the bishop's elegant bookcases, valuable books and a Gainsborough portrait. The chapel was decorated by Henry Keene and one bedroom, with a canopied bed, was prepared for George IV as Prince of Wales. Part of the castle is now the Worcestershire County Museum.

YORKSHIRE
Burton Agnes Hall

This very handsome house of brick with stone dressings is reached through a charming, turreted gatehouse, and was built by Sir Henry Griffith who died in 1620. It has descended to Mr M. Wickham-Boynton. The ceilings, wainscoting, staircases and chimneypieces are a joy. The Great Hall screen (with the Sybils, Evangelists and twelve tribes of Israel), and the alabaster carving of the Wise and Foolish Virgins over the nearby fireplace are outstanding; the long gallery a brilliant restoration. Many family pictures are complemented by a collection of Impressionist, Post-Impressionist and Surrealist paintings. Near the house are the remains of a Norman manor house and a church with family monuments. There are beautiful formal gardens.

Burton Constable

Originally an Elizabethan mansion, the house was greatly altered by Robert Adam, Thomas Lightoller, and James Wyatt. The interior is of tremendous impressiveness with a richly stuccoed hall (the original Great Hall raised in height), chapel, gallery with gilded Restoration chairs, and a silk-lined ballroom with noble mirrors. Equally fine is the superb staircase hall, the Blue Drawing Room and the Chinese Room. Important 18th-century furniture. Gardens with statuary, Irish yews and an orangery, adjoin a park with a brick-lined lake. Burton Constable is the home of the Chichester-Constables, the Lords Paramount of the Seignory of Holderness.

Castle Howard

Designed by Vanbrugh in conjunction with Hawksmoor, this huge, wonderfully situated Baroque palace, which even Horace Walpole found 'sublime', was chiefly built for the third Earl of Carlisle with whose descendants it has remained. Sir Thomas Robinson, the Earl's son-in-law, designed the later west wing and the chapel was remodelled last century. Fire destroyed the dome and part of Pellegrini's mythological paintings in 1940, but restoration has been effected and other damaged work made good. The contents include Soho

Burton Agnes, Yorkshire: the entrance front and forecourt from the gatehouse.

below. Burton Agnes: the Chinese Room decorated with early 18th-century lacquer-work.

Castle Howard, Yorkshire: the great hall, Bagutti and
Plura's stucco chimneypiece, c.1710.

Castle Howard: the centrepiece of the entrance front.

Castle Howard: the park with Vanburgh's Temple
and Hawksmoor's Mausoleum.

tapestries, Roman, Greek and Egyptian sculpture, Chelsea, Meissen, Derby and Delft ware, paintings by Holbein (Henry VIII), Rubens, Tintoretto, Van Dyck, Lely, Zuccarelli, Romney, Reynolds and Gainsborough. There is French, Italian and English furniture, the last including marble-topped tables and damask-upholstered chairs made when the house was built. A terrace ascends to Vanbrugh's lovely temple of the Four Winds. The magnificent mausoleum is chiefly by Hawksmoor.

Ebberston Hall

Whereas most of the houses here described are large and magnificent, Ebberston is a tiny jewel. The architect, Colen Campbell, a pioneer of Palladianism, is best known by such contrasting edifices as Houghton in Norfolk and Mereworth Castle in Kent. Built in 1718 it is in the grand manner reduced to the scale of its setting within a small wooded valley. The highly formalised water garden, only some of which remains, is typical of the period and was in due proportion. The interior, also in the grand manner but comparably diminished, is superbly and elaborately decorated by the distinguished band of craftsmen working in Yorkshire at that period; much of the furniture also is contemporary.

Harewood House

Robert Adam and Carr of York were responsible for this grand house of the Lascelles family who have held the Earldom of Harewood since 1812. Many consider the building to have been considerably spoiled by Sir Charles Barry, who also designed the formal layout to the south, overlooking Brown's lake. The gallery, with wooden pelmets simulating drapery (Chippendale) and the Music Room (with musical motifs in its decoration and paintings by Kauffman and Zucchi) are two of the most beautiful rooms, but one must not forget the austere, but magnificent, Entrance Hall and the Rose Drawing Room. There is much furniture by Chippendale, but the famous writing table is now at Temple Newsam.

Newby Hall

Sir Edward Blackett began the brick house in Queen Anne's day. It passed from his family to William Weddell around the middle of the 18th century. He engaged Robert Adam to enlarge and alter it as a setting for his numerous art treasures. Weddell's Boucher/Neilson tapestry from the Gobelins factory is still in the room Adam designed for it; the handsome sculpture gallery contains the Barberini Venus; and the library (Adam's dining room) has ceiling and other paintings by Angelica Kauffman. The plasterwork is by Rose and the works of Kneller, Batoni, Raeburn, Romney, Lawrence and Annibale Carracci are represented. The great gardens are justly famous and there are imposing Adam stables.

Nostell Priory

In 1733 Sir Rowland Winn, fourth baronet, engaged James Paine to design a new house. Parts of this have vanished, but the main block and kitchen wing survive, with an important addition by Robert Adam. Apart from grand decoration in stucco, the house is particularly celebrated for its furniture by Thomas Chippendale, which was made for Nostell and for which the bills are preserved. Among the four hundred and more pictures are works by Rembrandt, Van Dyck, Hogarth, Gainsborough and Richard Wilson, but special mention must be made of Holbein's magnificent painting of Sir Thomas More and his family. Nostell Priory now belongs to the National Trust, the Winns remaining in occupation.

Ripley Castle

This very charming mansion in an equally lovely setting of lakes, park and walled gardens, goes back in part to the 16th century, but the Ingilbys have held the estate far longer. The Knight's Chamber has Tudor wainscoting, and the Tower Room a Jacobean ceiling said to commemorate a visit of James I, while its floor was originally the deck of a frigate first moved to a now-demolished mansion near Thirsk and then to Ripley in 1927. Sir John Ingilby – later to rebuild the village in French style – rebuilt most of the castle in about 1780. There is attractive Georgian plasterwork in the drawing room, which has a statue of Venus by Canova.

Ebberston Lodge, Yorkshire: Campbell's miniature
mansion.

Harewood House, Yorkshire: Barry's 19th-century
front and terrace.

Nostell Priory, Yorkshire: the state bedroom with
ceiling to James Paine's design, c.1745.

Rudding Park, Yorkshire: the entrance front of the Regency house.

below. Sledmere, Yorkshire: view from the south.

Ripley has family portraits and late 18th-century and other furniture.

Rudding Park

Rudding, begun in 1805, was finished by Sir Joseph Radcliffe when he bought the estate in George IV's reign. Elegant, almost austere, the bow-windowed stone house (cleverly designed to catch maximum sun) has interiors of great distinction. One notes the restrained, effective plasterwork, the hall paving, the graceful stairs, a rich flock paper in the Blue Drawing Room, the Brussels tapestries and English Savonnerie carpet of the Yellow Drawing Room. Magnificent furniture includes—one picks at random—William Kent coffers, a Louis XV bureau of exceptional importance (ascribed to Bondurand), a *Régence* commode, Rococo mirrors and a Chippendale suite. There are Italian, Dutch, French and English pictures, fine glass, silver, Chinese porcelain and French Terracotta. The gardens, in themselves, are of major importance.

Sledmere

A somewhat earlier house was incorporated in the mansion built by Sir Christopher Sykes in 1750. This elegant building, with its magnificent Rose plasterwork, was burnt in 1911, but rebuilt and greatly enlarged, the stucco decorations being reproduced. The additions have since been removed. Some plaster panels come from Wormleybury in Hertfordshire. The Great Library is 120 feet long and was probably inspired by the baths of Diocletian and Caracalla. Fine Georgian furniture survived the fire and there is good porcelain and antique statuary. The Romney portrait of Sir Christopher and Lady Sykes was painted 1786. Lawns, trees, statuary and the Yorkshire Wolds, form a setting of great beauty.

Sledmere: the great library.

below. Sledmere. the late-Georgian entrance hall.

SCOTLAND

Culzean Castle, Ayrshire

Superbly placed above the sea and incorporating older work, Culzean owes much of its present form to Robert Adam, though some changes have since been made, particularly in 1879. The romantic exterior, with its towers and turrets is in marked contrast to the interior where nothing of the 'Gothic' intrudes. Among the delightful rooms may be noted the Round Drawing Room in which most of the fittings are from Adam's design; so probably is the carpet said to have been made at Maybole. His Oval Staircase, with Corinthian and Ionic columns, is very grand and various rooms have his typical ceilings and chimneypieces. Door furniture and mirrors appear to be by Matthew Boulton. The pictures include a Batoni of David Kennedy, tenth Earl of Cassillis, from whom Culzean descended to the fifth Marquess of Ailsa who gave it to the National Trust for Scotland. There are beautiful grounds. The castle contains a flat provided for General Eisenhower in 1946 as a token of gratitude for his services as Supreme Commander of the Allied Forces in the Second World War.

Mellerstain, Berwickshire

This is a curious mansion for the flanking wings were constructed before the main house was built. William Adam designed the wings about 1725 and these, with formal avenues, lake and estate, were inherited by George Baillie in 1759. He engaged Robert Adam to design the embattled centre block which contains very fine stucco decorations, the library, with its moulded friezes over the bookcases, being an outstanding room. A strange feature is the unfinished Adam gallery at the top of the house. Roubiliac was responsible for the bust of the Scottish heroine, Lady Grisell Baillie, from whom the Earl of Haddington, owner of Mellerstain, is descended. There are family portraits by Gainsborough, Raeburn and Allan Ramsay and important furniture. Formal gardens were laid out by Sir Reginald Blomfield, and there are views to the Cheviots.

Brodick Castle, Bute

Once a royal possession, the castle of red sandstone on the Isle of Arran goes back in part to the 14th century. There is 16th and 17th-century work and an addition of 1844 was made for a future Duke of Hamilton who married Princess Marie of Baden. The castle is particularly notable for its European and other porcelain and there are treasures from the collection of William Beckford of Fonthill whose daughter married the tenth Duke. In addition to many family portraits, one may note a Clouet painting of the Duc d'Alençon once in Charles I's collection, and landscapes by Thomas Gainsborough. The Red Gallery contains watercolours by Thomas Rowlandson, the dining room panelling from Suffolk and the drawing room Italian marquetry and French furniture. The magnificent gardens were laid out by the Duchess of Montrose aided by her son-in-law, Major Boscawen.

Lennoxlove, East Lothian

The origin of Lethington Tower, as Lennoclove was once prosaically known, is uncertain, but the oldest part may be a 15th-century rebuilding. Certainly, John Maitland, Earl of Lauderdale, enlarged the windows and made other improvements in 1626, his son later adding considerably to the structure. Further work was undertaken by John Maitland, only Duke of Lauderdale, and in 1703 the estate was acquired, after her death by the trustees of 'La Belle Stewart', Frances, Duchess of Lennox, for her kinsman and heir, Walter Stewart, Master of Blantyre, 'and she desired whatever estate was purchased to be named and called Lennoxlove.' It remained unsold until the Duke of Hamilton bought it in 1947. The house now contains a good collection of pictures by Van Dyck, Lely, Kneller, Gavin Hamilton, Raeburn, de Laszlo and Augustus John. There are Epstein busts, English, French, and Dutch furniture and in the impressive banqueting hall is displayed a death-mask of Mary Queen of Scots, and the casket of the 'Casket Letters'.

Falkland Palace, Fife

The south range of this ancient and romantic hunting palace of the Stuart monarchs, with its close

Lennoxlove, East Lothian: the great hall.

connections with Mary Queen of Scots, has been described as 'the finest work of its period in Scotland', though the French renaissance façade of James V's time is later than the building itself. The east range, now roofless, shows changes made by the same King; that on the north was burnt when occupied by Cromwell's soldiers and only foundations remain. The south range contains the Chapel Royal which has its original entrance screen; the third Marquess of Bute as Hereditary Keeper (the office is now held by his grandson, Major Crichton-Stuart) restored the royal pew and pulpit and did other notable work at Falkland. The gatehouse, with its flanking towers surmounted by pointed roofs, survives as does the Cross House where the King's Bedchamber has been beautifully restored in collaboration with the National Trust for Scotland. In it is the 17th-century Golden Bed of Brahan, a splendid piece of Dutch craftsmanship.

Crathes Castle, Kincardineshire

Sir James Burnett of Leys gave Crathes—owned by his family since the second half of the 16th century—to the National Trust for Scotland in 1952. Alexander Burnett began the castle in 1553; further work was done by his great-grandson and there is an 18th-century wing. The most remarkable feature of the building is undoubtedly the tempera painted ceilings in the Chamber of the Nine Muses and the Green Lady's Room. The long gallery has a panelled ceiling described as 'unique in Scotland'. Among the furniture at Crathes is a grand bed made for Alexander Burnett and his Gordon wife, with their armorial bearings, fine hangings and the date 1594. The portraits include examples of Hoppner and Allan Ramsay and there is Burnett silver. The very lovely gardens owe much to the late Sir James and his wife, but were originally laid out in the early years of the 18th century, when lime walks and yew hedges (the latter today over twelve feet high) were planted.

Kinross House, Kinross

Sir William Bruce, the architect and politician (in the former capacity he designed part of Hopetoun), built this very impressive sandstone house for him-

Crathes Castle, Kincardineshire:
the south side of the tower.

self at the end of the 17th century, but he was never able to finish the interior as he had planned. Externally it displays giant pilasters and some elaborate carving probably from the hands of Dutch craftsmen. A very lovely view extends over a modern formal layout to Lochleven. There are fine stables, garden pavilions and the grand 'Fish Gate' – adorned with cupids, cornucopias and fish – surviving from Bruce's days. George Graham bought the estate in 1777 and it has descended to the present owner, but in recent times Sir Basil Montgomery restored the near-derelict mansion which had long been empty. The house, with portraits and good furniture, and its setting, are now of exceptional charm.

Blair Castle, Perthshire

Blair, the seat of the Stewarts and of the Murrays, Dukes of Atholl, was rebuilt in the mid-18th century on a grand scale under James Winter. The exterior was remodelled and given turrets and battlements by David Bryce 100 years ago for the seventh Duke. Comym's Tower dates from 1269, and Blair was the last castle in Great Britain to be besieged – in 1746 by Lord George Murray, a son of the first Duke, who afterwards joined the Young Pretender in Rome and died in exile in Holland. The interior is noted for its Rococo plasterwork, chimneypieces and woodwork, including two fine staircases. There is a great array of 17th and 18th-century portraits, as well as Mortlake tapestries, furniture, china, lace, armour and Jacobite relics.

Traquair, Peeblesshire

Reconstructed in 1695 by the Earl of Traquair, this most romantic mansion incorporates a 14th-century tower. Standing beside the River Quair, it has been described as a house 'whose magic . . . brooding over its memories works a spell that long haunts the senses of everyone who goes there' (Oliver Hill). Traquair was given by James II of Scotland to a favourite who sold it to James Stuart, Earl of Buchan, whose descendant, Sir John Stuart became Earl of Traquair in 1633. The present owners, the Maxwell-Stuarts, are descended from the fourth Earl. The Bear Gates have never been opened since Prince Charles Edward passed through

them in 1745, the legend being that they were to remain closed until he returned as King. Mary Queen of Scots was here with Darnley, and some of her needlework is to be seen.

The Binns, West Lothian

This remarkable and historic house was restored by Thomas Dalyell in the early years of the 17th century and there have been subsequent additions. In the last century the architect William Burn added the battlements and did away with crow-stepping and the pointed roofs of turrets. Dalyell's magnificent, bold plasterwork remains, that in the King's Room including medallions of David and Alexander and a fine frieze of pomegranates and other fruits, while that in the Sea Room incorporates family portraits. There are many paintings of the Dalyells and relics of General Tam Dalyell, a staunch Royalist who, after escaping from the Tower of London, where he had been incarcerated by Cromwell, entered the Czar of Russia's service, helped to reorganise his army (in which he fought) and was made a Noble of Russia. Back in Scotland he was to become Lieutenant-General of the Forces in that country, and first Colonel of the Royal Scots Greys.

Hopetoun House, West Lothian

Now one of the grandest of Scottish houses, Hopetoun underwent a gradual growth. It was begun by Charles Hope, first Earl of Hopetoun, to Sir William Bruce's design. Between 1721 and 1746, it was enlarged by William Adam and was completed by his sons in the second half of the 18th century. The exterior is splendid with balustrades and urns, steps, colonnades and pavilions. Early wainscoting with carving in the Gibbons manner survives in the Bruce building. The Yellow and Red Drawing Rooms have Adam Rococo decoration and beautiful damask wall coverings. Many of the pictures were acquired last century, the fine collection including works by Rubens, Van Dyck, Allan Ramsay, Raeburn and Gainsborough, and there are Flemish and English tapestries and a chimneypiece by Rysbrack. The magnificent setting of lawns and parkland is near the Forth bridges.

Kinross House, Kinross: Sir William Bruce's house
from the north east.

Traquair, Peebleshire: the grass-grown avenue and forecourt.

below. Hopetoun House, West Lothian: the east façade by William Adam

WALES

Chirk Castle, Denbighshire

This grand and imposing pile was possibly started by Edward I and certainly owes much to Roger Mortimer who completed his work here in the early 14th century. Among various later owners were Thomas Seymour, husband of Queen Catherine Parr, and Robert Dudley, Earl of Leicester. It passed to the Myddletons in 1595 and (the name carried on in the female line) a Myddleton still owns it. Huge round towers remain from medieval times; there are also Tudor buildings while the east range was taken in hand by A. W. N. Pugin last century. There is a grand suite of rooms in the Adam style, the Saloon having mythological subjects in a blue and gold ceiling, as well as Mortlake tapestries, family portraits and English and French furniture of note. A long gallery of late Stuart date was the work of Thomas Dugdale and is finely panelled in oak. Topiary adorns the gardens and the really magnificent entrance gates to the park were made early in the 18th century by Robert and Thomas Davies of Bersham, near Wrexham.

Penrhyn Castle, Caernarvonshire

Designed by Thomas Hopper for George Hay Dawkins Pennant, this vast pile, with towering Hedingham-like keep and vaulted hall, is one of the most extraordinary mock-medieval structures we have, rightly deserving the description, 'stately, massive and stupendous'. The elaborate 'Norman' (sometimes Arabic) decoration and furniture has to be seen to be believed. Of the library, once again echoes the words of the guide book, 'the room creates the effect of some cavern where natural forms have run wild.' There are Morris wallpapers and bed-hangings, good pictures and china. A Bed (like some of the other furniture) is of slate; it weighs four tons. The gardens and setting in general are of great beauty. The castle and the estate of 40,000 acres now belong to the National Trust.

Cardiff Castle, Glamorgan

This is a fantastic place in the centre of the city with Roman remains in the outer walls, which were built by the fourth Marquess of Bute last century, and a Norman shell-keep. The first Marquess employed Lancelot Brown here, but a vast restoration was carried out by the third Lord Bute who had the assistance of William Burges here, as he did at Castel Coch. Some of the results are more curious than beautiful. The Banqueting Hall is adorned with frescoes by H. N. Lonsdale. Its fireplace is in the form of a castle from which Robert, Earl of Gloucester (who owned Cardiff), is being seen off to battle by his spouse and others, while the imprisoned Robert, Duke of Normandy looks out from his cell window. There are winter and summer smoking rooms in the lofty clock tower and also an Arab Room.

Castell Coch, Glamorgan

This extraordinary, and highly effective, building arose from the scanty remains of a medieval castle in the last quarter of the 19th century. The architect who supplied the third Marquess of Bute with impressive round towers (crowned by conical roofs), drawbridge, portcullis and galleried courtyard was William Burges, who also worked at Cardiff Castle. Burges died before the fairy-tale castle was finished and final touches were supervised by a man called Frame. The rich carving, gilding and colour must be seen to be believed, as must Lady Bute's domed bedroom and her castellated washstand with towers for hot water. Lord Bute attempted to grow grapes on a large scale near Castell Coch, which has a romantic wooded setting, but the experiment was not a success. The fifth Marquess made over the property to the Ministry of Public Building and Works in 1950.

Fonmon Castle, Glamorgan

Fonmon may be the oldest inhabited house in Wales. The St John family held it from the 12th to the 17th century, but such features as the Georgian windows tend to disguise its vast antiquity. However it is to their successors, the Jones family, that the embattled structure owes its finest architectural possession. This is Robert Jones's splendid library, or drawing room, which, like the staircase hall, contains some exceptional plaster decoration, possibly by Thomas Stocking, and almost certainly of

Penrhyn Castle, Caernarvon: the great hall, 1827-37.

Castell Coch, Glamorgan: the drawing room
decoration executed after Burges's death in 1881.

Bristol workmanship. The room, with its gilded fireplaces and mirrors, is one of the finest 18th-century rooms in the country. In 1932 Fonmon Castle passed by inheritance to Lady (Seymour) Boothby, and Boothby and other family pictures, once at Ashbourne Hall, Derbyshire, were added to the collection here. There is a charming old garden.

Powis Castle, Montgomeryshire

A medieval red stone castle, much altered internally, Powis is set with marvellous effect above terraced gardens with huge, clipped yews, lead figures, balustrades and excellent planting. An inlaid staircase is decorated with murals by Lanscroon, and a frightening state bedroom was evidently created as a memorial to Charles I who stayed here. The Elizabethan gallery has a delightfully moulded ceiling, and panelling painted to represent bevelling. The dining room (by G. F. Bodley) has Dance's portrait of Clive of India whose family (now called Herbert after their maternal ancestors) became Earls of Powis. A National Trust property in the occupation of the present Earl.

IRELAND

Castlecoole, Fermanagh

Finished in 1798, the Neo-Georgian Castlecoole was built by the first Earl of Belmore using specially imported Portland stone. Colonnaded wings terminate in pavilions, but James Wyatt, who adapted earlier designs, may never have seen his finest composition. Fireplaces and other features were sent from England, and much original mahogany furniture – made on the spot – remains. There is a superb staircase hall and Dublin-made furnishings in the grand circular Saloon, as well as a fine stuccowork by Rose. A state bedroom, the bed in flame silk, was prepared for George IV who never came. The house was acquired in 1951 by the National Trust with funds made available by the Northern Ireland Government.

Castletown House, Co. Kildare

Alessandro Galilei (who designed a new façade for the church of St John-in-Lateran, Rome) was the architect of this important house, built or begun, by Speaker Conolly in 1722. Progenitor of all Irish Palladian houses, it consists of a great central block with curving colonnades and pavilions. Later and striking decoration is due to Lady Louisa Conolly, and of her time is the very lovely Francini stuccowork in the staircase hall, as well as the curious staircase itself, with its brass balusters, the Pompeian splendour of the gallery and the charming Print Room, unique in Ireland today. Rescued from impending ruin, the house is now the headquarters of the Irish Georgian Society, and family pictures, statuary, furniture and Venetian chandeliers formerly belonging to the house have been returned.

Castleward, Co. Down

The first Lord and Lady Bangor built the present house in about 1770, using Bath stone, but the architect's name is unknown. One front is Palladian; the other (Lady Bangor's choice) in the 'Gothic' manner, and there are classic and 'Gothic' rooms. The stucco decoration is very handsome, and the Music Room – originally the entrance hall – also has yellow scagliola columns and (surprisingly)

Caroline relics which belonged to Jane Lane, including a bit of the Boscobel Oak! There are family pictures and the situation by Strangford Lough is quite beautiful. The property was made over to the Northern Ireland Government, in payment of Death Duties and conveyed to the National Trust.

Florence Court, Fermanagh

The home of the Florence Court yew, and set close to Upper Lough Erne, the mansion is named after Florence, wife of John Cole, grandfather of the first Earl of Enniskillen. The architect is unknown, and it seems uncertain which of the Coles built it, but it is thought that the house was finished in 1764. Long colonnades and charming pavilions flank the central structure which has a grand and heavily rusticated main façade overlooking a park. A serious fire in 1955 damaged or destroyed the important and elaborate plasterwork, but most of this has been beautifully restored or replaced. Shortly before the conflagration, the late Viscount Cole, son of the fifth Lord Enniskillen, gave the house to the National Trust. The pictures and furniture are still family property.

Riverstown House, Co. Cork

Smith's *History of Cork* (1750) describes Riverstown, built by Bishop Jemmett Browne, as 'beautified with several curious pieces of stucco by the Francini brothers,' while, in 1826, Brewer's 'Beauties of Ireland' speaks of gardens watered by the Glanmire and serpentine canals and 'a pleasant park well stocked with deer.' The deer and canals have gone, but the room with the very important classical plasterwork (the ceiling shows Time rescuing Truth from the assaults of Discord and Envy) has been restored by the Irish Georgian Society and furnished to represent as far as possible a bishop's dining room in 1750. Paul and Philip Francini were brought over in 1738 by the Earl of Kildare and their ceiling at Carton depicting the Courtship of the Gods has been rightly called 'the finest in Ireland'. The first to introduce fully sculptured figures into this type of decoration, the two Italian brothers exercised a profound influence on Irish Stuccoists.

Castleward, Co. Down: the Palladian facade, *c*.1765.   *below*. Castleward: the north-east Gothic front.

LUDOVICI XV. JUSSU
FLORE ET CONSILIO
SABELDI DUCTU
STAT HÆC MOLES

Biographical Index

Geoffrey Beard

PRINCIPAL ARCHITECTS and CRAFTSMEN

In compiling these lists some words of Dr Samuel Johnson have been constantly in mind. 'It is impossible' he said 'for an expositor not to write too little for some, and too much for others. He can judge what is necessary for his own experience, and how long soever he may deliberate will at last explain many lines which the learned will think impossible to be mistaken and omit many for which the ignorant will want his help. These are censures merely relative and must be quietly endured.' Where the names are those which most often occur in a consideration of country-house architecture and decoration, the biographies are of necessity brief. Reference should be made to the various biographical dictionaries referred to in the reading list (page 262). Where appropriate, mention is made within each biography of further sources of information, but it must not be assumed that each house is of necessity open to the public. Reference should be made to *Historic Houses, Castles and Gardens* (annual: Index Publishers), and the Guide in this book.

The Adam Family, Architects

It may well be that some fortunate star saw to it that the Adam family, most celebrated of 18th-century architects, should appear first in these lists. William Adam (1689-1748), father of more famous children was one of the first strictly classical architects produced by Scotland and the family seemed to be ever in the ascendancy, borne up by patrons who demanded their talents and energies. At the time when Lord Burlington and Colen Campbell were erecting Palladian houses in England, William Adam was busy at Hopetoun, Mavisbank, Mellerstain and a host of other Scottish houses. He owed a little to the cool disciplined architecture of Sir William Bruce (q.v.) but the chronology of his work has been obscured by the posthumous, indeed overlate, appearance of his pattern book *Vitruvius Scoticus* in 1810, and by the greater fame of two of his sons, Robert and James. We need concern ourselves less with the eldest, John, and the youngest, William, although they helped with the administrative side of the partnership even in their father's lifetime.

It is not easy to chart the achievements of Robert Adam (1728-92) involving as it does the erection or alteration of at least 45 country houses from the late 1750s to his death. After four years' study in Italy, pursued at great extravagance, he moved to London to take up newly found friendships and contacts. By 1760 he was Joint Architect—with Sir William Chambers—to George III and was ready to launch the Neo-classical style and to control and direct each commission so that no small part was allowed to go unheeded and without design. The practice grew, with the dilettante assistance of James (1732-94), who had also had the opportunity of three years in Italy and meetings with the leading exponents of Neo-classicism. Whereas they inspired James to intellectual theorising, they inspired Robert to action and his bank account at Drummond's bears testimony, in copperplate silence, to his great success.

Such patronage as was now to be his demanded a talented team of craftsmen to put his ideas into effect. He early made use of the family firm of Rose for the execution of plasterwork and used them almost without exception. His carvers, John Gilbert, John Linnell (also a successful cabinet-maker) and Sefferin Alken, were at work almost from his early commissions at Croome and Kedleston in the 1760s. The masons, ormolu workers, carpet weavers and statuaries appear in our lists. Drawing on youthful memories of Scottish architecture and the advantages of knowledge garnered in Italy, Robert welded them into his 'regiment of artificers'. It is these men who hold part of the credit for the exact realisation of his bold ideas and who lay to the winds the oft-quoted tale that 'Mr Adams [sic] carved this doorcase' or 'Adam came here in my great grandfather's day to make this Drawing Room chimneypiece'. Come he may have done, but in fine silk coat, powdered wig, rolled batch of coloured drawings at the ready and a precise mind, financial backing and a proud social standing to go with it all.

We may commend the following buildings as providing visual evidence of his great enterprise, in the 1760-70 period: Kedleston, Derbyshire; Osterley and Syon House, both in Middlesex and Nostell Priory, Harewood House and Newby Hall, all in Yorkshire. In Scotland, Mellerstain, Berwickshire, is an example of a house begun by William Adam and completed by his sons. Their rare use of Rococo motifs appears at Hopetoun, West Lothian, in the plasterwork executed by Thomas Clayton (q.v.)

Reading: J. Lees-Milne, *The Age of Adam,* 1947; John Fleming, *Robert Adam and his Circle in Edinburgh and Rome,* 1962.

Thomas Archer (?1668-1743), Architect

One of the principal exponents of the Baroque style of architecture in England, Archer is perhaps better known for his St Philip's Church, Birmingham (1710-15, now the Cathedral) than his country house work. He made an Italian journey in 1691 and undoubtedly studied the churches in Rome by Borromini for features; in particular, the Italian architect's use of capitals with in-turned volutes were carried into his work. With a voluptuous use of curves, heavily incised stone, dramatic towers (in his churches) and an unerring sense of site and drama, Archer brought a touch of Italy into England. His Cascade House and the north front at Chatsworth are his best known works, but he was probably involved in the design of Bramham, Yorkshire, and the remodelling of Aynho Park, Northants. He is buried at Hale, Hampshire, where he built a house for himself, now much altered.

Reading: Marcus Whiffen, *Thomas Archer,* 1950.

Giuseppe Artari (1697-1769), Stuccoist

Born at Arogno near Lugano in Switzerland, Artari was the son of a stucco-worker and came to England about 1720. He seems to have been the junior partner to Giovanni Bagutti (q.v.) but these niceties of involved research do little to indicate the Baroque, and later, Rococo riches of Artari's swirling stucco. He used a lime composition which was given its fine white finish by adding ground marble dust, and the churches of Switzerland and southern Germany abound in excellent examples of its use. Trained in these traditions, Artari worked particularly for James Gibbs (q.v.) at Ditchley, Oxfordshire, 1725, Ragley, Warwickshire, 1759, and at St Martin-in-the-Fields. His English work has been listed but there is little doubt that he paid frequent visits abroad to work on commissions, and he finally entered the service of the Elector of Cologne and died in that city in 1769.

Reading: Geoffrey Beard, *Georgian Craftsmen and their Work,* 1966.

William Atkinson (c. 1773-1839), Architect

Most of Atkinson's work is found in Scotland and the visitor to Scone Castle, Perthshire, or Tulliallan, Fife will be able to see what this pupil of James Wyatt could do. Both houses are of the early 19th century, a period that was sympathetic to the use of Gothic. Atkinson was much patronised by the Marquis of Bredalbane and Lord Mulgrave and allowed to work in this style, which in castellated form was far removed from his book of 1805, *Picturesque Views of Cottages.*

Giovanni Bagutti (active 1685-c. 1735), Stuccoist

This talented worker, born at Rovio near Lugano in Switzerland was in England by 1709 and was working for Sir John Vanbrugh (q.v.) at Castle Howard. He was responsible for the stucco chimneypiece in the Great Saloon. After this early commission and in partnership with Giuseppe Artari (q.v.), he worked for James Gibbs at St Martin-in-the-Fields and the Senate House, Cambridge. His best work (based on a statement on a drawing in the Gibbs collection (iv. 24) at the Ashmolean Museum, Oxford) is at Moor Park, Hertfordshire, c. 1730. He was patronised by the Duke of Chandos, and may have provided the complex stucco-work at Clandon Park, Surrey, as well as that at Mereworth Castle, Kent, and Great Witley Church, Worcs. Compounded of the elements of Baroque, with random hordes of mythological gods and goddesses, there is no doubt that while to some eyes Bagutti's work is florid, it was competently done. He disappears from England a little after 1730 and probably returned to his native Switzerland.

Giuseppe Artari, in conjunction with Vassali and Serena: saloon ceiling at Ditchley, *Flora with zephyrs, c.*1726.

Robert Bakewell (1685-1752), Wrought-iron Smith

'Robert Bakewell of Derby, in the County of Derby, Gatesmith' in the terse phrase of his will of October 13, 1752 indicates one of Bakewell's principal tasks, making entrance gates for country houses and churches. His activity was for the most part confined to the Midlands and Derbyshire in particular. The visitor to Derby can see many examples of his work in the cathedral and adjacent to the public library. But let him go a little further out from Derby to Melbourne and there is Bakewell's great gilded 'Birdcage', c. 1708, which was recently restored to the gilded splendour befitting the finest garden arbour in England. We know from a letter of December 1749 that when Rowland Cotton wanted a drawing of the west door of Tutbury Church he 'apply'd first to Bakewell, famous all over England for Iron work & who Drawes to perfection'. His delicate metal tracery is a joy to behold and his characteristic wavy bar within a rectangle is found on many gates. He was buried on October 31, 1752 at St Peter's Church, Derby unheralded by any monument.

Thomas Banks (1735-1805), Sculptor

When Queen Charlotte and her daughters joined the enthusiastic visitors to an exhibition of sculpture at Somerset House in 1793 they are said to have been deeply moved by the simple marble figure of a sleeping child. This monument by Banks, commemorating Penelope Boothby, is now in Ashbourne Church, Derbyshire, and being his most admired monument has obscured wet eyes to his importance as a Neo-classical sculptor. The works which remain, mostly monuments, are of unequal quality, but as many busts and casts were dispersed at the sale of his effects held by Mr Christie on May 22, 1805, they may come to light when a visitor, tired of the informative but monotonous drone of his guide, peers into the dark understairs of some porticoed country house.

Reading: C. F. Bell, *Annals of Thomas Banks,* 1938.

Sir Charles Barry (1795-1860), Architect

The visitor to Manchester Art Gallery may not realise he is entering a building designed by Charles Barry in 1824 but when he enters the Houses of Parliament he perhaps troubles to enquire. The point is, however, that Barry is better represented in Manchester and its neighbourhood by churches and public buildings than any area outside London. After the usual travels abroad, but this time unusually including Egypt and Syria, a rapid 'course' in Gothic, and his Manchester work he turned to his country-house alterations. Interspersing work on these between the twenty years of attention to the Houses of Parliament, Barry's Italian-style terraces steadily surrounded his houses. His work for the Duke of Sutherland at Dunrobin Castle in Scotland, Cliveden House, Buckinghamshire and Trentham, Staffordshire, alterations at Harewood House, Yorkshire, and his recasing and internal remodelling of Kingston Lacy, Dorset, all followed fast on each other in the 1840s. He beset them with varying styles, and moved his own from 'Mr' to 'Sir' when knighted in 1852. His closest friend J. L. Wolfe, whom he had met in Italy, said that Barry 'seemed to think that enrichment could never be overdone'. He achieved his final resting place in Westminster Abbey.

The Bernasconi family, Stuccoists

Bernato Bernasconi and his son (?) Francis may seem unlikely names to encounter in English country house decoration but in the first thirty years of the 19th century they had no equal for Gothic plasterwork and work in *scagliola*. In the grand stairhall at Taymouth Castle, Perthshire, the vaulted heights of Eastnor Castle, Herefordshire, at Blithfield Hall, Staffordshire, and Garnons, Herefordshire, they dominated the scene and bring before us accurately and with precise line exactly what the Gothic revival was all about. They decorated the royal palaces and worked in particular at Windsor under the architect Wyatville (q.v.). 'Angels with plain shields, elliptical soffits, enriched spandrels, Gothic mouldings' run across the pages of their accounts and when James Wyatt died in 1813 he owed them £2000. They had worked for him and Lord Bridgwater at Ashridge, Hertfordshire, and

Robert Bakewell's iron arbour at Melbourne Hall,
*c.*1708.

one can see and remember them all, looking at the plaster fan-vaulting in the chapel there.

Matthew Brettingham (1699-1769), Architect
Who designed the great Palladian house of Holkham for the Earl of Leicester in Norfolk may never be decided if one only looks at the plans and elevations of the house published in 1761. Brettingham claimed himself there as the 'architect', and while this ignores the contributions of William Kent, the owner, and his friend Lord Burlington, it did assure him patronage by those distinguished 'for their love of *Palladian* Architecture', and he undoubtedly supervised the actual building of Holkham.

In Palladian mood one might visit Marble Hill, Twickenham, a lovely precise house of 1724-5, but while altered internally by Brettingham in 1750-1, all trace of his work was removed in 1909. One would therefore find no Brettingham, only his beloved Palladian style, and this would perhaps be apposite for he is a ghost architect, flashing plans here, said to have been ignorant of drawing or measuring, possibly involved at Langley, Norfolk, superseded at Kedleston, and even his son, another Matthew (1725-1803) is recorded in the terse words 'little is known of his architectural work . . .'.

Charles Bridgeman (?-1738), Royal Gardener
Bridgeman, despite his position as Royal Gardener to George II, is less well known than Brown or Repton (q.v.). The detailed story of the development of the English landscape park has been partly told, but not enough emphasis has been placed on Bridgeman's share in it. He is a shadowy figure, and whilst his connection with Lord Harley's circle and the St Luke's Club of artists brought him influential friends we know all too little of his private life. Gardens however, were his creation and Dr Peter Willis has listed his participation in at least 36 in he period 1709-1738.

Stowe, Buckinghamshire, is the most important but while Bridgeman was working there for most of his active life, providing, as Walpole said, 'inexpressible richness', he was at Blenheim as early as 1709. Here at the great house rising as the nation's

gift to the 1st Duke of Marlborough he worked under Sir John Vanbrugh. Five royal gardens also came under his care, but today few of his layouts survive. At the Vanbrugh house of Eastbury we can trace him a little, but the best pilgrimage will be to Stowe, armed with the *Views of Stowe,* which his widow Sarah published in 1739. He is the originator of English landscape gardening and his importance has steadily emerged in recent years.

Lancelot 'Capability' Brown (1716-83), Landscape Gardener: Architect
The setting to any house is important and brief mention needs to be made of the most successful and best known of the 18th-century landscape gardeners, Capability Brown. He is said to have earned his nickname from a habit of referring to the 'capabilities' of the park layouts that he was asked to improve. It is often forgotten that he swept away may late 17th-century formal gardens and when these are tabulated against the perspective engravings of Kip and Knyff (as depicted in *Britannia Illustrata,* 1708-20) the loss is seen to be real. To dwell on this, however, is to deny Brown the success which came as a result of his undoubted ability, and particularly after he had moved to London in 1751. The clumping of trees, the serpentine line of walk and lake, as approved by Hogarth, led the eye a wanton kind of chase and enhanced the settings. But Brown was not above designing the house as well and the most successful fusions of his joint talents are at Croome Court, Worcestershire, and Claremont, Surrey, where he was assisted by his future son-in-law, Henry Holland (q.v.). The rolling parks of Blenheim (his greatest work), Harewood and Longleat enable one to see the formula of his improvements.

Reading: Dorothy Stroud, *Capability Brown,* 1950.

Sir William Bruce (*c.* 1630-1710), Architect
We still await a detailed study of Sir William Bruce – two are promised – but it is clear that what Colen Campbell did for classical architecture in England Bruce did, and earlier, in Scotland. When classical architecture reached Scotland after the Restoration Bruce stood in high favour and eventually became

Overseer of the Royal Works in Scotland. His most important work that can be seen by the public is the remodelling he carried out at Thirlestane Castle, Berwickshire, in the early 1670s. His patron here was the 2nd Earl (later Duke) of Lauderdale, the chief favourite of Charles II in Scotland, who is known (from correspondence in the Scottish Record Office) to have sent Dutch workmen North from Ham House, the Lauderdale's residence at Richmond, near London. As a result of this patronage Bruce also remodelled the palace of Holyrood House, Edinburgh, and had a share in the early conception of Hopetoun House.

Reading: J. G. Dunbar, The Historic Architecture of Scotland, 1966.

William Burges (1827-1881), Architect
The collaboration between patron and architect rarely reached a higher point than that which existed between the 3rd Marquess of Bute and William Burges. It resulted in the transformation of the remains of the medieval Cardiff Castle into 'a romantic Victorian palace' and work at nearby Castell Coch. This, also a long-ruined castle, was recreated between 1875 and work was still incomplete when Burges died at the age of 53. His debt to High Gothic and the exuberance of his decorations marked him out as no ordinary architect. Anyone who has seen the architect's house in Kensington, or his fine church at Studley Royal, Yorkshire will never efface the interior decorations from his mind. The bronze doors, mosaics, star-painted ceilings, black, red and green marble, all combine to provide a unique display of High Victorian art.

Reading: Charles Handley-Read 'William Burges', in Victorian Architecture, ed. Peter Ferriday, 1964.

Richard Boyle, 3rd Earl of Burlington (1694-1753), Architect
In 1714, ten years after Lord Burlington had succeeded to his father's estates, he set out on a Grand Tour with Italy as his ultimate destination. It would be wrong to suggest that the course of English architecture was destined to change at his journey. Indeed on his first visit he took little note of the villas of Andrea Palladio. At his return to England there were the lavish folios by Leoni and Campbell, which not only published Palladio but set many crisp elevations before the eager patrons bent on imitating the Italian master. In the summer of 1719 Burlington set out again for Italy, this time eager to study Palladio and to acquire as many of his drawings as he could find.

It was on this second trip that Lord Burlington met William Kent (q.v.) the architect, decorator and landscape gardener with whom his name is now always linked. They returned from Italy together and Kent was soon to be involved in the decorations for Lord Burlington's own Palladian villa at Chiswick. By 1726 or so Burlington had established a leading position and persons of taste were ready to take what he and Kent had to offer; this patronage, as Burlington's of Kent, assured their joint success. In this year Leoni (q.v.) published his translation of Alberti's Architecture with its praise of Burlington for establishing the classical sequence back through our own 17th-century architect Inigo Jones (q.v.) to the Italian Palladio. It was natural that in these years he had become the centre of a group sympathetic to his ideas and to his position as 'the Apostle of the Arts'. As the scholar he provided the inspiration, and his protégé Kent realised the dreams. Between them they were capable of works of great virtuosity, they enjoyed the friendship of Alexander Pope, and the admiration – in Burlington's case at least – of Horace Walpole.

The Palladian style which Burlington revived lasted almost to his death, but in the last ten years of his life he had almost retired. There were the memories of designing and seeing built the York Assembly Rooms, of houses such as Kirby Hall built for his friend William Aislabie, of managing his large estates in Yorkshire and Ireland and meddling with Hawksmoor's designs for the great Mausoleum at Castle Howard. He died at Chiswick on December 3rd 1753.

Reading: James Lees-Milne, Earls of Creation, 1962.

William Burn (1789-1879), Architect
A pupil of Sir Robert Smirke (q.v.), Burn was most

Stucco portrait of Colen Campbell at Compton Place, Sussex.

active in Scotland, but he shunned publicity, never exhibited his drawings and yet he prospered. To his buildings he brought a modesty and good sense, and occasionally a sense of grandeur. The fine exterior, and the 'Jacobethan' plasterwork of the interior of Falkland House (1839) have few equals in a house of its scale, and his Carstairs, Lanarkshire, is also stylish in a form of 'Tudor Gothic'. Later in his life his office included as assistants William Eden Nesfield and Norman Shaw who both emerged as successful architects in their own right.

Colen Campbell (1676-1729), Architect

Of recent years Colen Campbell has been regarded as one of the most important of the early 18th-century architects but some doubt still surrounds his origins and training. Born in Scotland, seemingly in 1676, he seems to have practised as a lawyer until about 1710. He appears in the Padua University Registers as a visitor in 1697 and it was probably on this Italian trip that he laid the secure knowledge he undoubtedly later possessed of Palladio's build-

ings. In architecture he made his first bow in 1710 with a house in Glasgow and gradually the transition from lawyer to architect took place. He may have received some training under James Smith (?-1731) the Overseer of the Royal Works in Scotland, a post formerly held by Sir William Bruce (q.v.).

Whatever the genealogical and formative influences were, Campbell launched himself firmly on London society in 1714-15 with the publication of the first volume of the eventual three volume, *Vitruvius Britannicus*. It was this first volume that played so important a part in arousing Lord Burlington's interest in Palladianism, and Campbell collaborated with the Earl in erecting Burlington House in Piccadilly. But it is in Kent that one sees the mature Campbell at Mereworth (1723). The house is a direct adaptation from Palladio's Villa Rotonda and the Swiss stuccoist Giovanni Bagutti (q.v.) was used, along with the decorative painter Francesco Sleter to enrich the proportioned interiors. A group of over two hundred of Campbell's drawings came to light in 1967 and are now in the library of the R.I.B.A.

Even if the country house visitor does not examine these he will recognise the splendours of Mereworth, Houghton, the great Walpole house (1721) in Norfolk and the centre block at Stourhead (1722) in Wiltshire as the work of a masterly hand. As the probable master of Roger Morris (q.v.), the friend of noblemen and the purveyor of an important architectural style in precise three-dimensional terms his importance is unquestioned; his choice of fine craftsmen unequalled. He died at his house in Whitehall on September 13, 1729.

Reading: H. E. Stutchbury, *Colen Campbell,* 1967.

John Carr (1723-1807), Architect

While John Carr designed interiors in an Adamesque style he did not use the sophisticated and famous decorators used by the Scottish-born architect. Very little painted decoration is to be found in a Carr house of the mid-1760s but his favourite plasterers, Giuseppe Cortese (q.v.) and James Henderson, spread their Rococo stucco-work across the walls and ceilings. Carr was born at Horbury, near Wakefield and it is in this West Riding of Yorkshire village that he is burried in the church he designed.

Carr had an extensive practice, being involved with at least sixty commissions, including an uncounted number of York town houses. Most of his work lay in the northern counties and apart from architecture he served as an alderman and Lord Mayor of York. Visitors to Harewood House, Leeds look at a Carr designed house, modified by Adam, and again in the 19th century by Sir Charles Barry (q.v.). It is however at Wentworth Woodhouse in South Yorkshire that his splendid stable block and the Mausoleum, in memory of Charles, 2nd Marquess of Rockingham, bring home the extent of his friendships and patronage. The Mausoleum is filled with marble busts of the Marquess's friends and the statue of Rockingham by Carr's friend Nollekens is dominant. At Cannon Hall, near Barnsley, Carr attended on four occasions, spread over forty years (1767-1807) to alter the house. It is a plain good house and in nearly all his designs one can see this honest approach, the use of competent York craftsmen and a correct relationship between economy and show. It ensured success and he left property worth £150,000 to his nephews and nieces.

Sir William Chambers (1723-96), Architect

Chambers was born in Sweden and at the age of 16 he went back there, after an English education, to enter the service of the Swedish East India Company. This is a key to his split career, for travelling out to Bengal and China gave him a unique knowledge of Oriental art. Our space only allows brief mention of the succession of studies in France and five years in Italy. The initiated will know that this rich experience in the first 30 years of his life—he returned to England in 1755—well fitted him to enter architectural practice at a time when society was eagerly involved in the vogue for Chinese decoration and pagoda-like garden buildings.

After arrival in London, Chambers was recommended to Lord Bute as a person fitted to become architectural tutor to the Prince of Wales, and when that young man became King George III it was Chambers (with his rival Robert Adam) who was appointed one of the Architects of His Majesty's Works. A publisher of important books on Chinese buildings, a founder member and first Treasurer of the Royal Academy, knighted in 1770, Comptroller of the Works, and later first Surveyor-General—the man was all-important—but what of his works? At least eight public buildings, including Somerset House, country houses, London town houses, bridges, monuments, churches, give plenty of choice. They show his command of the orders, his nice use of decoration in a style, as he flattered himself, more akin than that of Robert Adam to the principles of the ancients in Rome, and his knowledge of men and manners. The visitor to Kew Gardens with its orangery, temples and pagoda designed by Chambers for the Princess Dowager of Wales will not easily forget him. He outlived this commission of 1757-62 by over thirty years. Royal favour ensured his burial in Westminster Abbey–but without a monument.

Sir Francis Chantrey (1781-1841), Sculptor

Francis Legatt Chantrey was born at Norton, near Sheffield, as was Joseph Rose (q.v.) the successful Adam plasterer; and like Rose he left, almost at the end of his apprenticeship, to try his fortune in London. His rise to fame was a precarious and uncertain one and he was 32 before a bust of his exhibited at the Royal Academy brought the commissions tumbling in for attention. From this time and for the next 30 years he worked on some 270 commissions. All the world is represented from George IV, William IV, Queen Victoria, the Duke of Wellington and Sir Walter Scott, to the classical relief of 'Penelope's Reluctance to Produce the Bow of Ulysses', and the crowded 'Signing of the Reform Bill'.

He left his large fortune to his wife and, after her life interest, to the Royal Academy. It founded the Chantrey Bequest. He was buried at Norton beneath a tomb of his own design.

Sir Henry Cheere (1703-1781), Sculptor

The bank account which Henry Cheere kept at Drummond's Bank shows him to have had a most successful practice. For the visitor to country houses it is his chimneypieces which are most noteworthy. At Ditchley and Kirtlington, Oxfordshire, Wallington, Northumberland, Longford Castle, Wiltshire, they delight by their incorporation of Rococo detail. He was at first in partnership with his brother John, who had a successful business in moulding lead garden figures. Henry had probably been a pupil of John van Nost (q.v.), who also specialised in this sort of work. After the interlude with his brother he again entered another partnership, with Henry Scheemakers. All this varied experience gave him a full and busy life, a share in the founding of the Royal Academy and a knighthood.

Thomas Chippendale (1718-1779), Cabinet-maker

For one whose name is almost universally known, Chippendale has had to endure posthumously the great burden of having much that was unworthy of his skill credited to him. Born in 1718 at Otley, Yorkshire, Chippendale showed enough promise, after training (presumably) under his father, to leave eventually the Yorkshire town for London. Indeed we know hardly anything of him before his marriage on May 19, 1748 at St George's Chapel, Mayfair to an equally obscure Catherine Redshaw. It may well be he was financed in London by the Fawkes family, on whose estates his family had lived since the 17th century, but, whatever the truth, he prospered. By 1753 he had moved to premises in St Martin's Lane and in 1754 the first edition of his famous pattern book, the *Gentleman and Cabinet-maker's Director* was issued. Of recent years he has been given an increasing share of the credit for making the designs himself, rather than using the services of Matthias Lock and Henry Copland, two talented carvers and draughtsmen. Scholars have also sorted out his relationship to Robert Adam and the problems of our anticipation of the French in the question of Neo-classical furniture. While Chippendale made a journey to France in 1768 we do not know what for and it clouds the issue hardly at all if we look with appreciative eyes at the furniture itself, rather than the shadows of his life.

If we assume that at the time of a fire at his premises in 1755 Chippendale employed 22 men (that number of workmen's tool chests are mentioned) it is obvious that for most of his active career (1750-1775) he headed a large and busy workshop. As far as is known, however, he never received the patronage of the Crown as did his contemporaries William Vile, John Cobb, William Hallett, William Ince and John Mayhew. In the early years of the first *Director,* Chippendale, as with most of his contemporaries, must have concentrated on Rococo pieces, many intended for gilding. By the time of the third edition of 1762 he replaced many designs for new ones. It was not until the 1765-70 period, when he was in his fifties, that the finest work was created, such as that at Nostell Priory, Yorkshire, (the great library-table is alone worth the visit) and the pieces he made for the Lascelles family at nearby Harewood House. At these houses documentation exists for the pieces that survive. It cannot be stressed too strongly that in Chippendale's case this applies to a handful of examples only. What is frequently referred to as 'Chippendale' may mean in the style of the published plates of the *Director* pattern book and may merely be a vague ascription of inferior material to a well-known name. The case is only convincing where the furniture is undeniably the work of a skilled craftsman and is surviving in a house where the 18th-century owner was a subscriber to one or more editions of the *Director*.

The patronage that Chippendale enjoyed—although some of the letters sent to him by Sir Rowland Winn of Nostell Priory are outspoken about shortcomings—was eventually extended to his son, Thomas Chippendale the younger (1749-1822). He had been born a year after his father's arrival in London and marriage and, being brought up in his father's business, continued it, after the eminent man's death, with Thomas Haig, who had long been in partnership with them. Haig withdrew from the business in 1796, the year in which Chippendale provided furniture to the Lascelles family at Harewood as his father had done over twenty years before. It is however at Stourhead, Wiltshire, that the younger Chippendale's achievements can best be seen, in furniture which survives in pristine condition. The surviving accounts show that furniture was provided over 25 years from 1795 to 1802, with many notable purchases, including elegant satinwood armchairs in 1802. Together father and son dominated the Rococo, Neo-classical and revived Greek styles for seventy years during a period which knew when quality was being provided, and even more acutely when it was not.

Reading: Anthony Coleridge, *Chippendale Furniture,* 1968.

Giovanni Battista Cipriani (1727-1785), Decorative Painter

In 1750 Cipriani, a Florentine by birth, met Sir William Chambers (q.v.), who was on his Grand Tour. Each recognised in the other the means to enhancing a livelihood and Cipriani returned to England with Chambers in 1756. He remained here for the rest of his life and played a vital part in establishing Neo-classical painting as a proper subject for the enrichment of classical houses. He is perhaps best known for the painted panels for George III's state coach, designed by Chambers, and still in use on royal occasions. He was a founder member of the Royal Academy and his style may best be judged by work at Syon House and Osterley, both in Middlesex.

Thomas Clayton (active 1740-76), Stuccoist

One of the best known of the 18th-century workers in Scotland, Thomas Clayton worked for both William Adam and his famous son Robert. He specialised in a Rococo form of plasterwork and this may be seen at Hopetoun House, West Lothian and Blair Castle, Perthshire, (his most important commission). It would seem that Clayton was not Scottish, although he had a yard at Leith, near Edinburgh. In 1771-2, he or his son did ceilings with Coney for Sir Lawrence Dundas's house in St Andrew's Square, Edinburgh (now the Royal Bank of Scotland).

John Cobb (?-1778), Cabinet-maker

Apart from being a skilled cabinet-maker and a contemporary of Chippendale, Cobb was one of the proudest men in England, and haughty and successful to a corresponding degree. The finest achievements of his firm in the late years are the marquetried commodes of which that of 1772 at Corsham Court, Wiltshire, with its vase stands of unusual design, is the most noteworthy. His earlier achievements are noted under the description of his partner, William Vile. He combined with him to about 1765 and then continued the business alone and, as his bank account at Drummonds shows, most successfully, until his death in 1778.

William Collins (1721-1793), Sculptor and Stuccoist

As a pupil of Sir Henry Cheere (q.v.) Collins had a good training but his true worth is difficult to recognise. He worked firstly as a conventional sculptor providing chimneypiece panels, pediment

Thomas Clayton's plasterwork in the dining room at Blair Castle, Perthshire, c.1755.

carvings, altar-pieces and medallions. And then he entered the lucrative business of providing plaster casts of a classical nature. These were eminently suitable for the Neo-classical interiors being created by Adam and Chambers, and may be seen in the form of full length figures and medallions at Kedleston, Derbyshire, and in a large panel at Burton Constable, Yorkshire. He has been credited with the stuccowork in the Music Room of Norfolk House (re-erected in the Victoria and Albert Museum). If he did it we must view him in the dimension of an artist of incredible talent. Only time and the growing availability of documentation will sort truth from half-truths.

Giuseppe Cortese (?-1778), Stuccoist
Working principally in Yorkshire, Cortese had an extensive practice as a stuccoist and he may well have been active at Gilling Castle, Yorkshire, before 1730. He worked there in later years, and at Fairfax House, York, Newburgh Priory (1765) and Somerset House, Halifax. Most of his known work is in a capable Rococo style and he worked on occasion for John Carr (q.v.) and with James Henderson (q.v.). He died in 1778 and Henderson and Edward Elwick, a competent cabinet-maker of Wakefield, acted as his executors.

Thomas Cubitt (1788-1855), Architect
Cubitt's fame came late in life when a long and suc-

cessful career was crowned by his being given the commission in 1848 to build Osborne House for Queen Victoria. He started life as a carpenter, but quickly became, with his brother Lewis (the 'architect' of King's Cross Station), a speculative builder on a large scale. The employer of labour on a permanent wage basis, he developed extensive areas in Bloomsbury, Pimlico, Clapham and Camden Town.

George Dance, Junior (1741-1825), Architect
The master of Sir John Soane (q.v.). His fame rests on competent house restorations and public buildings. The interior of the best of them, Newgate Prison, is, needless to say, little known.

Robert Davies (c. 1675-1748), Wrought-iron Smith
This talented Welsh smith was already famous at the age of 24 and, working in a style made fashionable by Jean Tijou (q.v.), provided splendid gates in the North-West. His most celebrated achievements include the gates at Chirk Castle, Denbighshire, at Eaton Hall, near Chester and at Leeswood, Mold, Flintshire. The White Gates and Screen at Leeswood, over thirty yards in length, are among the finest in Europe, and were erected in 1726 with the assistance of his brother John.

Roger Davies (active 1682-1709), Master Joiner
One of the talented workers in the London City churches Davies was employed by both Wren and his scientist friend, Robert Hooke. He worked at Ragley Hall, Warwickshire, Boughton House, Northamptonshire, and extensively in London. A William Davies, seemingly a relative, also worked at Chatsworth.

John Devall (1701-74), Mason and Sculptor
With his son, another John (1728-1794), Devall was one of the most important craftsmen working in the 18th century. They worked for all the major architects from James Gibbs to Robert Adam, and apart from their ability as masons and master-builders they made many chimneypieces and marble tables.

Archibald Elliot (1761-1823), Architect
The castellated Gothic style, which at the beginning of the 19th century in England had its champion in the person of Sir Robert Smirke (q.v.), was represented in Scotland by Archibald Elliot and his brother James (died 1810). Their best work is at Taymouth Castle, Perthshire, where the Elliots were given the task, from 1806-10, of completing the house in their favourite style. The interior was enriched with a fan-vaulted staircase hall with plasterwork by Francis Bernasconi (q.v.).

The Etty family of York (17th-18th cent.), Carpenters and Builders
York had always been an important building centre, with a Company and Fellowship of Carpenters which started in the reign of Edward IV. In later years activity revolved around the Etty family. As his monument states, John Etty (1634-1708/9) 'acquired great knowledge of mathematics, especially geometry and architecture in all its parts far beyond any of his contemporaries in this City'. He would be the Etty who showed the youthful Grinling Gibbons (q.v.) around the City in about 1667 when the young man first came to England.

William Etty (died 1734) had a very successful patronage and was to be Sir John Vanbrugh's clerk of works at Seaton Delaval and Castle Howard; he was also to be associated with the gentleman architect William Wakefield (died 1730), and with Colen Campbell (q.v.) at Baldersby Park, Yorkshire. When he died the architect Nicholas Hawksmoor (q.v.), attending as best he could to the progress of the Castle Howard Mausoleum in Yorkshire from distant London, wrote to Lord Carlisle: 'I am very much concerned to hear of the Death of Mr Etty, his loss will be felt by his family more than by anybody else, but as he was a usefull man to the world they will almost certainly miss him . . . .' As a family they were involved in most country house building around York in the late 17th and early 18th centuries.

John Flaxman (1755-1826), Sculptor
Another son of York was Flaxman, but he was taken away south to London by his parents when he was only six months old. His father, John, was a sculptor of note who produced many reliefs for

Josiah Wedgwood's Staffordshire potteries to copy. He joined in this work and had a long and satisfactory association with the master potter. It is however more in the role of a sculptor of monuments for family churches adjacent to his patron's houses that he will be encountered by the country-house visitor. There are at least 170 of them spread across the period 1780–1825 when Neo-classicism and the revived Greek taste held sway.

Reading: W. G. Constable, *John Flaxman*, 1927.

Henry Flitcroft (1697–1769), Architect

It is said that Flitcroft came to the notice of Lord Burlington (q.v.) when he fell from a scaffold and broke his leg whilst working as a 'journeyman carpenter' in 1720 at Burlington House, Piccadilly. Whatever the truth of the story, Flitcroft was taken into the Earl's service and worked as a draughtsman and surveyor on various of the Palladian designs in hand. In 1726 'Burlington Harry' as he had become known, became, with his master's help, an important figure in the Office of Works and over the next twenty years he rose to the positions of Master Carpenter, Master Mason and Deputy Surveyor and finally Comptroller of the Works. His principal country house work was the rebuilding of Woburn Abbey, Bedfordshire. He produced plans and sketches over four years, 1747–51, and then the craftsmen assembled to work at various jobs until 1763.

The Devall family (q.v.) were the masons and Portland and Purbeck stone was used. The whole story, set out in the late Gladys Scott Thomson's *Family Background* (1949) gives a fascinating insight into the building of a grand country house. The account books show that £84,970 6s. 8d. was spent on the reconstruction. The fourth Duke of Bedford outlived the completion of the work by eight years.

Paul and Philip Franchini (active 1730–60), Stuccoists

Most of the English work of these two Swiss Stuccoists has no documentation to support it and it is principally in Ireland that their frothy Rococo style should be studied. In 1739 they were at Carton and the year after executed a very fine variant of this ceiling at 85, St Stephen's Green, Dublin. Riverstown, Tyrone House, Dublin, Castle Saffron in County Cork and Castletown were also all given swirling foliage and mythological figures and panels in soft yielding stucco. They laid the foundations whereby the extensive Dublin Guild of Plasterers could fuse into their work some of the new fashionable trends.

Reading: C. F. Curran, *Dublin Decorative Plasterwork*, 1967.

Grinling Gibbons (1648–1721), Wood and Stone-carver

Born in Holland of English parents, Grinling Gibbons came to England about 1667 and early went to York where he was with (but not apprenticed to) John Etty (q.v.). He then left for London and is said to have been discovered and introduced to Charles II by John Evelyn. He was appointed Master Carver in wood to the Crown, a position he held until the reign of George I. In these terms his career is one of bare facts. What must forcefully emerge from our brief discussion of him is the amazing virtuosity he brought to his wood and stone-carving, but as with all outstanding artists many works are attributed to him which are unworthy of his art. It is also frequently said that his wood carving may be distinguished by the presence of an open peapod. We can do no better than quote his most recent and precise biographer, David Green (*Grinling Gibbons*, 1964).

Mr Green writes: 'Certainly it is more than high time that the hoary peapod fable was buried . . . If there were in fact any such signature or sign-manual to be relied on, it need hardly be said the student would be thankful: for Gibbons' imitators were in his own lifetime industrious, and though many of their works show poverty of spirit as well as of invention, others at their best run him so close that a copyright peapod, exclusive to Gibbons, would be more than welcome. As it is, one might just as reasonably accept the acanthus leaf, especially in scroll form, as his favourite motif, both in marble and in wood; but that he annexed from ancient Rome . . . .' An hour before the authentic

The west overmantel in the saloon at Belton House,
possibly carved by Grinling Gibbons.

Grinling Gibbons: a detail from the Carved Room at Petworth House.

carvings at Petworth, or looking at his stone and marble carvings at Blenheim Palace will do more to etch Gibbons on the mind than any frantic and needless hunt for peapods.

Gibbons also worked extensively in Wren's St Paul's with the Oxford carver, Jonathan Maine (q.v.), at Trinity College, Oxford, Badminton House, Gloucestershire and Burghley House, Northamptonshire. He died in 1721 and is buried at St Paul's, Covent Garden. It was left until 1965 to provide a memorial to him in the form of a lime-wood wreath of flowers which Gibbons had carved for St Paul's Cathedral. It was generously presented to the church by the Dean and Chapter of St Paul's

and affixed to the wooden church screen.
Reading: David Green, *Grinling Gibbons,* 1964.
James Gibbs (1682-1754), Architect
At a time when Lord Burlington and Colen Campbell were immersed in the strictures of the Palladian style James Gibbs was pursuing an individual path with every mark of the Italian Baroque revolving about him. Scottish born, he travelled to Italy in 1704 and became a pupil of Carlo Fontana, the Pope's surveyor. A study of the Gibbs drawings at the Ashmolean Museum is in itself a rewarding experience, especially when one encounters those Gibbs did in Rome. Imaginative groupings of columns, figures and fragments of buildings fill the

paper and almost rise from it. With this secure training, possessed by hardly any of his contemporaries, he returned to England in 1709, and set about securing a strong Tory patronage for himself.

In 1728 Gibbs published his *A Book of Architecture* dedicated to the Duke of Argyll. He indicated that he had taken the 'utmost care that these Designs should be done in the best Tast[e] I could form upon the Instructions of the greatest Masters in Italy . . .'. One hundred and fifty designs lie on the crisp pages and, as with all his publications, they had a great influence on architectural design in England and America, particularly the plates concerning St Martin-in-the-Fields (1722-26). With his public buildings at Oxford and Cambridge, his work as one of the surveyors to the Commissioners for Building Fifty New Churches in London, and his country-house practice, Gibbs was busy and successful. His designs for houses are best seen in the compass of Ditchley, Oxfordshire, Sudbrooke Park, Surrey, the Octagon House at Twickenham, Wimpole Hall, Cambridgeshire, and Fairlawne, Kent. In most of them he employed Swiss stuccoists (principally Giuseppe Artari), although in some of his London work Isaac Mansfield (q.v.) the London and York plasterer assisted. In his early years a Roman Catholic, Gibbs turned to the Established Church and was buried at 'Marylebone Chapel' (St Peter, Vere Street) on August 9, 1754. He had designed the church in 1723-4 for the Earl of Oxford using all the 'skill in architecture', noted on his simple pedimented memorial tablet.

Reading: Bryan Little, *The Life and Works of James Gibbs*, 1955.

Edward Goudge (active late 17th, early 18th-century), Plasterer
One of the most talented of late Renaissance workers in England, Goudge seems to have had an early connection with Nicholas Hawksmoor (q.v.). Vertue records that Goudge did 'some frett-work ceilings at Justice Mellust's in Yorkshire', where Hawksmoor was a clerk, and it seems that Goudge, recognising the young man's abilities, introduced him to London architectural circles. As for Goudge

himself, the architect William Winde (q.v.) told Mary Bridgeman in 1689 that he 'is now looked on as ye beste master in England in his profession as his works atte Combe, Hampstead & Sir John Brownlowe's will Evidence'. This last refers to Goudge's fine plasterwork at Belton House, Lincolnshire, c. 1687. A number of his designs are preserved (principally in the Bodleian Library) but by 1702 he lamented that his business was dwindling away occasioned by war and the rise of ceiling-painting.

James Gillespie Graham (c. 1777-1855), Architect
Starting life as a joiner, Graham with Scottish tenacity of purpose became a leading Scottish architect, married well, and had a most successful practice. With Crace he decorated much of the interior of Taymouth Castle, Perthshire, and his castellated houses show his ability to devise imaginative Gothic residences. He was however capable of the occasional classical job as his dignified buildings of 1822, columned and porticoed, in Moray Place, Edinburgh, prove.

Nicholas Hawksmoor (1661-1736), Architect.
Born in Nottinghamshire Hawksmoor was early in the service of Samuel Mellish of Doncaster as a clerk. He was there 'discovered' by Edward Goudge (q.v.), taken to London and introduced to Sir Christopher Wren. From this time on Hawksmoor acted as clerk of works, supervisor and general 'domestic clerk' to Wren. He worked on drawings for all the major buildings, became Clerk of Works at Kensington Palace, and at Greenwich Hospital and it was here that he came into contact with Sir John Vanbrugh (q.v.) who was then Comptroller of the Works and who used his services, particularly at Castle Howard and Blenheim. Hawksmoor's independence and knowledge swung him well beyond the normal role of assistant and he provided the technical knowledge necessary to carry Vanbrugh's restless pencillings into effect. His own buildings, particularly Easton Neston (1702), his six London churches, and the Castle Howard Mausoleum, show his mastery of the orders and his knowledge of the work and theories of other major architects. Some of this was in a Gothic style,

Nicholas Hawksmoor's Mausoleum at Castle Howard,
1729-42.

and some in the style of Roman architects of the High Renaissance such as Donato Bramante.

Reading: K. Downes, *Nicholas Hawksmoor,* 1960.

Henry Herbert, Earl of Pembroke (1693-1750), Architect

Like his contemporary, the 3rd Earl of Burlington, Lord Herbert was an important gentleman architect, and an ardent advocate of the Palladian manner. Living at Wilton House (as his descendants still do), Pembroke was able to witness the work of Inigo Jones in the Double Cube Room. He was in a position to choose the occasions when he would design and build, but he was greatly assisted, as Wren and Vanbrugh were by Hawksmoor, by Roger Morris (q.v.). Together they erected several notable buildings, particularly Marble Hill for George II's mistress, Henrietta, Countess of Suffolk. The beautiful Palladian Bridge of 1736-7 at Wilton itself is however perhaps their finest achievement. It spans the little River Nadder, and when Lord Oxford visited Wilton in 1738 it was complete and he was able to describe it as 'a most beautiful bridge over the river'. The mason was John Devall (q.v.).

Reading: James Lees-Milne, *Earls of Creation,* 1962.

James Henderson (active 1755-78), Plasterer

Best known for his association with the architect John Carr (q.v.), Henderson had a successful practice established in York in which he was assisted by his son Thomas. They probably had a working relationship with the Swiss stuccoist, Giuseppe Cortese (q.v.), since Henderson acted as one of the executors to his will. Henderson's list of work is a long one and in essence it may be said that if the house is by Carr, the plasterwork is probably by Henderson. He was equally adept at the Rococo and Neo-classical styles.

Henry Holland (1745-1806), Architect

It is as Capability Brown's son-in-law that Holland is often known, but he had a successful and independent style (which blended Greco-Roman themes), and which soon brought him to the notice of the Prince of Wales. He enlarged Carlton House, London and built the Marine Pavilion at Brighton (turned into the 'Royal Pavilion' by John Nash (q.v.)) for the Prince. His private houses included Berrington Hall, Herefordshire (1778), the outbuildings including the delightful Chinese Dairy at Woburn Abbey, Bedfordshire, reconstructions at Althorp, Northamptonshire, and Southill House (1795) for the Whitbread family. In the Library at Southill is a bust of him by George Garrard. It has engraved beneath it a verse by Samuel Whitbread which concludes:

> Farewell! in life I honoured thee;
> In death they name respected be.

Reading: Dorothy Stroud, *Henry Holland,* 1965.

Robert Hooke (1635-1703), Scientist, Architect

Like his great contemporary Sir Christopher Wren Robert Hooke was a prominent member of the Royal Society and for some time its Secretary. As a scientist with a fertile, inventive mind it was natural that in an age where science and architecture were hardly separable as careers, Hooke should make designs for friends and clients. Much of his work has been destroyed but his contribution to the exterior of Ragley Hall, Warwickshire c. 1680 (it has a later portico), can still be discerned.

Reading: H. M. Colvin, *Biographical Dictionary of English Architects,* 1954.

William Ince and John Mayhew (active 1755-1810), Cabinet-makers

Important yet little-known may be the conclusion we have to draw on the activities of these two cabinet-makers. Dr L. O. J. Boynton has recently shown that they provided an important cabinet for the Duchess of Manchester (now in the Victoria and Albert Museum), which had ormolu fittings provided by Matthew Boulton's Birmingham manufactory. He has also shown that their book-keeping was lax and their business methods conducted on a vague basis. However, their reputation was high and their book of designs entitled the *Universal System of Household Furniture,* while not as important as Chippendale's, was useful enough and dedicated to a grand enough patron, the Duke of Marlborough.

John James (c. 1672-1746), Architect

While he started work as a carpenter James worked

hard, equipped himself with a wide practical knowledge under Matthew Bancks, Master Carpenter to the Crown, and was soon joint Clerk of Works with Nicholas Hawksmoor (q.v.) at Greenwich. It was with this group of builders that he was associated until his death, but he moved easily from one post of authority to another. At Wren's death in 1723 he became Surveyor to the Fabric of St Paul's. He was also Surveyor to the Dean and Chapter of Westminster Abbey, and succeeded Hawksmoor in other positions at the older man's death in 1736. To these routine jobs which required competence without virtuosity he was admirably suited. It is hard to realise therefore that he was the architect of the very competent Appuldurcombe House, Isle of Wight (now a ruin under the care of the Ministry of Public Building and Works).

Thomas Johnson (1714-1778?), Carver
Among the leading exponents of the Rococo style in England, the name of Thomas Johnson has long been included. The style was so quickly eclipsed by Neo-classicism that only Johnson's published works and work in the style of the published plates drew attention to the work of this gifted carver. An able boy could readily learn the craft of carving in the years which saw the rich creations of Lord Burlington and William Kent, and the important designs published by French and English engravers. Chief among these to have an influence on Johnson were the various editions of *Aesop's Fables* with Francis Barlow's engraved illustrations. These last were also used by the Rococo plasterers, Giuseppe Cortese (q.v.) among them, as well as by the Oxford plasterer, Thomas Roberts (q.v.), and the young Johnson. By the mid-1750s he was a foremost designer and carver and a close study of his *One Hundred and Fifty New Designs* of 1761 shows the close approximation of many Rococo mirrors and tables to his mercurial style.
Reading: Helena Hayward, *Thomas Johnson and English Rococo*, 1964.

Inigo Jones (1573-1652), Architect
English classical architecture might on occasion seem to be pedantic and wanting in invention, but when it is realised that Inigo Jones introduced it to a country still in the realms of Gothic survival and half-timbering, its importance may be allowed. He became Surveyor of the King's Works in 1615 and for the next thirty years was employed in this service. It allowed him to follow the ideals and principles of Andrea Palladio, the Italian architect whose buildings he had studied on his tours. His Queen's House at Greenwich and the Banqueting House in Whitehall introduced a new dimension to English architecture of the 1620s. He brought poise and elegance and combined it with an English vernacular which, in the case of the Banqueting House, was further enriched by the great ceiling paintings by Rubens.

The style he set out was continued, particularly at Wilton House, by his pupil and nephew by marriage, John Webb (q.v.) and, eighty years after his death, by Lord Burlington and William Kent. His important stage designs for Italianate masques may be seen among the drawings at Chatsworth. They draw attention to the rich diversity of his talent, which he used according to the rules, but occasionally broke beyond them with a dash of brilliance. In consequence he has been credited with much work he would have known better not to design.
Reading: Sir John Summerson, *Inigo Jones*, 1966.

Angelica Kauffmann (1741-1807), Decorative Painter
A Swiss immigrant, Angelica Kauffmann was one of the two women chosen as founder members of the Royal Academy. She had arrived in England in 1766 after several years spent studying in Italy, eager to look up the friends she had made abroad. Her self-portrait at Burghley House, Northamptonshire, depicts her as assured and bright-eyed and half London seems to have taken her to their hearts and not a few were ardently in love. Nathaniel Dance she spurned for the attentions of Sir Joshua Reynolds, but these were more academic than serious. Henry Fuseli also paid her court, and was as unavailing in love with her as Mary Moser, Angelica's fellow Academician, was in love with him.

Angelica Kauffmann, R.A.: portrait by Nathaniel
Dance R.A. (Collection of the Marquess of Exeter).

But the elusive qualities of love need not be sought in her easel and decorative ceiling paintings. There are less of these room decorations than may be supposed, and 'in the style of Angelica Kauffmann' is a safer phrase. The entrance hall decorations at the Royal Academy are undeniably hers but documented work by her is rare, and often confused with that of her second husband, Antonio Zucchi (q.v.). She left England for Italy with Zucchi in 1781, having spent fifteen successful years in London, patronised by Robert Adam and a host of his clients. When she died Rome mourned and the sculptor Canova supervised preparations for a grand funeral. It took place on November 7, 1807, far from the little Swiss village where her eventful life had begun.

Reading: Lady Victoria Manners and Dr G. C. Williamson: *Angelica Kauffmann,* 1924.

Henry Keene (1726-76), Architect

Apart from Horace Walpole and his Committee of Taste who met to discuss the Gothicising of Strawberry Hill, there were a few other architects, Sanderson Miller and Henry Keene among them, who were proficient at erecting the tumbling ruin and battlemented wall. The visitor to Arbury, Warwickshire, encounters Gothick spread across forty years, from its beginnings in 1750 by Henry Keene. The fact that he died in mid-career at the age of fifty has blunted appreciation of his buildings. They are swept by the winds at Uppark where his Vandalian Tower stands high, and have been destroyed at Bowood House and Hartwell Church. In classical mood however he can be appreciated in his Oxford work at Worcester College, and his association with the Newdigate family of Arbury continued with work for them in the Gothic style at University College.

William Kent (1685/6-1748), Architect, Painter, Gardener

The sharply contrasting friendship between Kent, a coach-painter's son from Hull, and Lord Burlington with his extensive estates and a grand London house, is only understood in its original context. That is that Lord Burlington recognised in the other, when they met in Italy, a talent and a gift for communication and ideas akin only to his own, and which had already won Kent the Pope's prize for painting in 1713. With such prodigous talent locked within a person of impulsive outlook it is perhaps surprising that they remained friends. For thirty years after his return (with Burlington) from Italy Kent was disciple and friend, not only of his peer, but of the irascible Alexander Pope. Although he practised painting, furniture designing, landscape-gardening and architecture, he is perhaps most important in the history of landscaping. Horace Walpole wrote that Kent 'leaped the fence, and saw that all Nature was a Garden', and the rebellion against formality which was already under way in the work of Charles Bridgeman (q.v.) was given a sharp stir to ferment it.

For most of his English years Kent lived at Burlington House, and interior decorations were pencilled out not only for its decoration, but for many other Palladian houses. At Houghton and Holkham in Norfolk one can see his rich interiors, and at Stowe, Buckinghamshire, his garden buildings are all important. Add to that some thirty other commissions as varied as designing the Royal Barge (1732), plate, candelabra and even, it is said, a lady's dress, then the 'Signior' of the Burlington circle becomes a moonbeam in the hand—whimsical, mercurial, friendly, talented, almost impossible to define. He was buried in his patron's vault at Chiswick. His patron's long length was laid to rest two hundred miles away from his own vault.

Reading: Margaret Jourdain, *William Kent,* 1948.

The Knibb family (17th and 18th century), Clockmakers

An early clockmaking family the Knibbs, the best known of whom was Joseph (born 1640) based themselves at Oxford. Joseph moved there with his younger brother John in the 1660s and found employment at Trinity College. But London was the centre of artistic activity and Joseph returned to set up business at the sign of 'The Dyal' in Suffolk Street. Here, as one of the earliest of long-case clockmakers, he worked in a traditional way. The

Chimneypiece in the parlour at Rousham House,
designed by William Kent, c.1740.

narrow cases, the Roman system of striking and the spade-like hour hands may have been old-fashioned but he was appointed clockmaker to King Charles II and afterwards to King James II. His brother John remained in Oxford.

Reading: R. A. Lee, *The Knibb Family*, 1964.

Louis Laguerre (1663-1721), Decorative Painter
This French decorative painter was born to greatness for his father was keeper of the royal menagerie at Versailles and the godfather to the young Laguerre was the King himself, Louis XIV, 'Le Roi Soleil'. He came to England about 1684 as an assistant to Antonio Verrio (q.v.) and it was not long before he branched out on his own. He has been recorded as working on 27 separate commissions and notably, among surviving examples, at Blenheim Palace, Oxfordshire, in the Saloon, (*c.* 1720), at Chatsworth, Derbyshire, 1689-94, and Petworth House, Sussex, after 1714. He was less able than Verrio and this sometimes emerges in a large-scale work. Their particular styles of all-embracing decorative painting whereby wall and ceiling fused into one mass of goddesses, foliage, architecture and angelic putti, the galloping horses and chariots of the Sun God, or the debaucheries of the court of Bacchus, were popular with patrons. They earned the oft-quoted praise of Alexander Pope who, in writing of Timon's villa (said to have been the great house of Canons which was built for Laguerre's patron, the 1st Duke of Chandos), said of its interior, 'where sprawl the saints of Verrio and Laguerre . . .'

Laguerre married Eleanor Tijou, daughter of the famous French wrought-iron smith, Jean Tijou (q.v.). They had a son John, who achieved some fame as an actor and scene-painter. Laguerre died suddenly while watching his son perform at Lincoln's Inn Theatre on April 20, 1721.

Reading: Edward Croft-Murray, *Decorative Painting in England*, 1537-1837, *Vol. I*, 1962.

Pierre Langlois (1738-1805), Cabinet-maker
Of French extraction, and trained presumably in Paris, Langlois came to England as a young man. In the 1760s he worked from an address in Tottenham Court Road, London and as his trade-card stated he made 'all Sorts of Fine Cabinets and Commodes . . . inlaid in the Politest manner with Brasse & Tortoishell & Likewise all rich Ornamental Clock Cases, and Inlaid work mended with great Care . . .'. His splendid commodes may be found at Woburn and the Lady Lever Gallery, Port Sunlight and a splendid pair was sold at Christie's on April 21, 1966 for 19,000 guineas. It has been stated that Langlois, in England, 'counted among his clients the Dukes of Montagu and Bedford, Horace Walpole, John Chute and probably the Marquess of Salisbury and Sir Laurence Dundas'.

After this successful career he left England for France about 1771, was made a *maître ébéniste* in 1774, and died in Paris on November 5, 1805.

Giacomo Leoni (?1686-1746), Architect
Leoni was born in Venice about 1686 and was not only educated to appreciate the architecture of Italy's great architect, Andrea Palladio, but 'was more likely a product of the studio of Andrea Tirali who initiated a late 17th-century Palladian revival in Venice'. He was in Germany by 1710 but came to England about 1714 to superintend an edition of Palladio. Together with Colen Campbell's *Vitruvius Britannicus*, Leoni's edition was to give a literary impetus to the revival of Palladianism in England and it also brought work to its author.

His work may best be seen at Lyme Park, Cheshire, and Clandon Park, Surrey, and the east part of the south front at Knowsley, Lancashire, may be his. Towards the end of his life, however, patrons were turning away from Palladianism to the Gothic, Chinese and Rococo styles. Leoni seems to have fallen on to hard times and was in part supported by his patron, Lord Fitzwalter. He was buried at St Pancras Old Churchyard, London, in 1746.

Thomas Leverton (1743-1824), Architect
A worker in the Adam style, some of Leverton's buildings may often be mistaken for that of his more eminent peers in architecture. He designed many London interiors, particularly in Bedford Square, and his best-known country house is Woodhall Park, Hertfordshire, (1777-82). It has a Staircase Hall decorated in the Etruscan taste and com-

partmented with plaster panels.

Luke Lightfoot (?1722-1789), Carver

It was only in 1966 that Lightfoot's career was precisely established. His name had been associated with the Rococo carving at Claydon House, Buckinghamshire, (c. 1768), since the publication, in 1926, of a series of letters from Sir Thomas Robinson (q.v.) to Ralph, 2nd Earl Verney, the owner of Claydon. Unfortunately Lightfoot overstepped himself in his work and charges for Verney and with the mounting opposition of the Earl's architect, Sir Thomas, soon found himself facing lawsuits in the Court of Chancery. 'In all he was charged with having received over £30,000 in money and materials, whereas all the work and materials sent to Claydon and elsewhere were worth at the highest valuation only £7000 or so'. This, however, does little to deny us the splendour of the Claydon carvings, the one exuberant expression of Lightfoot's eccentric career.

Reading: L. O. J. Boynton, 'Luke Lightfoot' *Furniture History Society, Journal,* II, 1966.

John Linnell (c. 1737-1796), Cabinet-maker

William Linnell was a succesful cabinet-maker in the first half of the 18th century, and when he died in 1763 his son John took over the business which was well patronised by the ' Quality'. He became one of the most important furniture-makers in the second half of the 18th century, and at least nine hundred of his drawings have survived (Victoria and Albert Museum). They charged their clients dearly for what they provided.

Reading: Patricia Kirkham, 'The Careers of William and John Linnell,' *Furniture History Society, Journal,* III, 1967. See also *Vol. V,* 1969.

Robert Lugar (c. 1773-1855), Architect

In the years that followed the Napoleonic Wars the Greek Revival style of architecture became popular and all-pervading. Those who wanted a change often turned to Robert Lugar of London who, in picturesque style, provided them with castellated Gothic houses. His best-known essays in this mood are at Balloch Castle, Dumbartonshire (1809) and Swinton Park, Yorkshire (1821-4).

Sir Edwin Landseer Lutyens (1869-1944), Architect

The Edwardian years saw Lutyens at his best in satisfying the whims of patrons who built in a mood of expansion and exuberance not unlike that of their 18th-century predecessors. He designed the last of the grand country houses, and his imperious touch can also be seen in the Viceroy's House at New Delhi and the Cenotaph in Whitehall. He used fine materials and good craftsmen and had much in common with Gertrude Jekyll, whose house he designed and whose gardens often surrounded his creations. He clung to classicism, even when ornamenting it with decoration that no Palladian would own and his puckish personality became a legend.

Reading: Christopher Hussey, *The Life of Sir Edwin Lutyens,* 1959.

Isaac Mansfield (active before 1697-1739), Plasterer

The son of Samuel Mansfield of Derby, also a plasterer, Isaac became one of the foremost workers in the early 18th century. His association with Sir John Vanbrugh both at Castle Howard and Blenheim meant that he had both London and York connections. He became Sheriff of York in 1728-9. His best-known work is the ceiling of the Long Library at Blenheim Palace. He worked for James Gibbs at the Cambridge Senate House, had a house near the architect's in Henrietta Street, and with his son Isaac subscribed to Gibbs's *A Book of Architecture.*

Edward Martin (active 1657-99), Plasterer

The visitor to Arbury, Warwickshire, will not only encounter the Gothickising activities of Henry Keene (q.v.) but a Wren chapel with plasterwork of 1678 by Edward Martin. He had worked in the London City churches for Wren, at Burghley House, Northamptonshire (where all the enriched ceilings are presumably his work) and, as a prominent member of the Worshipful Company of Plaistererers, became its Master in 1699.

Hugh May (1622-84), Architect

Connected with the Royalist cause, the friend of the painter Sir Peter Lely and of John Evelyn the diarist, Hugh May was a well-known figure in London court circles in the 1660s. He was appointed Comptroller of the Works, and architect to Windsor Castle. Among private commissions he worked for the Earl of Clarendon at Cornbury House, Oxfordshire, where the stables and chapel (1663-4) are his earliest surviving buildings. He built Eltham Lodge, Kent, in 1663-5 for Sir John Shaw and its neat elevations indicate that May probably learned his architecture in Holland. He is known to have been there in the 1650s in the service of the Duke of Buckingham.

Reading: Oliver Hill and John Cornforth, *English Country Houses, Caroline, 1625-1685,* 1966.

Jonathan Mayne (Maine) (active 1680-1704), Carver

Mayne, with Gibbons, Pearce, Roger Davies and Thomas Young (all included in this Dictionary) was one of the most important woodcarvers of the late 17th century. He worked at several London City churches and at St Paul's Cathedral, Eton College and Christ's Hospital. For private patrons he worked at Burghley House, Northamptonshire (1682-4), and in Oxford at Trinity College Chapel. He became a Liveryman of the Joiners' Company in 1694.

Sanderson Miller (1717-80), Architect

The 'dear San' of a talented literary circle, Miller was much in demand, albeit it as an amateur architect, for the erection of 'ruins' in the Gothick taste. Settling in Warwickshire after an Oxford education, he experimented with architecture in a picturesque mood and the resulting structures were among the earliest in the revived Gothic taste. His principal structures in the classical style, to which on occasion he was forced to adhere, are Hagley Hall, Worcestershire, and the Warwick Shirehall. In a ruined state his Castle above Hagley (1748) and his work in the Gothik style at Lacock Abbey, Wiltshire (1754-5) must be his main monuments. The extensive correspondence to and from his friends (now in the Warwickshire County Record Office) was partly printed in 1910 under the title of *An Eighteenth Century Correspondence.*

Peter Mills (c. 1600-1670), Architect

In 1653 Mills designed Thorpe Hall, near Peterborough for one of the principal Commonwealth officers, Oliver St John, the Chief Justice. He was mainly a bricklayer rather than an architect, but his versatility was the product of an age that bred invention and competence. With Sir Christopher Wren, Hugh May and Sir Roger Pratt, he was one of the four surveyors appointed to supervise the rebuilding of London after the Great Fire and Plague, 1665-6.

Thomas Moore (active 1756-1778), Carpet-weaver

Moore's trade-card shows him to have resided at Chiswell Street, Moorfields, London, and it is as a maker of many carpets for Adam houses and to the architect's design that he is best known. One of his finest carpets is the signed one (1769) at Syon House, Middlesex. He won the Society of Arts premium in 1757 for a carpet 'in many respects equal, and in some respects superior to those imported from Persia and Turkey'. In consequence he made one for that arbiter of taste, Horace Walpole.

Roger Morris (1695-1749), Architect

With his architect patron, Henry Herbert, Earl of Pembroke (q.v.), Morris was responsible for many buildings in a correct Palladian taste. There is some reason to think that after his birth in London he moved to Yorkshire and that he acted as assistant to Colen Campbell (q.v.). Whatever the niceties of exact research eventually decide, what is certain is that his Palladian style may be judged at Marble Hill, Twickenham, the Palladian Bridge at Wilton, Wiltshire, and in the Gothic way at Inveraray Castle, Argyllshire. He became 'Carpenter and Principal Engineer to the Board of Ordnance', which brought him to the notice of the Duke of Argyll and of Lord Pembroke.

His kinsman Robert Morris was an important architectural writer and theorist.

William Morris (1834-1896), Designer

It is difficult to fit Morris into any one particular category for he designed books, textiles, carpets, wallpaper, furniture and stained glass. He began as a

The Red House, Bexley Heath, designed by Philip Webb for William Morris in 1859.

divinity student, followed in quick succession by interests in architecture and painting, but in 1861 he founded his own firm and set off through the confused pattern of Victorian artistic life. He abhorred the Machine Age of Progress that surrounded him, and looked backward to the medieval concept of hand-work by traditional methods. The problem he never resolved was that work under these circumstances was expensive and could rarely be, as he wished, an art 'by the people for the people'.

His friend Philip Webb designed the Red House at Bexley Heath for him, and there, with his large circle of friends, he urged and strove for better design and a socialist creed of universal betterment.

As an influence he was all-important and the founders of the German Bauhaus movement in the 1920s, particularly Walter Gropius, owed much to his early example. His wallpaper and textile designs have also enjoyed a popular revival in recent years.
Reading: Paul Thompson, *William Morris,* 1967.

Robert Mylne (1734-1811), Architect
A little younger than Robert Adam (q.v.) and outliving him by twenty years or so, Mylne spent most of his active years reliving his earlier successful ones. Born in Scotland (his ancestors had provided many Master Masons to the Crown) he went to Rome in the same years as Adam, and won First Prize at the Academy of St Luke.

He came back to England however to make his mark as a designer of bridges, canals, dockyards and mills. His principal country-house work was the refitting of several rooms at Inveraray Castle, Argyllshire. He is buried near Sir Christopher Wren in the crypt of St Paul's Cathedral.

John Nash (1752-1835), Architect

When James Wyatt died in 1813, John Nash was given his place as Surveyor-General 'by direct command of the Prince Regent'. It is fitting to look at him well into his successful career, for as our greatest town-planner he was poised in this year to dazzle London with his daring terrace-schemes. He remodelled the Royal Pavilion at Brighton, designed Buckingham Palace, and set enough grand patterns in motion almost to earn a knighthood. Only the enmity of his contemporaries and the death of George IV prevented it.

The seeker after John Nash, 'Architect of the Picturesque' will however eschew the grand London layouts and go to Blaise Castle, near Bristol. Here he will find Nash's orangery, thatched dairy and estate cottages set in and near the deep valley landscaped by Humphry Repton (q.v.). The cottages are grouped around a small village green, each thought out in relation to its neighbour and the sky-line silhouette. It is almost too cloying, yet is saved from complete sentiment by its isolation and the skill of its architect.

Reading: Sir John Summerson, *John Nash*, 2nd edn., 1949.

William Andrews Nesfield (1793-1881), Garden Designer

A friend of the romantic painter Turner, Nesfield specialised in waterfalls and garden layouts in the Italian manner. He worked endlessly and at Drayton, Northamptonshire, Great Witley, Worcestershire, Grimston, Yorkshire, and at Trentham, Staffordshire, his layouts can be seen. The last, now a pleasure-garden, gives untold enjoyment to thousands of visitors who know nothing of Nesfield and his grand schemes for grander patrons.

His son, William Eden Nesfield, achieved fame as an architect, as his uncle, Anthony Salvin (q.v.)

had done. For a time he was in partnership with Norman Shaw (q.v.).

Joseph Nollekens (1737-1823), Sculptor

There is a game which knowledgeable country-house visitors play. When weary of painted wall and family trees they slide their hands at the sides and back of the sculptured heads of noblemen. There they often find the deeply incised signature of Joseph Nollekens whose sitters numbered both George III and most of the titled *cognoscenti* of the Regency. His reputation has suffered not a little from the candid and inaccurate biography by his pupil J. T. Smith.

As a successful Academician however, with (according to Smith) a mean streak in him and a meaner wife, he prospered to the point of leaving a fortune of £200,000 at his death. Discern his skill in the bust of William Weddell at Ripon Cathedral (1789) and the large monument to the Earl of Gainsborough at Exton, Rutland (1790). Compounded of sensitivity and created against the background of Neo-classicism they are masterly exercises. Since he spent most of his life working hard (and saving harder) there are plenty more to choose from.

John Van Nost (active 1686-1729), Sculptor

The visitor who comes unexpectedly on John van Nost's great Baroque monument to the Duke of Queensberry (1711) in Durisdeer Church, Dumfries will be eager to know more of the sculptor. The Duke reclines, weary of the world, on a tasselled couch while four putti hold aloft a scroll full of his virtues, extolled in Latin. Flanked by Corinthian columns of white marble he gazes at his Duchess, who had predeceased him by two years. It is an accomplished composition and, while somewhat lacking in fluency, is overwhelming in effect.

Nost's other great area of activity was in the creation of garden urns and lead garden figures and in producing a certain number of statues and equestrian figures. His George I, seated on an imperious stallion (now in front of the Barber Institute of Fine Arts, University of Birmingham) shows his mastery of the difficult stance such figures demand. His garden urns and figures at Melbourne, Derbyshire, are delightful essays of playful dexterity in a formal setting, and similar groups are well-sited in the important landscape-garden by William Kent at Rousham, Oxfordshire.

James Paine (*c.* 1716-1789), Architect
From his early work (possibly under another's direction) at Nostell Priory, Yorkshire, (1733), Paine remained a Palladian architect, but often introduced Rococo decoration to the interiors in the 1740s. He found ready encouragement for his talents, particularly from patrons in the North. He put it neatly in the Preface to his book of 1751, *Plans . . . of the Mansion House . . . Doncaster:* 'Having at that Time the Honour to be engaged in several Gentlemen's Buildings in that County, I was made choice of for their Architect . . .' The patronage which may be seen in the many crisp engravings in the two volumes of his *Plans* published in 1767 and 1783 respectively. The visitor to Chatsworth crosses Paine's bridge over the River Derwent, and the seeker after the 'lost' houses of the Dukeries suddenly encounters his red-brick Serlby for Viscount Galway. His most delightful essays are perhaps the Temple of Diana in Weston Park, Staffordshire, which only requires imagination to be a moonlit part of a Mozartian opera, and the chapel and mausoleum for George Bowes at Gibside, Durham. Each in its own way is superbly sited and of a scale befitting its task.

Edward Pearce (*c.* 1630-1695), Sculptor
The all-embracing nature of 17th-century craftsmanship means that Edward Pearce 'Baroque Sculptor of London' has been variously described as statuary, mason, stonecutter, carver and shopkeeper. He takes his place as all of them and, by his design of the Bishop's Palace at Lichfield, even took a polite nod at architecture. His fine marble bust of Sir Christopher Wren (1673) at the Ashmolean Museum, Oxford, reveals his Baroque sympathies, and it seems to have been Wren who recognised his talents. Among the country houses his richly carved wood foliage on the staircase at Sudbury Hall, Derbyshire (1676), and his ability in this work

and stone-carving encouraged Wren to employ him at several City churches and at St Paul's Cathedral.

Sir Roger Pratt (1620-1685), Architect
'Gentleman Architect' is a term sometimes used to indicate that the holder of the title was a polite amateur, usually well versed in such matters, but not dependent on it for his living. Pratt was descended from a family of Norfolk country gentlemen and after graduating at Oxford he left England on his foreign travels, aided by an income left him by his father. In consequence he was six years abroad and occupied most of his time studying architecture and all the best masters in its expression.

While most of his houses have been altered, or in the case of his finest, Coleshill, demolished (needlessly, to many minds) after a fire in 1952, Pratt's buildings had far-reaching influence and his writings on architecture are important. His own house in Norfolk, Ryston Hall, still stands (altered by Sir John Soane in 1784) and his portrait by Sir Peter Lely still gazes out on a world that has moved far from the period when it was normal to be 'an ingenious gentleman well versed in the best authors of Architecture'.
Reading: R. T. Gunther, *The Architecture of Sir Roger Pratt,* 1928.

Augustus Welby Northmore Pugin (1812-1852), Architect
In 40 years of tumultuous, overflowing life Pugin, a Roman Catholic convert, altered not only Catholic architecture, but the very measured pace of 19th-century Gothic itself. With overwhelming talent he was designing furniture and stage-sets before he was twenty, but many of the gilded dreams of his fertile mind never got beyond the drawing-board. But society noticed. Barry used him to work on the Houses of Parliament from 1844 until his death. Here was the chance to pour out his inexhaustible talents from the top rung of his Gothic ladder. How had he climbed there?

He wrote well and better than most contemporary architects, and came to notorious fame with the publication of *Contrasts* in 1836. Here was a brilliant argument comparing the vulgarity and meanness of contemporary building with the great riches of the Catholic past. With the support of wealthy patrons, particularly the Earl of Shrewsbury, Catholic churches were built as fast as he could design them. Lord Shrewsbury also employed him from 1836 onwards at his great Midlands palace of Alton Towers. Little remains today but the pleasure gardens which surround the ruins of the house and which, like his master Charles Barry's Trentham Gardens, are open to the public. Three times married, Pugin lost his mind a year before he died, and his epitaph may be his despairing comment to John Hardman in this year: 'My writings, much more than I have been able to do, have revolutionized the taste of England. My cause as an architect is run out . . .'.

Reading: Denis Gwynn, *Lord Shrewsbury, Pugin and the Catholic Revival*, 1946.

Daniel Quare (1649-1724), Clock-maker

A contemporary of Thomas Tompion (q.v.), Quare came from a Suffolk family of Quakers. He was admitted a Brother of the Clockmakers Company in 1671 and after a difficult time, as a Quaker, established his business in London. Although he refused to take the Oath of Allegiance to King George I, he became the King's Clockmaker and was one of the first makers of equation clocks. He specialised in long-case clocks, which ran for long periods between windings, several of them for a year. He was also noted for his portable barometers and his prowess brought him the Mastership of the Clockmakers Company in 1708.

Biagio Rebecca (1735-1808), Decorative Painter

Born in Italy, Rebecca spent most of his life away from it and lived and died in London. Starting life as a poor boy he steadily worked his way to an Associateship of the Royal Academy and was much patronised in the Adam period (c. 1760-90) as a painter of Etruscan-type ornament, and of easel-paintings. He worked for Sir William Chambers at Somerset House, at Audley End, Essex, for Robert Adam and at Heaton Hall, Lancashire, and Heveningham Hall, Suffolk, for James Wyatt. Mrs Montagu, writing of the panels he had done for her London house recorded: 'They are indeed exquisitely done and much surpass what they are meant to imitate . . . He is a wonderful master of light and shade and draws very finely . . .'.

Humphry Repton (1752-1818), Landscape Gardener

'Capability' Brown's death in 1783 left the way clear for Repton to provide patrons already conditioned to landscaping their estates with natural and picturesque settings for grand houses. His skill as a watercolourist also enabled him – in his famous 'Red Books' – to illustrate the proposed improvements. By an ingenious series of flaps, the owner could play about with the Red Book pages, arranging what was there to look as Repton intended it eventually would. He could also rarely resist suggesting improvements to the house itself. In all, he worked on the embellishment of some two hundred parks and gardens.

Reading: Dorothy Stroud, *Humphrey Repton*, 1962.

George Richardson (c. 1736-c. 1813), Architect

It is as the principal draughtsman to Robert and James Adam (whom he had accompanied on the Grand Tour) that Richardson is best known. However, in his publication of 1776, *A Book of Ornamental Ceilings,* he takes the credit for the design of the 1759 Hall ceiling at Kedleston, Derbyshire. He also acted as a drawing-master, and published about twelve books on architecture and ornament.

Thomas Roberts (1711-71), Plasterer

An Oxford plasterer with an extensive business, Roberts is best known for his work in several colleges, (e.g. Christ Church, St John's, Queen's and All Souls) and at Rousham, Oxfordshire (1764). He had a brief connection with the Danish sculptor-stuccoist Charles Stanley (q.v.) when they both worked at the Radcliffe Camera, Oxford in 1744.

Sir Thomas Robinson (c. 1700-77), Architect

Although Sir Thomas came from a good North Yorkshire family at Rokeby, he moved up the social scale when he married the eldest daughter of Charles Howard, 3rd Earl of Carlisle. The Earl had built Castle Howard to Vanbrugh's design and

Harewood House; the entrance hall with plasterwork
by Joseph Rose junior, 1767.

Robinson never ceased, as an ardent Palladian, to meddle with its late stages, and in particular Nicholas Hawksmoor's great Mausoleum there. The probable designer of his own house at Rokeby, Robinson travelled abroad, noting architecture and occasionally settling for a time to take posts such as Governor of Barbados. In designing a new house for Ralph, 2nd Earl Verney at Claydon, Buckinghamshire, he came into contact with the irascible wood-carver, Luke Lightfoot (q.v.) and for once met his equal at extravagant building without due permission. Years earlier Robinson had extended his official residence in the Barbados without permission of the Assembly.

Joseph Rose I (*c.* 1723-80), and **II** (1745-99), Plasterers

Uncle and nephew, both Joseph, joined by two Jonathans, have done much to blur the exact activities of the most important plastering firm of the 18th century. Jonathan and Joseph senior worked in Rococo style in the Yorkshire houses of James Paine (q.v.). Joseph was apprenticed to Thomas Perritt (1710-59) a successful York plasterer, and their work at Nostell Priory and the Doncaster Mansion House show their vast skill. Then Joseph and Jonathan were joined by their respective nephew and son, Joseph junior and Jonathan. They turned the attentions of the family firm to the Neoclassical style and faithfully carried out the instructions of Robert Adam at almost all his commissions. It is usually safe to say that if the house decoration is indisputably designed by Robert Adam the plasterwork is by Joseph Rose and Co. Most of the family are buried at Carshalton, Surrey where William Rose was Rector for 42 years.

Reading: Geoffrey Beard, 'The Rose family, with a catalogue of their work', *Apollo,* April 1967.

Louis François Roubiliac (?1705-1762), Sculptor

Born at Lyons in France Roubiliac was one of the most successful and talented of the group of sculptors (Scheemakers and Rysbrack in particular) who came to work in England. Roubiliac was engaged as an assistant about 1732 by Sir Henry Cheere (q.v.) and after some five years' work launched out on his own. He made a strong bid for his own fame by a successful statue of Handel for Vauxhall Gardens. His work, which was rarely surpassed, may be seen in several monuments and his mastery of the movement in figures may be held to go back to his youthful memories of the Rococo style in his native France. In Westminster Abbey the seven monuments by him include those to Lady Elizabeth Nightingale, the Duke of Argyll, and Handel. They demonstrate his skill that led to an extensive patronage. His portrait busts are to be found at Wilton and Mellerstain, while that of Alexander Pope (1738) is one of a group, best represented by the easily accessible version at Temple Newsam House, Leeds.

Reading: K. A. Esdaile, *Life of L. F. Roubiliac,* 1928.

John Michael Rysbrack (1694-1770), Sculptor

Possibly the finest portraitist between the death of Sir Godfrey Kneller and the arrival in London of Sir Joshua Reynolds, Rysbrack's influence in the development of the classical tradition in England was of the greatest importance. Born in Antwerp, the son of a painter, Rysbrack came to England in 1720 and soon won fame by his knowledge and ability. Whereas Roubiliac was a follower of Baroque and Rococo, Rysbrack was well versed in the classical style and the two were to be rivals for the available work.

The catalogue of his work is extensive but a study of his great chimneypieces at Clandon Park, Surrey (1729), Houghton Hall, Norfolk (*c.* 1730) and Hopetoun House, W. Lothian (1756), show his competence.

Reading: M. I. Webb, *Michael Rysbrack,* 1954.

Anthony Salvin (1799-1881), Architect

Of a family tracing itself back to the days of Edward I Salvin, the son of a general, had an excellent start to his career. It is not surprising that with a father inclined to a knowledge of battles and tactics, Salvin should become the outstanding authority on the fortification of medieval castles. His most important work is the exterior of Alnwick Castle and the supervision of the Italianate decorations by Canini within. But test your reactions on the fantasy

J. M. Rysbrack: marble chimneypiece in Hopetoun House, 1756.

below. Anthony Salvin: the west front of Harlaxton Manor, 1831-37.

of Harlaxton, Lincolnshire (1831-7), where after the overwhelming effect of the exterior has seared the mind the interior crushes all resistance. One steps into the rich Baroque hall from a dark vestibule and the effect is all theatre, with putti blowing hard on silent trumpets. The eyes are strained to focus on all the mass of decorative detail–some of this is by William Burn (q.v.) who replaced Salvin at the house in 1838–and from that moment Salvin's buildings either convert you to follow or urge you to reject his exuberant style.

When Salvin died in 1881 his nephew, William Eden Nesfield, supplied a list of his uncle's works to *The Builder*. Jumbled in the list along with castles are houses and churches, but most visitors will come across his name at Thoresby, Nottinghamshire, built in 1864-1875, without thought of expense. Lying in the Dukeries country Thoresby looks like a small fortified town with its cupolas, clock tower, and extensive outbuildings. The neighbouring church of St John, Perlethorpe, is also by Salvin.

Peter Scheemakers (1691-1781), Sculptor
Like Rysbrack, Peter Scheemakers and his brother Henry were natives of Antwerp who came to London in the 1720s. Peter's most successful work was the statue of Shakespeare in Westminster Abbey but his monuments and busts are scattered among many parish churches. The country-house visitor who goes to Stowe, Buckinghamshire, will find busts by Scheemakers in the Temple of British Worthies, and there are statues by him in the gardens at Rousham, Oxfordshire. He continued in England until 1771, and then returned to Antwerp where he died on September 12, 1781.

Henry entered into partnership with Sir Henry Cheere (q.v.) but left England some forty years before his brother and died at Antwerp in 1748. The visitor to Grimsthorpe Castle, Lincolnshire, should seek out Edenham Church with its Henry Scheemakers/Cheere monument (1723) to the 1st Duke of Ancaster and the Roubiliac (q.v.) one (1741) to the second Duke.

Richard Norman Shaw (1831-1912), Architect
A pupil of William Burn (q.v.), Shaw began his career in partnership with Salvin's nephew Eden Nesfield and then joined George Edmund Street's office as chief draughtsman. He became successful at Street's style and then spent much time working his way from that cloying mantle through a varied repertory of styles to which he added sensitivity and a sense of history. Bryanston, Dorset, which he designed in 1890 is an imitation of the Wren style in crimson brick and white stone.

Archibald Simpson (1796-1847), Architect
The best work by this Aberdeen architect has something of the monumental character of that granite city. A pupil of Robert Lugar (q.v.), Simpson followed the Grecian style of architecture. At Strathcathro, Angus (1827-30, now a Hospital) the interior is richly decorated in paint and marble.

Sir Robert Smirke (1780-1867), Architect
Although a pupil of Sir John Soane (q.v.) for a short time, Smirke's career owed his skill more to observations on his travels than to formal instruction. Given, however, that he made a good career the origins are perhaps unimportant. In the erection of great castles, such as Lowther or Eastnor, he showed his ability as an engineer and constructionist. In his classical buildings, of which the British Museum is the most monumental, he was often dull. An amalgam of the two however spelled success, and at the height of his career 'he is said to have declined commissions for work costing less than £10,000'. His control of craftsmen was exemplary. He intervened on their behalf to ask for money due to them, fluently explained his own charges and was often called in to settle disputes and extricate buildings from the muddled attentions of other architects. He was knighted in 1832 and retired in 1845 to enjoy another twenty years of life.

Francis Smith (1672-1738), Architect and Builder
More strictly a master-mason, Smith brought to his many country houses–sometimes working to the design of architects such as James Gibbs (q.v.)–a competent knowledge polished by frequent use of the same plan and motifs. As 'Smith of Warwick' he was involved in many Midland houses, and with the reconstruction of St Mary's Church, Warwick,

after the fire of 1694. He built Ditchley, Oxfordshire, to Gibbs's design and made the acquaintance of the Italian stuccoists. These he used in many of his own buildings such as Sutton Scarsdale, Derbyshire (now ruined) and (probably) Mawley Hall, Shropshire. He designed the north front of Stoneleigh Abbey, Warwickshire, and had connections with the architect Thomas Archer through his elder brother William Smith who had built St Philip's Church, Birmingham to Archer's design, and his own building of Archer's Heythrop House, Oxfordshire.

Robert Smythson (c. 1536-1614), Architect
Elizabethan architecture suffers from the silence of its creators—accounts and records are few—and the often bizarre nature of its creation and (later) repetition. Next to nothing is known of Smythson but he can be regarded as the designer of Hardwick, that great hilltop betowered house in Derbyshire, Wollaton, Nottinghamshire, with its fantastic façades and as the principal creator of Longleat, Wiltshire. Together with his son John and his grandson Huntingdon he designed and built these ingenious houses in the last thirty years of the 16th century. Hardwick is the centrepiece but the more minor houses such as Burton Agnes, Yorkshire, (1601-10), have a charm of their own. By 1612, when his son John started to create the unforgettable buildings of Bolsover Castle, astride another Derbyshire hill, Robert was an old man and he died in October 1614. He is buried in Wollaton Church, near to the great house he designed for Sir Francis Willoughby.
Reading: Mark Girouard, *Robert Smythson and the Architecture of the Elizabethan Era,* 1966.

Sir John Soane (1753-1837), Architect
Whether or not it was his humble origin as the son of a Berkshire bricklayer which spurred him to success, Soane was undoubtedly successful and original in style. He trained under Dance and Holland (q.v.), made the inevitable journey to Italy, met the friends and patrons most likely to be of future use to him, and finally married the niece of a wealthy builder. The current preoccupations with the revived Greek style (as practised by Smirke, and in Scotland by Alexander Thomson) and the medievalism of Gothic interested him hardly at all. He strived to distinguish himself in architecture and had an extensive country-house and public building practice. His own house, 13 Lincoln's Inn Fields (now the Sir John Soane Museum) best portrays his individual eccentricities.
Reading: Dorothy Stroud, *The Architecture of Sir John Soane,* 1961.

Charles Stanley (1703-1761), Sculptor and Stuccoist
Born in Copenhagen of British parents, Stanley had two careers, if not three. He trained as a stuccoist, came to England and worked at Compton Place, Eastbourne. He should however, be regarded only as part-author of the fine stuccowork at this house but whatever he did there led to financial and personal success for he married his landlady's daughter. There followed more work in Staffordshire, a few monuments, work with Thomas Roberts (q.v.) on plasterwork for the Radcliffe Camera, Oxford, and then a swift and unheralded return to Denmark to escape creditors in 1746.

Here he designed many ceilings, sculptures and ceramics, became court sculptor to Frederick V, and held the post until his death. His work in England has been endlessly extended by attributions and much of it should be accepted with caution. Documentation is scarce and the known commissions few.
Reading: Geoffrey Beard, *Georgian Craftsmen and their work,* 1966.

Thomas Stocking (1722-1808), Plasterer
Bristol and the West Country was Stocking's main sphere of activity and his most important commission the work at Corsham Court, Wiltshire (1763-6, for which he received £570). His son Thomas was apprenticed to him in 1764, and they were joined in about 1790 by Robert Harding, who carried on the business when Stocking senior retired.

James Stuart (1713-88), Architect
Known always as 'Athenian' Stuart, Stuart is

235

important more for his contribution to Greek Revival architecture in England than for the rest of his activity. His Temple of Theseus (1758) at Hagley, Worcestershire, is the earliest Doric Revival building in Europe and is evidence of the trip he made with Nicholas Revett to Greece (1751-55), and a forerunner of their *Antiquities of Athens,* published in 1762. He was however very unreliable and Mrs Montagu, for whom he designed Montagu (afterwards Portman) House in Portman Square, thought him 'idle and inattentive'. His park ornaments at Shugborough Park, Staffordshire, are his best surviving works. In the realm of interior decoration his early Neo-classical work, learned when he was in Rome (1742-50) is important, and some of the early furniture in this style which he designed is on loan to the Iveagh Bequest at Kenwood.

William Talman (1650-1719), Architect
In recent years Talman has emerged from an undeserved obscurity, and one which in his lifetime was made more complete by the success of Sir John Vanbrugh (q.v.). Talman was succeeded as Comptroller of the King's Works by Vanbrugh, and while he tried to regain the post in later years, he again lost to Vanbrugh. His houses were however influential in their effect and grand in their conception. He rebuilt the south and east fronts of Chatsworth and completed the interior of new buildings (working under Wren) at Hampton Court. He also had a share in Dyrham, Gloucestershire, and (possibly) Uppark, Sussex. His eldest son John (1677-1726) was a considerable traveller and collector of drawings and prints.

Sir James Thornhill (1674-1734), Architect, Decorative Painter
The ceilings and mural decorations by Thornhill at St Paul's Cathedral, Greenwich Hospital (particularly the Painted Hall), Blenheim, Hanbury and elsewhere made him England's best-known decorative painter. Looking deeper into his career he occasionally combined the work of artist and architect. He may have had a share in designing Moor Park, Hertfordshire, but Giacomo Leoni (q.v.) is another contestant here. He may also have been involved in the design of the west front of Chatsworth but most of his connections with architecture tend to be conjectural. It is said that his pretensions in this direction angered the officers of the King's Works. Thornhill tried to obtain the Surveyorship; instead he found himself passed over for the important job of decorating Kensington Palace. The task was given to William Kent (q.v.).

William Thornton (1670-1721), Carver
A carpenter and joiner of York who probably designed Beningbrough, Yorkshire and worked at the Treasurer's House, York. There are similarities in the staircases at both houses. Thornton worked at several grand northern houses and earned his epitaph as 'the best artist in England' (at joinery) by the elaborate framework he erected to restore the north front of Beverley Minster to the vertical. He was buried at St Olave's Church, York.

Jean Tijou (late 17th century-*c.* 1712), Wrought-iron Smith
Worked extensively at Hampton Court, St Paul's Cathedral and at country houses, such as Chatsworth, Drayton, Ampthill etc. He published his *A New Booke of Drawings* . . . in 1693 and, like similar publications in the latter part of the 18th century, it had a considerable improving effect. The title-page was designed by the decorative painter Louis Laguerre (q.v) who married Tijou's daughter, Eleanor. He left England about 1712.

Thomas Tompion (1639-1713), Clockmaker
Named the 'Father of English watch-making', Thomas Tompion's life is scanty and little-known; but his clocks and watches are world-renowned. His friend Robert Hooke wrote of him that he was 'a person deservedly famous for his excellent skill in making watches and clocks, and not less curious and dexterous in constructing and handworking of other nice mechanical instruments'. He introduced into his clocks many elaborate features (perpetual calendars etc.) and in the design of his clock faces he avoided excessive ornamentation which was a common fault of the age.
Reading: R. W. Symonds, *Thomas Tompion,* 1952.

William Thornton's staircase at Beninborough Hall, 1716.

Francesco Vassalli's signed stucco panel over a
fireplace at Hagley Hall, *c.* 1758.

Sir John Vanbrugh (1664-1726), Architect
Devoted lovers of the theatre will find it difficult to believe that the author of *The Relapse* and *The Provok'd Wife* was also the architect of Castle Howard and Blenheim Palace. In 1690 Vanbrugh was arrested in Calais for spying and subsequently imprisoned in the Bastille and his varied career of gentleman, soldier, dramatist and architect is one of the most compelling of his time. He was patronised soon after his return to England by the Duke of Manchester and the Earl of Carlisle and Castle Howard was his first recorded building. The third Earl of Carlisle was thirty years old when in 1699 he engaged Vanbrugh to design the house. Earlier plans had been submitted by William Talman (q.v.) but he demanded too high a price for them and Lord Carlisle refused to pay. The rivalry existing between Talman and Vanbrugh was to be given sharper emphasis at the death of William III when Vanbrugh succeeded Talman in 1702 as Comptroller of the King's Works.

Vanbrugh, perhaps the artist with the grandest conception of how to realise the splendours of Italian Baroque, owed much in his style and approach to Wren and to Nicholas Hawksmoor (q.v.). This was particularly noticeable over the long and involved commission that followed Castle Howard – the building of Blenheim Palace. The nation was to make it as a gift to its victorious soldier, the Duke of Marlborough, and the almost bottomless funds of the State were buttressing the task. With its romantic skylines and silhouettes, its honey-coloured stone and endless courts and colonnades Blenheim was, despite his quarrels with the irascible Sarah, Duchess of Marlborough, Vanbrugh's grandest house.

Devotees of Vanbrugh's style may however prefer the melancholy but impressive sight of his last masterpiece, Seaton Delaval, Northumberland. It was tortured by a tragic fire in 1822 and by its occupation during the 18th century by the 'Gay Delavals', the house having been built for Admiral George Delaval. It sprawls like a vast stage created by a dramatist for a theatre-loving family and at twilight one can believe that with a great grinding and squeaking the far-flung wings of the house will pivot in and out to the orders of some phantom stage-hand. It is this sense of 'movement in mass', the essence of Baroque, which makes Vanbrugh's houses the most exciting of all those in England.
Reading: Laurence Whistler, *The Imagination of Vanbrugh,* 1954.

Francesco Vassalli (*c.* 1700-after 1763), Stuccoist
One of the talented team of Italian *stuccatori* who worked at Ditchley, Sutton Scarsdale, Towneley Hall, Shugborough, Hagley and presumably a host of other English houses. His nicest achievements are the stucco and *scagliola* work in the Temple of the Four Winds at Castle Howard (1736), and his work at Hagley (1758) and Shugborough (1762-3).

Antonio Verrio (1639-1707), Decorative Painter
A Venetian painter in the grand style, Verrio's work is seen by every visitor to Hampton Court. As they ascend the King's Staircase full of wonderment at the all-enveloping painting over wall and ceiling, they may know little of Verrio and little of its date. Verrio came to England about 1672 at the invitation of the Duke of Montagu, and was soon at work for Charles II and his architect Hugh May (q.v.) at Windsor Castle (1675-84). This work stamped the seal of success on his career and in 1684 he was appointed as 'chief Painter' to the King, although at the Revolution of 1688 his appointment ceased. Eager patrons (such as the 5th Earl of Exeter) invited him to go to work in their houses. His work for Lord Exeter at Burghley House, Northamptonshire, is his best-known outside London. It was all finished before the Earl's death in 1700. The 'Heaven Room' in particular, with its feigned colonnades and rich riot of painting, shows the domination of the decorative painter in late 17th-century England. Their activities gradually depleted the livelihoods of plasterers such as Edward Goudge (q.v.) who could not compete with the bright palette of colours offered by the painters of the Verrio school.

William Vile (?-1767), Cabinet-maker
As senior partner of the firm of William Vile and

John Cobb (q.v.), Vile was involved in producing furniture of the finest sort. In 1761 the firm supplied Queen Charlotte with a handsome jewel cabinet in their capacity as cabinet-makers in chief to George III, and a number of articles made by them are in the Royal collections.

Reading: Ralph Edwards and Margaret Jourdain, *Georgian Cabinet-Makers,* 3rd revd. edn., 1962.

Isaac Ware (?-1766), Architect

Ware had close connections with Lord Burlington and he remained an uncompromising Palladian architect all his days. With a considerable amount of published work to his credit, including the solid *The Complete Body of Architecture* (1756), Ware had a reasonable career, but he dogmatically avoided experiment. While his main years saw the tumbled onrush of the Chinese, Rococo and Gothick styles he considered them debased and inferior. Wrotham Park, Middlesex (1754) is his principal building. His Chesterfield House with (despite his protests) a very rich Rococo interior was destroyed in 1937.

John Warren (late 17th-early 18th-century), Wrought-iron Smith

Worked at Denham Place, Buckinghamshire, and probably at Belton, Lincolnshire, and Powis Castle, Montgomeryshire. At Denham and Belton, William Stanton was master-mason and the architect William Winde (q.v.) had connections with Stanton and the houses of Belton and Powis.

Samuel Watson (1663-1715), Carver

Watson trained under the London carver Charles Okey, but his main reason for being known is the wood and stone-carving he carried out with others (mostly Thomas Young and Roger Davis) at Chatsworth, Derbyshire. He probably also worked at Melbourne in the same county, and at Burghley House, Northamptonshire. His native village was Heanor, Derbyshire, and he is buried in the church there. The epitaph on his monument reads:

'Watson is gone, whose skilful art display'd
To the very life whatever nature made.
View but his wonderous works on
Chatsworth Hall
Which are so gaz'd at and admir'd by all'.

John Webb (1611-1672), Architect

The pupil and nephew by marriage of Inigo Jones (q.v.). Webb worked with his master as Hawksmoor was to do with Vanbrugh. The discussion of their masters' ideas and the revolution of sketchy pencillings to ordered plan – these were the services rendered by the technically competent but less imaginative men of Webb's sort. His work at Wilton House, Wiltshire is thus intertwined with that of Jones, and his own hand is best seen at The Vyne, Hampshire, and Lamport, Northants.

John Wilkes (?-1733), Locksmith

John Wilkes resided in the Old Square, Birmingham, and was a maker of locks with elaborate mechanisms. These may be seen at Arbury Hall and Stoneleigh Abbey, both in Warwickshire, and at the Victoria and Albert Museum.

William Winde (?-1722), Architect

Born at an unknown date before 1647, Winde came to England from Holland (where he had been born to English parents) and after marrying entered the army. He conducted some of his architectural practice while in camp and on military duty, and yet managed to control a large number of commissions (particularly for Lord Craven) and talented craftsmen.

There is reason to suppose that his was the guiding hand at Belton House, Lincolnshire, (1685-87), and his early Buckingham House (the forerunner of Buckingham Palace) was a prototype of far-reaching influence.

Reading: Oliver Hill and John Cornforth, *English Country Houses: Caroline,* 1966.

John Wood, Senior (1704-1754), Architect

There is now some reason to think he may have been born in Yorkshire where he found his early patronage, but the popular image of John Wood and his son John (1728-1791) is as the creators of the townscape of 18th-century Bath. This is certainly their monument, but seekers of a more intimate glimpse of such talent will trace John Wood the elder to his chapel at Capesthorne Hall, Cheshire.

Reading: W. Ison, *The Georgian Buildings of Bath,* 1948.

Antonio Zucchi: part of the ceiling of the Tapestry
Room at Nostell Priory, *c*.1770.

Sir Christopher Wren (1632-1723), Architect

As the best known and probably the greatest of English classical architects, much country-house work has been credited to Wren and without, unfortunately, any good reason. University buildings, Royal Palaces, City churches, St Paul's Cathedral, all these certainly but of houses there are few exact details. A door at Arbury, the house at Winslow, Buckinghamshire (1699-1702); Marlborough House, St James's—one is almost done. The range of Wren's abilities exceeded the vast literature about him, and when he died aged ninety-one so ended a life that had made 'some figure in the world' and that has now entered the comfortable perspective of greatness.

Reading: Sir John Summerson, *Sir Christopher Wren,* 1954.

James Wyatt (1746-1813), Architect

Wyatt first came to the attention of polite society when he erected a copy of the Pantheon in London in 1772. The problem that dogged most of his active career, however, was the disapproval at his cathedral restorations and his own unbusiness-like ways. He is most difficult to evaluate because his career intermingled with that of many relatives, of whom the closest was his architect brother Samuel (1737-1807). He tried to eclipse the Adam style, to revive Gothic and to build a practice on the vague platform of bursts of misguided enthusiasm and a negative approach to visual values. Heveningham, Suffolk, contains some of his most successful interiors, and the Orangery there and the Mausoleum at Brocklesby Park, Lincolnshire, have a lyrical quality which defies expression. Belvoir Castle, Leicestershire, shows his capabilities at Gothic.

Reading: Antony Dale, *James Wyatt,* 1956.

Sir Jeffrey Wyatville (1766-1840), Architect

Wyatville specialised in the design of Gothic and Tudor revival buildings and as his active years coincided with the active revival of these styles he had a large practice. His enormous works at Windsor Castle are a picturesque outline that hide extensive suites of rooms and galleries. His country houses and alterations to them are almost legion. His competence may be judged in the north wing and tower at Chatsworth, Derbyshire, and reconstructions at Longleat House, Wiltshire.

Thomas Young (late 17th-century), Carver

A London carver who worked as master-carver at Chatsworth until 1692. He was assisted by Samuel Watson (q.v.).

Antonio Zucchi (1726-95), Decorative Painter

Zucchi probably met Robert Adam in Italy in 1757 and accompanied him, and later his brother James, on several expeditions to archæological remains. At Adam's invitation he came to England and was much visited by patrons intent on enriching their houses with decorative painting. His work may be seen at Nostell Priory, Yorkshire, Saltram, Devon, and Kenwood, Hampstead. He was married to Angelica Kauffmann (q.v.) and while their styles are similar and confused, it is Zucchi who appears most consistently in Adam's bank account, who provided the coloured drawings to which the carpet-weaver Thomas Moore (q.v.) worked and who is best regarded as the painter associated with the Adam style.

Glossary
Geoffrey Beard

Illustrated by Colin Wilson

Some Terms Defined

Abacus
The flat slab on the top part (capital) of a column.

Acanthus
A formalised design based on the much divided, spiny leaves of a plant so named and particularly associated with the Corinthian order (q.v.).

Alcove.
A recess in a wall or room, usually semi-circular in plan.

Amphitheatre.
An elliptical or circular building with seats rising in tiers around a central arena.

Andiron.
A fire-dog; one of a pair of horizontal iron bars in a fireplace on which to rest the ends of logs.

Anthemion.
A Greek ornament based on the honeysuckle.

Apse.
A wing or recess, either semicircular or polygonal, of a building, usually having a vaulted roof.

Arabesque.
A fanciful scroll design based on flowing curves usually carved in low relief or painted as decoration.

Arcade.
A series of free-standing arches supported on columns; when attached decoratively to a wall, it is known as a blank or blind arcade.

Arch.
A curved structure either bearing a weight or merely ornamental bridging an opening, consisting of wedge-shaped stones, called voussoirs, supported by their mutual pressure and finally held in position by the stone at its apex, the keystone. The outer surface is the extrados, the inner the intrados or soffit. Arches take numerous forms according to the centres from which their curves are struck. (See fig. 1).

Arcuated.
Structures using the arch (q.v.).

Architrave.
The lowest division of the entablature, i.e. the part resting on the column, in classical architecture (see fig. 13); today the parts around a door or window.

Ashlar.
Masonry built from large, clean-cut blocks of stone regularly arranged.

Astragal.
See mouldings.

Attic.
A low room in the roof of a house.

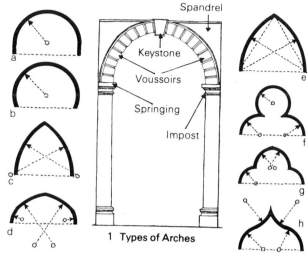

1 Types of Arches

a semi-circular   b horse-shoe   c lancet   d four-centred
e equilateral   f trefoil-round   g trefoil-pointed   h ogee

2 Barge-board

Ball-flower.	See mouldings.
Baluster.	A small shaft of varying diameters when round or widths when rectangular.
Balustrade.	A series of balusters carrying a hand rail or coping.
Banqueting house.	Usually a small detached building in a garden used for eating.
Barge-board.	A wooden board, usually decorated, hanging under a gable and hiding the projecting roof timbers (see fig. 2).
Baroque.	The exuberant, and solidly magnificent style principally associated with Bernini and Borromini in Italy during the 17th century. Full of emotion and drama, it affected Britain for a generation only, its greatest exponents being Archer, Hawksmoor and Vanbrugh (q.v.).
Basement.	A storey (q.v.) partly below ground.
Battlement.	A notched parapet originally intended as a defence, later used decoratively. The notch is the crenelle (hence crenellated) or embrasure, the part on either side of it the merlon.
Bay.	An opening in a wall, especially between two columns; an internal recess formed by causing a wall to project outwards beyond the general line for the reception of some feature, e.g. a window.
Bead.	See mouldings.
Bay-window.	A projecting window, usually polygonal or semicircular (bow-window) in plan. See also oriel.
Bolection.	See moulding.
Bond.	The overlapping of stones or brickwork in the courses of a wall. See brickwork.
Bracket.	A projecting support. See also cantilever, console, corbel and modillion.
Bressumer.	A beam in a timber-framed building to support the projecting superstructure.
Brickwork.	In early work, the bricks were smaller than those used today and less regular. They were laid, jointed by mortar, in two methods or bonds. In English

bond, one row was laid across the direction of the wall, the next along its length, and so on. In Flemish bond, each layer consists of a pair of bricks laid lengthwise, then one crosswise, and so on. In the layer above, the pattern is the same but placed so as not to coincide with the joints below. Those bricks whose end only is visible on the surface of a wall are *headers*; those laid so that their long side alone shows, are *stretchers*.

3 Brickwork

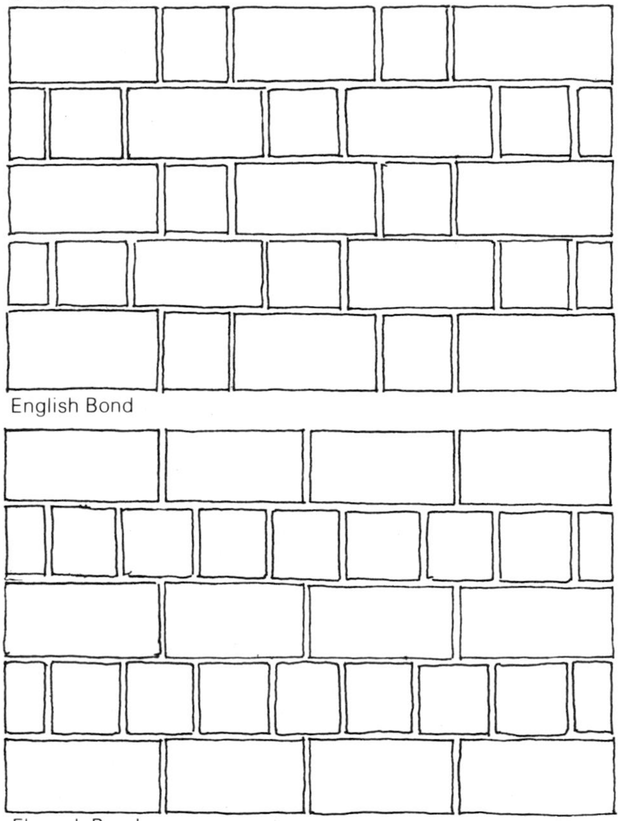

English Bond

Flemish Bond

Buttery.	A room for storing provisions or liquor.
Buttress.	A structure built up against a wall (or a short distance away from, and connected to it by an arch) to strengthen it, or to take a sideways or oblique thrust.

Campanile.	A free-standing bell tower.
Canopy.	A roof projecting from a wall to protect a doorway, statue or other object.
Cantilever.	A bracket.
Capital.	The top part of a column.
Cartouche.	A tablet imitative of a sheet of paper with the edges rolled up, usually bearing an inscription.
Caryatid.	Carved figure used as a column or support.
Casement.	A window opening on hinges.
Castellated, castellation.	Decorated with battlements (q.v.).
Ceiling.	The lining of the inner roof of a room, often decorated by plaster-work or painting.
Cellar.	An underground room usually used for storage.
Chamfer.	The cutting-off of a solid corner to make a third surface.
Chequer-work.	Walling built of two materials, e.g. brick and flint, arranged to make a chess-board pattern.
Chinoiserie.	A free, imitative and not authentic adaptation of Chinese elements first popular during the early 18th century.
Circus.	(i) A row of houses built on the arc of a circle; (ii) a meeting-place of streets.
Classical, classicism.	Architecture in the manner of the Greeks or Romans, or subsequently inspired by or derived from it.
Cloister.	A covered way.
Cob-wall.	A wall built of blocks made from unburnt clay or chalk mixed with straw.
Coffer.	A deeply sunk panel in a ceiling, vault or dome.
Collar-beam.	See roof, timber.
Colonnade.	A row of columns bearing an entablature rather than arches.
Column.	A support consisting of three main elements: the base, the shaft and the capital. See orders.
Conduit.	A cistern, or pipe conveying water.
Console.	A deep bracket formed from two reversed volutes (q.v.).

Coping.	The covering on top of a wall, etc., to protect it from the weather.
Corbel.	A substantial bracket projecting from a wall to carry a weight.
Corinthian.	See orders, classical.
Cornice.	The crowning moulding projecting from the top of a building or part of it; in classical architecture, the top section of the entablature (see orders).
Court, courtyard.	A space enclosed by buildings.
Cove.	Concave under-surface.
Crenel, crenellation.	See battlement.
Crescent.	A curved row of houses.
Crocket.	A decorative feature placed on the sides of spires, gables, etc.

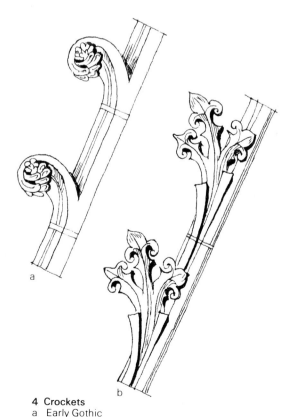

4 Crockets
a Early Gothic
b Late Gothic

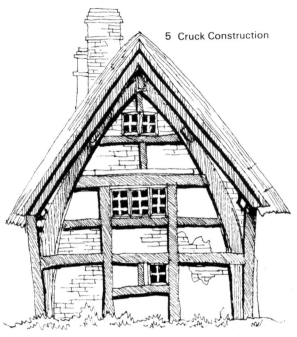

5 Cruck Construction

Dog-tooth. An ornament consisting of a row of pyramids, the sides of which are split open (see fig. 12).

Dome. A roof or ceiling of hemispherical shapes formed from a series of self-supporting concentric circles. The transition from its square base is made by bracket-like structures called pendentives first devised by the Byzantines (*c.* 300-500 A.D.).

Door. The barrier to an entrance, set in a door-case: the hinges, locks etc. are

Cruck. An arch-like or angular beam naturally formed from the trunk or branch of a tree used in the framing of houses.

Crypt. A room under a building.

Cupola. A crowning dome (q.v.) often of bulbous or pointed shape (see fig. 6).

Cusp. A pointed member projecting from within a Gothic arch. (See fig. 1).

Dado. Decorative covering (painting, paper or panelling) of the lower part of a room wall.

Dais. A raised platform usually at the end of a room, particularly in the medieval hall.

Decastyle. Having ten detached columns, e.g. in a portico.

Demi-column. A column partly sunk into the wall.

Dentil. An ornament consisting of small projecting rectangular blocks. (See fig. 11).

Diaper. A pattern carved or painted on a wall or ceiling consisting of squares or other simple shapes each one of which contains a flower or other ornament.

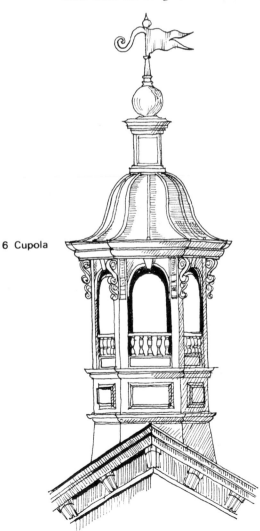

6 Cupola

the door-furniture. All have long been treated decoratively.

Doric. See orders, classical.

Dormer. A window inserted in the sloping roof of a building, with a gable above.

Drawing-room The room to withdraw into after dining, or used for a reception.

Eaves. The edges, usually projecting, of a roof.

Embrasure. See battlement.

Encaustic. See tile, floor.

7 Fanlight *c.* 1820

Entasis. The slight belly-like swelling of a column designed to overcome an optical illusion of narrowness if its sides are parallel.

Entresol. See mezzanine.

Escutcheon. (i) A shield with armorial bearings upon it; (ii) the plate on a door from which the handle hangs or through which the key is inserted.

Exedra. Originally a place for assembly, hence the apsidal (q.v.) end of a room.

Extrados. See arch.

Facade. The front of a building.

Fanlight. A rectangular window over a square-headed door, the division of the panes radiating fan-wise (see fig. 7).

Fascia. A flat face or band, originally restricted to that used in the architrave of the entablature in the classical orders (q.v.) but now of much wider application.

Fenestration. The arrangement of windows in a building.

Festoon. A carved garland of foliage, flowers and often fruit, suspended at each end.

Fillet. See mouldings.

Finial. A finishing ornament on a gable end, pinnacle, canopy, bench, etc.

Fireback. A cast-iron plate usually decorated in relief, placed behind the fire in a grate of the 17th and 18th centuries.

Flèche. A small wooden spire.

Flemish bond. See brickwork.

Flint. Hard, steel-grey stones used, usually after being 'knapped' with a hammer, as a material for walls, particularly in south-east England.

Flint-and-stone work. Decoration of stone sunk into flint work.

Foliated. Carved or otherwise decorated with leaf-shapes.

Freestone. Stone which can be easily shaped or carved by a chisel, as distinct from that which is so hard that it can only be roughly dressed.

Fresco. Painting done on fresh, damp plaster.

Fret. A decoration using a key-pattern (q.v.) on a flat surface.

Frieze. Strictly, the middle division of the classical entablature, but now usually referring to a band of decoration below the cornice of a room, either carved, painted, or in plasterwork.

Gable. The end of a steeply pitched roof: the Dutch gable has curved sides crowned by a pediment; the shaped gable has sides of several curves; the crow-stepped, a series of steps, sometimes carrying ornaments. (See fig. 8).

Gadroon. The decorative treatment of the edges of inverted (i.e. convex) fluting.

Gallery. (i) A roofed space, one side open, in which to walk: (ii) a long upstairs room; the 'long gallery' found in Elizabethan and Jacobean houses.

Gazebo. A small garden building so placed that its windows (usually in an upper storey) overlook a view.

Gesso. A hard, fine-grained plaster.

Gothic. The medieval style of architecture in

8 Gables

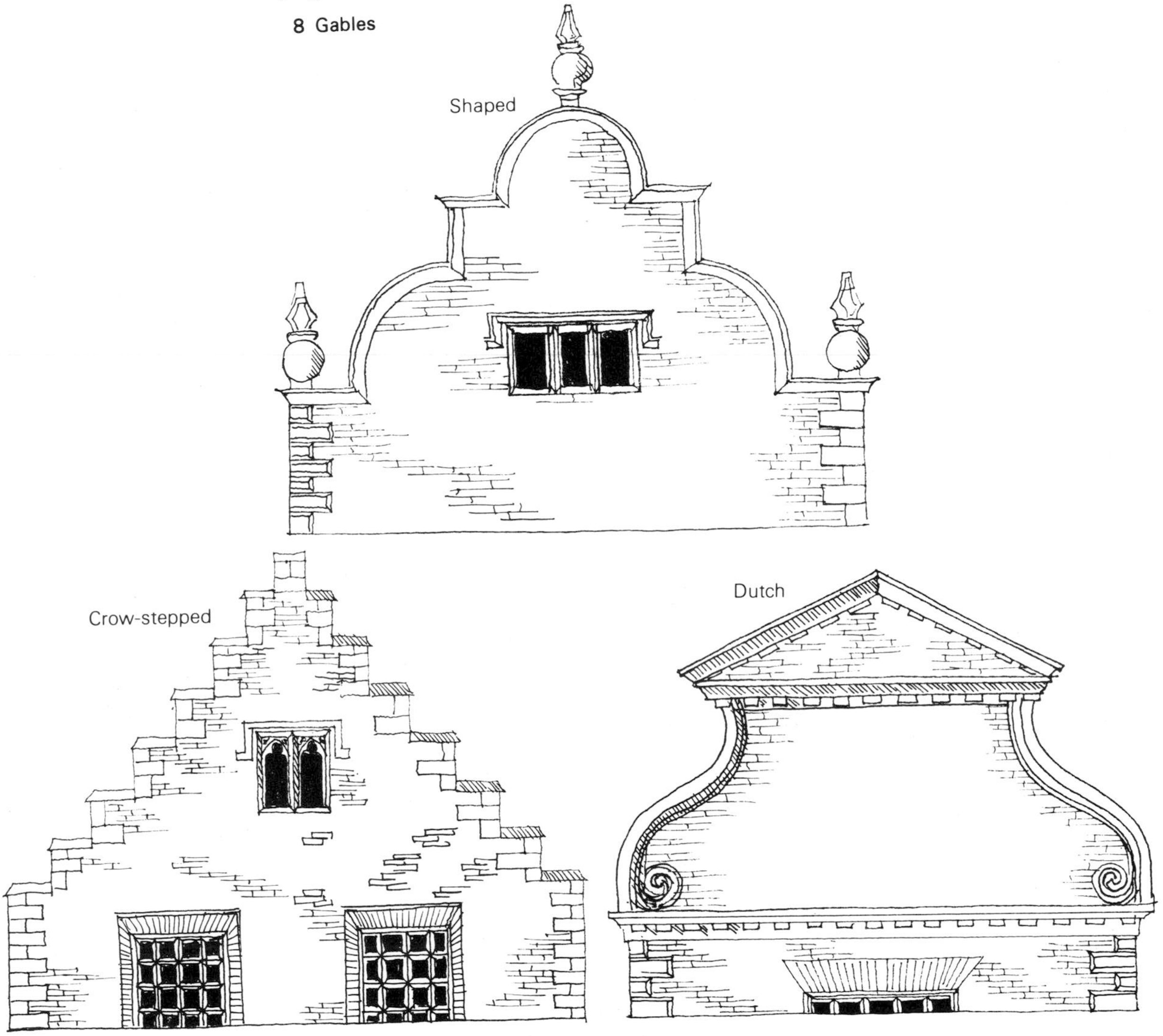

Shaped

Crow-stepped

Dutch

	which the pointed arch is a fundamental feature.
Gothic revival.	The 19th-century revival of architecture on the principles, often greatly elaborated or enlarged, of medieval Gothic building.
Gothick.	A term now applied to a style of architecture in the late 18th and early 19th centuries superficially imitative of the true Gothic style but without an understanding of its fundamental structural principles.
Grotesques.	Fanciful, often weird, decorations.
Grotto.	An artificial, ornamental cave.
Guilloche.	See mouldings.
Half-timber.	Applied to timber-framed buildings when the beams and studs are exposed to view, so that the outer surface is about half-and-half timber and plaster (or brickwork).
Hammer-beam.	See roof, timber.
Herring-bone work.	The use of bricks, stones or tiles placed diagonally instead of flat.

9 Linenfold Panelling

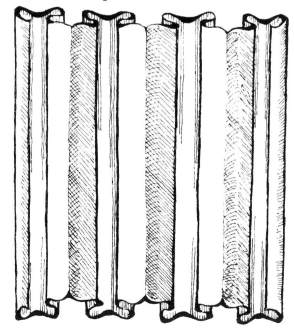

Hexastyle.	Having six detached columns, e.g. in a portico.
Honeysuckle.	A pattern much used in Greek architecture. (See fig. 11).
Inglenook.	A built-in seat by a fireplace.
Ionic.	See orders, classical.
Jamb.	The side masonry or woodwork of the openings of arches, doors, windows, etc.
Joists.	The timbers in a floor upon which the floor boards lie.
Key-pattern.	A pattern favoured in classical architecture. (See fig. 11).
King post.	See roof, timber.
Linenfold.	Tudor panelling carved in a pattern resembling a piece of folded linen.
Lintel.	A horizontal stone or wooden beam placed over a door or window or between columns to support the weight above.
Loggia.	A colonnade (q.v.) recessed into a building; a small building with open arches forming a shelter.
Lunette.	A small round or oval window.
Majolica.	Ornamental glazed earthenware.
Marquetry.	Surface decoration of inlaid wood or ivory.
Mausoleum.	A private building to contain tombs, named after the famous building at Halicarnassus in memory of Mausolus, king of Caria, who died in 353 B.C.
Mezzanine.	A low floor above the ground storey, yet included within its classical order: also known as an entresol.
Module.	A unit of measure regulating the proportions of a structure, e.g. the classical orders (q.v.).
Mortice and tenon.	A rigid joint formed by the shaped end of one piece of wood being firmly fitted into a hole in another.
Mosaic.	A pattern or picture made with small pieces of different-coloured stone or glass, sometimes found on floors.
Mouldings and ornaments.	From early times it has been the practice to shape projecting angles of buildings into contours, a feature extended to window and door frames,

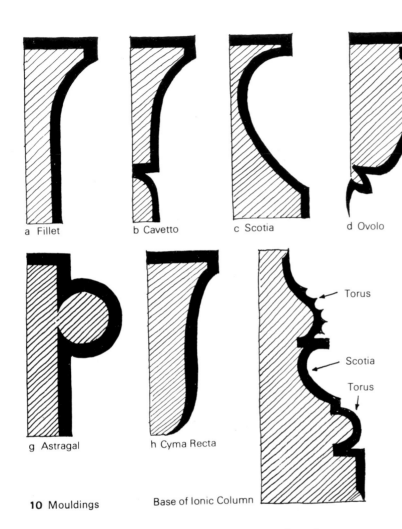

a Fillet　　b Cavetto　　c Scotia　　d Ovolo　　e Ogee　　f Torus

g Astragal　　h Cyma Recta

Torus

Scotia

Torus

10 Mouldings　　Base of Ionic Column

panelling, furniture and similar objects. The Greeks took particular advantage of this—the shadows cast by the bright Mediterranean sun making them particularly effective. The patterns they used, sometimes elaborated by the Romans, have been widely followed and, with their names, virtually standardised. Some basic examples are shown in fig. 10 *a* to *h*. The fillet (*a*) is a plain, narrow band frequently used to separate one moulding from another. The ogee (*e*), an elaborated s-shape, is a widely

used form of decoration not only in mouldings. Another common shape is the astragal or simple bead (*g*), which, when used in numbers closely together, is described as reeding. The scotia moulding (*c*) is so called from the dark shadow it casts.

These mouldings were frequently ornamented with carving, of which some well known examples are shown and named in fig. 11. These designs, and variations of them, are frequently used also as decoration on flat surfaces in the interior decoration of houses of the classical manner.

Gothic mouldings are much more elaborate and inconsistent. They are inevitably associated more with ecclesiastical than domestic architecture until the Gothick and Gothic revivals. Typical ornaments are shown in fig. 12.

Mullion. The vertical division in a window, generally of wood but formerly of stone, sometimes decoratively treated, e.g. with mouldings.

Newel. The central post in a winding or circular staircase.

Niche. A shallow recess.

Nogging. Brickwork or other filling of the space in a timber-framed wall.

Obelisk. A tall square pillar tapering towards the top and ending in a pyramid.

Egg & Tongue

Leaf & Tongue
or Tongue & Dart

Anthemion or
Honeysuckle Pattern

Guilloche

Dentils

Bead & Reel

Key Pattern

An Ionic Capital
involving three
mouldings

11

12

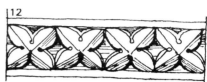
Dog Tooth
(Early English)

Stiff Leaf Foliage
(Early English)

Ball-Flower
(Decorated)

Tablet-Flower
(Decorated)

Vine
(Perpendicular)

Tudor Rose
(Perpendicular)

11 and 12 Mouldings and Ornaments

Octastyle. Having eight detached columns, e.g. in a portico.

Œil-de-bœuf. A small, round or oval window.

Ogee. See mouldings.

Orders, classical The columnar features of classical temples and similar buildings. Originally used in Greek construction, which was trabeated (i.e. formed by erect posts and horizontal beams, arches being absent) on examination they show their origin to have lain in straight lengths of timber. The Greek orders are of three major kinds, Doric, Ionic and Corinthian. Their details varied. Later, their principal elements were widely used, much altered and adapted particularly by the Romans who introduced them into arcuated structures (i.e. incorporating arches to bridge a space). Also, whereas the Greeks used them structurally to carry a roof, the Romans often used them as little more than ornament. This use was, of course, also widespread later during the Renaissance and particularly in Georgian and Victorian architecture.

The proportions of all the major parts of an order were based on a module, a unit such as the basal diameter of column (e.g. in the Ionic order this is taken as 8 units, and the various parts are either multiples or simple fractions of this figure).

The *Doric* is the simplest of the orders (see fig. 13). From the ground upwards, its constituent parts were as follows. The platform, so to speak, is the *stylobate*. Directly on this stands the **column**, designed with an *entasis* (a slight bellying-out to correct an optical illusion of narrowing if the sides remain parallel). It is fluted. Upon this is the capital, consisting of two parts, the lower round and increasing in diameter, the upper a rectangular block, the *abacus*.

These complete units are arranged

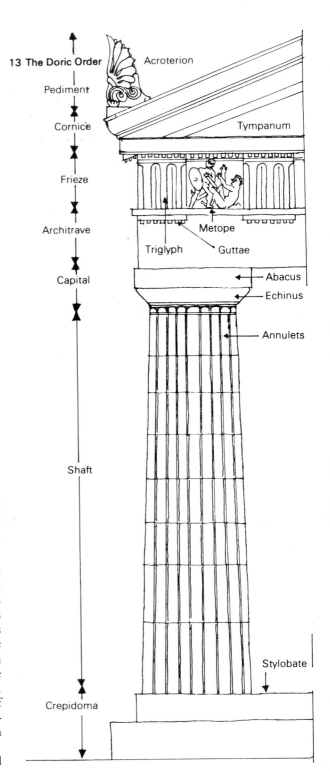

13 The Doric Order

Acroterion

Pediment

Cornice

Tympanum

Frieze

Architrave

Metope

Triglyph

Guttae

Capital

Abacus

Echinus

Annulets

Shaft

Stylobate

Crepidoma

along the sides of the building, and carry the *entablature*, a deep, beam-like structure, which extends all round the building and is the framework carrying the roof. It is divided into three parts. The lowest is the *architrave*. Above it is the *frieze*, decorated with carvings. Finally, the projecting *cornice*, whose undecorated, flat vertical band is the *fascia*. At one end of the building above the cornice is placed the shallowly triangular pediment, with a carved panel at its centre.

The *Ionic* order (fig. 14) varies more in its form from example to example than the Doric. However its divisions are the same – stylobate, column, entablature, etc. with the important exception that the column stands on a base. The capital takes the form of two spiral scroll-shaped ornaments, *volutes* (at each corner there are three). The architrave is three-stepped, the frieze richly carved.

The distinctive feature of the Corinthian order (fig. 15) is the capital. This is a formalised version (so the story goes) of the leaves of an acanthus plant which sprang up from under a basket which had inadvertently been left upon the root. The abacus, too, is more elaborate.

A scholarly knowledge of the details of the numerous orders, particularly the proportions and even the buildings from which they came, was a *sine qua non*, particularly during Georgian times, of the connoisseur of architecture.

Oriel, oriel window.	A bay-window (q.v.) on an upper floor only (see fig. 16).
Ornaments.	See mouldings.
Ovolo.	See mouldings.
Pagoda.	An ornamental pyramidal tower, the design derived from the Chinese.
Palimpsest.	A wall-painting in which a new piece

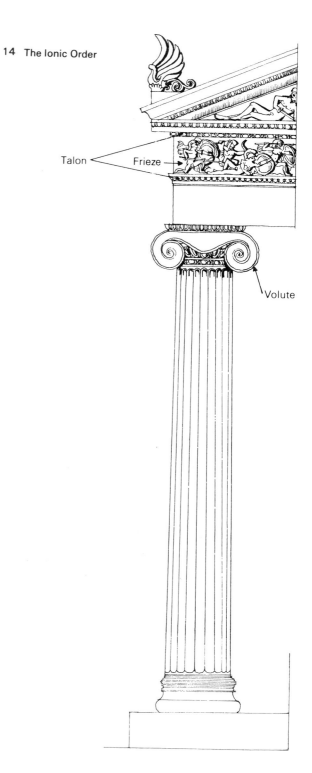

14 The Ionic Order

Talon

Frieze

Volute

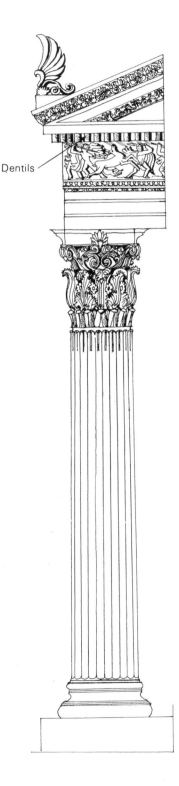

15 The Corinthian Order

Dentils

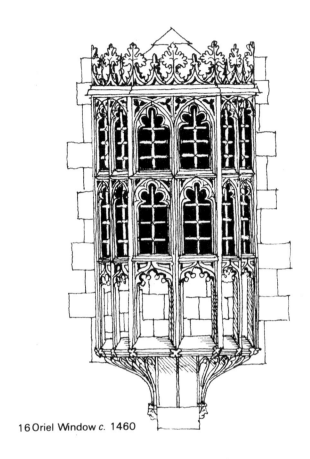

16 Oriel Window *c.* 1460

of work overlaps and covers an earlier one.

Palladian. A severe yet elegant style conforming to rules laid down by the Italian Andrea Palladio (1518-80), a student of Roman (Vitruvian) principles. In Britain, associated with the Earl of Burlington (1695-1753).

Pantile. See tile, roofing.

Parapet. The upper portion of a roof above the guttering.

Pargetting. Decoration in relief or carved on plasterwork.

Parlour. Family sitting-room.

Pediment. Originally a low-pitched triangular structure over the end of a building in classical style, the equivalent of a gable; later widely used also over doors, windows etc. The sides may also be curved. In a broken pediment

255

Pendentive.	the centre part of the base is missing; in an open pediment, the meeting point of the sloping sides is absent. A concave spandrel (q.v.) enabling a circular dome (q.v.) to be carried on a rectangular base.
Piano nobile.	The storey of a house containing the main reception rooms.
Picturesque.	Originally, a design based on the pictures of the 17th-century landscape painters such as Claude, Salvator and Poussin. Later widened to include buildings that would make a charmingly pretty picture.
Piazza.	A public square.
Pier.	A mass of supporting masonry or brickwork.
Pilaster.	A rectangular, shallow pillar attached to a wall.
Pillar.	A detached support.
Pinnacle.	A turret narrowing towards the top.
Plasterwork.	The modelling of decorative features such as ceilings, cornices, fireplaces etc.—a craft that was highly developed during Georgian times.
Plinth.	A low block on which a column stands, or the projecting surface at the base of a wall.
Porch.	A shelter placed over and often around the entrance to a building.
Portcullis.	A heavy gate rising and falling in vertical grooves, often placed at the entrance of castles.
Porte cochère.	A porch large enough to permit the entrance of a carriage.
Portico.	Centrepiece of a building with a pediment supported by classical columns. When of four columns, tetrastyle; of six, hexastyle; of eight, octastyle; of ten, decastyle.
Principals.	See roof, timber.
Pugging.	The filling of spaces between the timbers of a building with a mixture of clay and straw.
Purlin.	See roof, timber.
Putti.	Decorations consisting of figures of small naked boys.
Quarry.	A square stone, tile or brick used for

	making hard-wearing floors.
Queen post.	One of two vertical tie posts in a trussed rafter roof. See roof, timber.
Quoin.	The angle of a building formed of dressed stones.
Rafter.	See roof, timber.
Reeding.	See mouldings.
Renaissance.	The revival of interest, at first in Italy, early in the 13th century, of the thought and art of the ancient Greeks and Romans, which greatly affected architecture. Its ideas first reached Britain at about the time of Henry VIII.
Respond.	A half-pier let into a wall and carrying one half of an arch.
Rococo.	An elaborate, airy and light-hearted, fanciful style, sometimes associated with late Baroque (q.v.) in the 18th century; not commonly used in Britain.
Romanesque.	The heavy massive style of architecture current principally in Europe during the 11th and 12th centuries, associated in the British Isles with the Norman period, and preceding the Gothic style.
Romantic.	A style which favoured the dramatic, picturesque and emotional, with literary overtones looking back to the past as opposed to the calm reason of the classical; it was particularly in vogue during the late 18th and 19th centuries.
Roof.	*Hipped:* roof with sloping instead of vertical ends; *mansard:* roof with two slopes, the lower being steeper and longer than the upper; *timber:* the timber roof is a particular and important feature of British domestic architecture. Structurally, it has to solve two problems. Firstly, the strong tendency of the two halves to become squashed out flat by the weight of the roof, and secondly, the dangerous sideways thrust that this weight brings to bear upon the walls, which to resist it would have to be excessively thick.

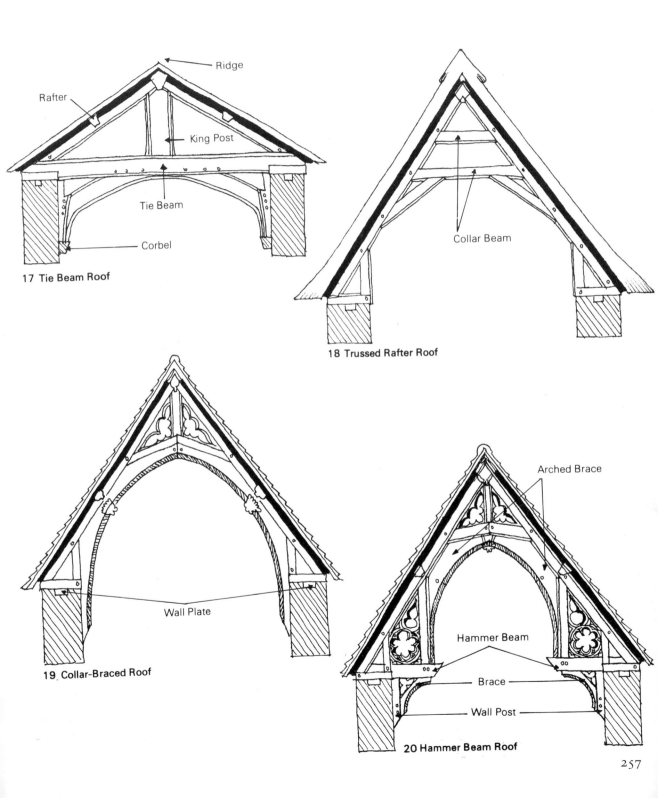

17 Tie Beam Roof

Ridge

Rafter

King Post

Tie Beam

Corbel

18 Trussed Rafter Roof

Collar Beam

19 Collar-Braced Roof

Wall Plate

20 Hammer Beam Roof

Arched Brace

Hammer Beam

Brace

Wall Post

All roofs include the *rafters,* which run from the ridge to the eaves, and usually are of two kinds: the principals, which are strong structural features, and the thinner *common rafters* upon which are laid the tiles or slates.

In a longitudinal direction run the *purlins.*

The simplest method of overcoming spread and thrust is by means of a tie-beam between the base of the rafters, which is always in tension. The resultant low-pitched roof needs another vertical member to secure rigidity and this is called the *kingpost.* Often, a carved and decorated angle piece is added, while the triangular space within the truss may be filled with open, carved woodwork (see fig. 17).

Apart from its flat pitch, the tie beam gives little head-room with the consequent need for higher and stronger walls. This, to some extent, is overcome in a *trussed rafter roof* (see fig. 18). It is of lighter construction and is applied to each individual rafter. The triangular element at its base diverts the thrust downwards.

The *collar-braced roof* (see fig. 19) is dependent on the use of massive collars, whose size is dependent on the availability of suitable timber. Again, the triangulation at the base avoids side thrust.

These basal triangles are again important in the *hammer-beam roof* (see fig. 20), which is often seen in our largest halls. It consists of three major triangles. That supporting the ridge consists of two upper principal rafters, a collar beam with a king post at its centre. Below it, on either side, are the two other triangles. Each has a broad base overhanging the wall on either side, i.e. the hammer beam. A hammer post rises vertically to the base of the upper triangle. The result is a very stable structure, giving much more space far higher above the tops of the walls than other roof structures. The hammer beams are often richly carved and ornamented.

Rotunda. A building of circular plan.

Roughcast. Course plaster mixed with fine stones applied to the exterior of buildings.

Rustication. Masonry giving prominence by contrasting surfaces and emphasis on the joints.

21 Rustication – Inigo Jones' Queen's House at Greenwich

Scagliola. A plaster-like substance with a mixture of colours somewhat like marble in appearance not common in Britain until the mid-18th-century. Used for columns, flat pictures, tabletops, etc.

Screen, screen passage. The medieval house was entered by a passage on one side of which was a screen dividing it from the hall with its dais at the far end and on the other doorways to the kitchen, pantry etc.

The screen in time was elaborated with carving and often had a gallery above (see fig. 22).

Sgraffito. A pattern incised into plaster.

Shaft. The main part of a column excluding the base and capital.

Shingle. A tile made of split wood, usually oak in the past, now often western red cedar (*Thuja plicata*).

Sill. The lowest horizontal element in a window frame.

Skirting. A low plinth or base at the base of

or, in more substantial slabs, for building.

Solar. An upper chamber of a medieval house kept for the use of the owner, his family and friends.

Span. The space between supporting walls or pillars.

Spandrel. The triangular space between the curve of an arch (q.v.) and the right-angle enclosing it, often decorated.

Spire. The tapering roof of a tower, turret or pinnacle as distinct from the body

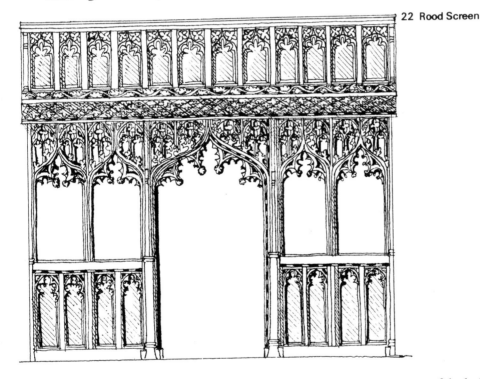

22 Rood Screen   Rood Loft

Section

walls within a room placed there primarily to prevent damage to the plaster.

Slatehanging. A wall covered by slates hanging from a timber structure.

Soffit. The underside of an architectural member, e.g. of an arch (q.v.) cornice or lintel.

Slate. Thin sheets split from the greyish rock of that name used to cover roofs

of the building itself.

Splay, splayed A broad surface oblique to the vertical surface of a wall, particularly of the jamb of a window.

Splocket. A piece of wood joined to and making an extension to the rafter of a roof so as to form a projection of the eaves if overhanging the wall.

Springing. The point at which an arch (q.v.) breaks away from its supports.

Squinch.	An arch built across the angle of a tower, to carry a polygonal or round superstructure on a square plan.
Staccato.	Literally, a musical term meaning notes or phrases sharply detached or separated; used by architectural writers to indicate a feature sharply emphasised.
Staircase.	A flight or series of flights of stairs with their supporting framework, balusters, etc.
Still-room.	A room in which preserves, cakes, liqueurs, perfumes, etc. were prepared or kept.
Stone, Austin's.	An artificial stone that could be cast, used from about 1828 to 1860 for statuary, fountains, chimney pots and other ornaments.
Stone, Coade.	An artificial stone that could be cast, used from about 1770 to the early 19th century for a great variety of external ornaments, statuary, etc.
Storey.	The set of rooms on one level.
Strapwork.	A tracery design applied to a surface in Elizabethan times, usually in ceilings or on parapets.
Stringcourse.	A projecting course of bricks or decoration in a wall.
Strut.	A structural element that keeps two others apart and is in compression – the opposite to a tie (q.v.).
Stucco.	(i) A fine white plaster used for the making of moulded decorations; (ii) a thin plaster used to cover external walls to give an appearance of stone.
Studs.	The upright timbers in a timber-framed house.
Stylobate.	In classical architecture the platform on which stand the columns in front of or around a building. (See orders).
Tapestry.	A patterned woven textile formerly used as a wall covering, hung from tenterhooks.
Terminal figures, termini.	Piers or pilasters narrowing towards their bases out of which grow the upper part of a human figure.
Tempera.	Painting on a thin ground of very fine hard, dried plaster (gesso) in transparent colours made from powdered pigment mixed with water and size.
Temple.	A place of worship, or the abode of a divinity.
Tenon.	The end of a piece of wood shaped to fit rigidly into a hole in another piece (the mortice) to form a mortice and tenon joint.
Tenterhooks.	The projecting hooks that carried tapestry.
Terrace.	(i) A raised promenade usually balustraded or walled, adjoining a house, sometimes forming a series at differing levels linked by steps; (ii) a continuing row of houses.
Terracotta.	A hard, unglazed fine pottery of brownish-red colour from which decorative tiles, bricks and ornaments are made. Extensively made in Italy from early times, imported into Britain in the early 16th century and from the middle of the 19th century made here and much used, particularly in towns, on account of its imperviousness to smoke and fumes.
Tesselated.	A floor made from small blocks (tesserae) as, for example, in a mosaic.
Tetrastyle.	Having four detached columns, e.g. in a portico (q.v.).
Thatch.	The covering of a roof with straw, reeds, heather or similar material.
Tie.	A structural element designed to draw two others together, as opposed to a strut (q.v.). See also roof, timber.
Tile, floor.	A flat tile usually but not always rectangular, laid as paving on a floor to give it a firm surface, either unglazed or glazed; when a glazed tile has a coloured decoration burnt in, it is described as encaustic.
Tile, roof.	A thin slab formerly made of burnt clay but now from a variety of materials. Tiles may be plain and flat, laid edge against edge in alternate rows so that the vertical joints meet on top of the body of those below (as also in a slate roof) or curved in

	various shapes (e.g. pantile) so that the edges overlap, thus securing a water-tight joint.
Trabeated.	Construction employing horizontal beams (post and lintel) as opposed to arches, as used in classical Greece.
Transom.	A horizontal bar across the opening of a window.
Trefoil.	A three-lobed leaf-shape decoration used in the 13th century.
Triglyph.	A decorative element of a Doric frieze consisting of a projecting block with two vertical grooves and chamfered on the vertical edges, one placed over each column, the other in each space, resembling the ends of wooden beams.
Trompe l'oeil.	A painting giving a deceptive illusion of reality.
Truss.	A system of timber or other framing that is self-supporting and used to bridge over a space, e.g. in a roof (q.v.).
Tudor flower.	A repetitive upright leaf decoration used in the 15th century.
Tympanum.	The enclosed space between the lintel and an arch, or between the entablature and sloping cornice of a pediment.
Vault.	An arched roof.
Verandah.	An open-sided portico or balcony with a roof on light, decorative (often metal) supports.
Vitrified.	Material given a hard, shiny, glass-like appearance.
Volute.	A spiral scroll-shape, particularly associated with the capitals of the Ionic order (q.v.).
Voussoir.	The wedge-shaped blocks forming an arch (q.v.).
Wattle-and-daub.	Early form of walling in which a structure of interwoven twigs is covered with an overlay principally of clay.
Weatherboarding.	Overlapping horizontal boards fixed over a timber frame.
Window.	*Sash:* one whose frames rise and fall vertically, counterbalanced by

weights hung over pulleys within 'sash-boxes', introduced in the latter part of the 17th century; at first these boxes were exposed giving a wider frame but owing to danger from fire

23 Sash Window

they were later concealed within the walls, so displaying a narrow frame (see fig. 23). *Venetian:* a window with three openings, the central one being the largest and with an arched top (see fig. 24).

24 Venetian Window

Bibliography

Special references in the text to periodical literature are not included.

The titles quoted will indicate that there is a certain overlapping of subject.

Since the literature of pictures, china and other ornaments is vast and international, it is not included.

General and Period Histories

Architecture in Britain. The Middle Ages
Geoffrey Webb, 1956
Architecture in Britain 1530–1830
Sir John Summerson, 1953
An Introduction to Elizabethan and Jacobean Architecture　　Marcus Whiffen, 1952
English Country Houses: Caroline 1625–1685
Oliver Hill and John Cornforth, 1966
English Baroque Architecture　　Kerry Downes, 1966
The Georgian Buildings of Bath　　W. Isons, 1952
The Georgian Buildings of Bristol　　W. Isons, 1952
English Country Houses:　　Christopher Hussey
　　Early Georgian 1715–1760　　1965
　　Mid Georgian 1760–1800　　1963
　　Late Georgian 1800–1840　　1966
An Introduction to Regency Architecture
Paul Reilly, 1948
Early Victorian Architecture in Britain
Henry Russell Hitchcock, 1955
Victorian Architecture　　ed. Peter Ferriday, 1964
English Architecture since the Regency
H. S. Goodhart-Rendel, 1953
The Historic Architecture of Scotland　J. G. Dunbar, 1966

Individual Architects

The Age of Adam　　James Lees-Milne, 1947
Robert Adam and his Circle in Edinburgh and Rome
John Fleming, 1962
Thomas Archer　　Marcus Whiffen, 1950
Annals of Thomas Banks　　C. F. Bell, 1938
Capability Brown　　Dorothy Stroud, 1950
Colen Campbell　　H. E. Stutchbury, 1967
John Flaxman　　W. G. Constable, 1927
Grinling Gibbons　　David Green, 1964
The Life and Work of James Gibbs　　Bryan Little, 1955
Nicholas Hawksmoor　　Kerry Downes, 1960
Henry Holland　　Dorothy Stroud, 1965
Thomas Johnson and English Rococo
Sir John Summerson, 1966
The Age of Inigo Jones　　James Lees-Milne, 1953

Angelica Kauffmann	Lady Victoria Manners and Dr. G. C. Williamson, 1924
William Kent	Margaret Jourdain, 1948
The Knibb Family	R. A. Lee, 1964
The Life of Sir Edwin Lutyens	Christopher Hussey, 1950
William Morris	Paul Thompson, 1967
John Nash	Sir John Summerson, 1949
The Architecture of Sir Roger Pratt	R. T. Gunther, 1928
Lord Shrewsbury, Pugin and the Catholic Revival	Denis Gwynn, 1946
Humphry Repton	Dorothy Stroud, 1962
Life of L. F. Roubiliac	K. A. Esdaile, 1928
Michael Rysbrack	M. I. Webb, 1954
Robert Smythson and the Architecture of the Elizabethan Era	Mark Girouard, 1966
Sir John Soane	Sir John Summerson, 1952
The Architecture of Sir John Soane	Dorothy Stroud, 1961
Thomas Tompion	R. W. Symonds, 1952
The Imagination of Vanbrugh	Laurence Whistler, 1954
Wren and His Place in European Architecture	Edward F. Seckler, 1956
Sir Christopher Wren	Sir John Summerson, 1954
James Wyatt	Antony Dale, 1956

Decoration

The English Interior	Ralph Dutton, 1948
Decorative Painting in England 1537-1837 Vol I	Edward Croft-Murray, 1962 (Vol II in preparation)
Georgian Craftsmen and their Work	Geoffrey Beard, 1967
Chinoiserie – The Vision of Cathay	Hugh Honour, 1961

Furniture

The Shorter Dictionary of English Furniture	Ralph Edwards, 1958
English Furniture	John C. Rogers, 1961
Georgian Cabinet Makers	Ralph Edwards and Margaret Jourdain, 1962
Chippendale Furniture	Anthony Coleridge, 1968
Regency Furniture	Ralph Fastnedge, 1965
Victorian Furniture	R. W. Symonds and B. B. Whineray, 1962
World Furniture	ed. Helena Hayward 1965

Structure

A History of the English House	Nathaniel Lloyd, 1949
The Pattern of English Building	A. Clifton-Taylor, 1962
A Documentary History of Building Down to 1540	L. F. Salzman, 1951
Timber Building in England	F. H. Crossley, 1951

Patronage

Earls of Creation	James Lees-Milne, 1962

Dictionaries and Glossaries

A Short Dictionary of British Architects	Dora Ware, 1967
English Medieval Architects, A Biographical Dictionary down to 1550	John Harvey and Arthur Oswald, 1954
Biographical Dictionary of English Architects, 1660-1840	H. M. Colvin, 1954
Dictionary of British Sculptors 1660-1851	Rupert Gunnis, 1953
The Country Life Pocket Guide to English Domestic Architecture	A. L. Osborne, 1967
Illustrated Glossary of Architecture, 850-1830	John Harris and Jill Lever, 1966

Index

Acknowledgments

Illustrations are from *Country Life* photographs, except those obtained from the following sources: Aerofilms Ltd. p 163; Ashmolean Museum, Oxford p 58 (left); Bill Bawden, Eagle Photos (Cheltenham) Ltd. pp 32, 105 (bottom), 139, 168 (top); British Travel Association p 38; Central Press Photos p 126 (bottom); Courtauld Institute, University of London pp 56, 58 (right), 61, 62, 65; English Life Publications Ltd. p 37 (bottom); Miles Hadfield p 182; A. F. Kersting, London pp 2-3, 5, 10, 14, 34 (left), 37 (top), 38, 90 (bottom), 102, 107, 108, 111, 119, 120 (top), 122, 129, 134 (bottom), 146 (top), 147, 154, 157 (bottom), 233; Keystone Press Agency p 72 (bottom); Paul Mellon Collection, Washington p 59; National Buildings Record p 208; National Gallery, London p 60; National Trust (L. & M. Gayton) p 82 (bottom); Royal Academy of Arts, London p 221; Vernon D. Shaw, Hale p 80; Edwin Smith, Saffron Walden pp 42, 52, 91; Victoria & Albert Museum, London p 72 (top).

The publishers gratefully acknowledge the helpful cooperation of the National Trust and the owners of the houses illustrated. The paintings on pages 56 and 65, and on page 62, are reproduced by kind permission of Mrs J. R. Fetherstonhaugh and the Earl Spencer respectively.